Royal Commission on Environmental Pollution

Chairman: Sir Tom Blundell frs FMedSci

Twenty-third Report

ENVIRONMENTAL PLANNING

Presented to Parliament by Command of Her Majesty
March 2002

Cm 5459   £25.00

Previous Reports by the Royal Commission on Environmental Pollution

22nd report	Energy – The Changing Climate	Cm 4749, June 2000
21st report	Setting Environmental Standards	Cm 4053, October 1998
20th report	Transport and the Environment – Developments since 1994	Cm 3752, September 1997
19th report	Sustainable Use of Soil	Cm 3165, February 1996
18th report	Transport and the Environment	Cm 2674, October 1994
17th report	Incineration of Waste	Cm 2181, May 1993
16th report	Freshwater Quality	Cm 1966, June 1992
15th report	Emissions from Heavy Duty Diesel Vehicles	Cm 1631, September 1991
14th report	GENHAZ - A System for the Critical Appraisal of Proposals to Release Genetically Modified Organisms into the Environment	Cm 1557, June 1991
13th report	The Release of Genetically Engineered Organisms to the Environment	Cm 720, July 1989
12th report	Best Practicable Environmental Option	Cm 310, February 1988
11th report	Managing Waste: The Duty of Care	Cmnd 9675, December 1985
10th report	Tackling Pollution – Experience and Prospects	Cmnd 9149, February 1984
9th report	Lead in the Environment	Cmnd 8852, April 1983
8th report	Oil Pollution of the Sea	Cmnd 8358, October 1981
7th report	Agriculture and Pollution	Cmnd 7644, September 1979
6th report	Nuclear Power and the Environment	Cmnd 6618, September 1976
5th report	Air Pollution Control: An Integrated Approach	Cmnd 6371, January 1976
4th report	Pollution Control: Progress and Problems	Cmnd 5780, December 1974
3rd report	Pollution in Some British Estuaries and Coastal Waters	Cmnd 5054, September 1972
2nd report	Three Issues in Industrial Pollution	Cmnd 4894, March 1972
	First Report	Cmnd 4585, February 1971

Information about the current work of the Royal Commission can be obtained from its website at http://www.rcep.org.uk or from the Secretariat at Third Floor, 5-8 The Sanctuary, Westminster, London SW1P 3JS

ROYAL COMMISSION ON ENVIRONMENTAL POLLUTION

TWENTY-THIRD REPORT

To the Queen's Most Excellent Majesty

MAY IT PLEASE YOUR MAJESTY

We, the undersigned Commissioners, having been appointed 'to advise on matters, both national and international, concerning the pollution of the environment; on the adequacy of research in this field; and the future possibilities of danger to the environment'; and to enquire into any such matters referred to us by one of Your Majesty's Secretaries of State or by one of Your Majesty's Ministers, or any other such matters on which we ourselves shall deem it expedient to advise:

HUMBLY SUBMIT TO YOUR MAJESTY THE FOLLOWING REPORT.

Our land mass and our population inevitably constrain us.

Rt Hon Tony Blair MP, January 2002

Nothing less than a comprehensive policy for the environment will suffice.

First Report of the Royal Commission, February 1971

CONTENTS

INFORMATION BOXES

TABLES

Key messages of our report

1   Economic and social objectives have to be achieved in ways that safeguard and enhance the environment. Alongside other legislation dealing with particular aspects of the environment, town and country planning is of central importance in ensuring this.

2   The present arrangements do not provide an integrated, accountable and transparent way of setting and achieving environmental goals at different levels. There is a complex variety of legislation. Responsibilities are divided between the UK government, the devolved administrations, local authorities and specialist agencies. There is a multiplicity of often overlapping and sometimes conflicting plans and strategies. Nowhere is the whole picture brought together and the respective responsibilities of all the different bodies clearly assigned. There is no succinct statement of priority objectives for the environment.

3   There is a widespread view that the town and country planning system is in need of reform. In the June 2001 UK election the three main parties all promised to reform it. There is much less clarity about the nature of that reform, or indeed about the objectives it should be designed to achieve. Business has a clear agenda, in that it wants quick and predictable decisions on planning applications. The government has accepted that view. As a result, attention has focused on development control, the regulatory dimension of the system, to the neglect of the other essential dimension, planning for the future. Yet a greater concern for the future of the environment is one of the major messages of sustainable development.

4   The town and country planning system is typical of many British institutions. Born of idealism at the end of the second world war, it now faces a very different world, to which it has yet to adjust. In the 1950s it had to confront a growing population, a severe shortage of housing, large areas of industrial dereliction and the beginnings of the new mobility brought by mass car ownership. Fifty years later the pressing problems we face include finding ways of living which require fewer natural resources, reducing carbon dioxide emissions from transport and other uses of energy, the growing numbers of small households, the difficulties of creating sustainable communities in inner cities and outer estates, and the future of a countryside now widely perceived to be in crisis.

5   Rather than being seen as an essential instrument for tackling such problems, town and country planning has come to be perceived in many quarters as a bureaucratic structure of doubtful relevance. Central government's priorities for the system have shifted repeatedly, and those operating it are no longer sure what they are expected to achieve. There is no clear statutory statement of its purpose. Planning policies are often obscure, inconsistent and out of date. Even where they are timely and relevant, they are not necessarily widely known or understood. Yet, if the town and country planning system had not existed, widespread damage to the environment would have occurred over the last fifty years, probably with serious economic and social consequences.

The Planning Green Paper

6   We welcome the recognition, in the Green Paper relating to England published in December 2001, that the planning system still has an important role. The foreword by the Secretary of State for Transport, Local Government and the Regions begins: 'Planning is fundamental to the way our cities, towns and villages look, the way they work and the way they relate to each other.' According to the Green Paper the two characteristics of a successful planning system are that it should 'fully [engage] people in shaping the future of their communities and local economies' and 'promote economic prosperity by delivering land for development in the right place and at the right time'.[1]

7   Government policy towards local authorities, however, has given more emphasis to community strategies and local strategic partnerships, largely as a way of integrating a host of area-based initiatives previously launched for specific purposes. In policies for the regions there has been more emphasis on economic strategies than on regional planning guidance.

8   The Green Paper adopts a narrow focus on people's views about their immediate environment and the effects of new developments on 'the surroundings in which they live and work.'[2] There is almost no reference to the wider environment or the value people attach to it. We are promised only that the planning system 'will value the countryside and our heritage while recognising that times move on'.[3] There is no recognition of the severe economic and social implications of ignoring fundamental constraints such as those analysed in our report on energy and climate change.[4]

9   The very few references to sustainable development do not acknowledge that it is an an environmental concept. Where a decision involves striking a balance, the Green Paper sees it as lying between 'our desire for economic development and for thriving communities'; environmental sustainability is not mentioned.[5] Yet a system for planning and regulating land use has effects on the environment which are at least as direct, and ultimately as important, as its effects on the economy or the community.

10   Although we share many of the Green Paper's concerns, we approach the planning system from a different standpoint. We agree that 'fundamental change' is necessary, but we believe it needs to go deeper and wider. We fear some of the proposals the government has put forward are unlikely to succeed because they proffer simplistic solutions to complex problems. Others may well lead to increased uncertainty, and therefore slow down the system by increasing the number of legal challenges to decisions, one of the major causes of delays. Our main difference with the Green Paper, however, is that we have addressed fundamental issues, which the Green Paper fails to acknowledge, about the purpose and nature of a land use planning system, and we have placed those issues in the wider context of achieving environmental sustainability.

The way forward

11 We have considered the requirements for environmental sustainability (chapter 3). We have concluded that present planning procedures in the UK do not have the coherence and effectiveness needed to meet those requirements (chapter 4). Dramatic changes in land use are in prospect in the countryside. Much needs to be done to reinvigorate urban areas. To reduce emissions of greenhouse gases, radical changes will be needed in the ways the UK obtains and uses energy. At the same time, extensive adaptations are likely to be necessary to cope with the changes in weather patterns and rises in sea level which now appear inevitable. It will be necessary to find more efficient ways of using other natural resources, especially water and minerals. The solutions to these problems will require new policies in many fields, and will certainly pose major challenges for the planning and regulation of land use. The town and country planning system needs to be modified and extended so that it can facilitate successful responses to a changing world, including changes which are longer-term and more far-reaching than those given attention in the Green Paper.

12 A basic weakness in present procedures is the lack of strong connections between town and country planning and the work of the specialist agencies dealing with pollution and conservation. By 2004 the EC Directive on Strategic Environmental Assessment has to be transposed into UK law. If the requirements of the Directive are applied in a formalistic way to the present plethora of partial, overlapping, and often inconsistent plans produced by various bodies, they could become a burdensome charade. We believe, however, that the Directive could be a positive and valuable influence. The recommendations we put forward in this report would create a framework within which it could bring real benefits.

13 Regulatory and planning systems are unlikely to contribute to sustainable development unless there is strong commitment to that overall goal extending across all sectors. A broad aim of sustainable development is to improve the quality of life. Nevertheless, there may be difficulties in making the transition to a world in which growth of the economy places progressively fewer demands on environmental and natural resources. There will be many gainers. But hard decisions will have to be made, including planning decisions, and inevitably some people will lose out in some ways. The system in which those decisions are made has to command public confidence as being open, fair and impartial, as well as accountable and effective.

14 Having looked in depth at the role of the planning system, we have concluded that, over and above the proposals in the Green Paper, and sometimes in conflict with them, action should be taken in six areas to increase efficiency and effectiveness. We see a pressing need for:

- clearer policies and objectives for the environment;
- statutory recognition of the central role of town and country planning in protecting and enhancing the environment;
- rationalising the overall system for environmental planning by introducing integrated spatial strategies covering all aspects of sustainable development;
- ensuring that strategies cover all forms of land use;
- much improved availability of information about the environment;

- further steps to engage a wider range of people in decisions about setting and achieving environmental goals.

We repeat here the key recommendations in this report under each of those headings. A complete list of our recommendations follows chapter 10.

Clearer policies and objectives for the environment

15   Although there are already wide-ranging environmental policies, these are not comprehensive, nor always mutually consistent. **We recommend that a concise and definitive statement of priority objectives for the environment be produced now for each part of the UK, and widely publicised** (8.7). **Wherever possible, this statement must include a quantified target or targets for movement towards the objective by a specified date** (8.7).

16   Protecting and enhancing the environment must be firmly and unambiguously accepted as the foundation for sustainable development. **The statements of priority objectives should be prepared on the basis that sustainable development is achievable only if the environment is safeguarded and enhanced** (8.10). The government should modify the main aims of the UK Sustainable Development Strategy to reflect its commitment to environmental improvement.

17   The objectives adopted will have to be consistent with European legislation and international commitments. As negotiating and complying with international agreements is a UK responsibility, **it will be necessary to produce a statement of priority environmental objectives for the UK as a whole, as well as for each of its parts** (8.9).

18   **It is essential that each objective for the environment is underpinned by a soundly based programme for achieving it** (8.13). These programmes must identify clearly the contributions expected from different policy instruments.

A clear purpose for town and country planning

19   We have highlighted the central role of town and country planning in safeguarding environmental sustainability. There has been much confusion about its role. A major reason for that is the failure of the Acts to say what its purpose is. For the future its importance in protecting and enhancing the environment must be made explicit, in a way that also recognises its other purposes. **We recommend that the town and country planning system should be given a statutory purpose and that, rather than use the term 'sustainable development', an appropriate purpose would be 'to facilitate the achievement of legitimate economic and social goals whilst ensuring that the quality of the environment is safeguarded and, wherever appropriate, enhanced'** (8.33).

20   The presumption in favour of development, which has been a strong implicit feature in the past, ought no longer to apply. To reinforce the new statutory purpose for the system, **legislation should also stipulate key aspects of the environment and natural resources as material considerations which should be taken into account in considering all planning applications** (8.36).

Rationalising the overall system for environmental planning

21   Although town and country planning is of central importance, we have emphasised that it is part of a wider system for setting and achieving environmental objectives, and effective arrangements for strategic planning must recognise that. **We recommend the introduction of integrated spatial strategies which take account of all spatially related activities and all spatially related aspects of environmental capacity. They should be four-dimensional, covering the atmosphere and groundwater as well as the land surface, and looking at least 25 years ahead** (10.21).

22   The integrated spatial strategy should be the dominant plan for the area it covers. That area must be meaningful to the public, but also large enough to provide a valid basis for strategic planning. It should not be any smaller than the areas for which structure plans are prepared at present.

23   We see integrated spatial strategies as the key instrument for rationalising the present plethora of plans produced by public bodies which either deal directly with, or have important implications for, spatially related aspects of the environment. They should cover the spatial implications of all government policies, including for example energy policies. To identify and address the problems of a particular area, the integrated spatial strategy should draw on a new form of environmental report which analyses both the current state of the environment and the pressures on it from current trends. Each strategy should also be required to incorporate appropriate contributions towards environmental and other targets set nationally.

24   **To ensure that all the relevant bodies contribute fully to preparation of the integrated spatial strategy, and are committed to its implementation, it should have a firm statutory basis, and the lead body should be clearly designated. All other public bodies should be placed under a duty to co-operate in its preparation and comply with it where it affects their activities** (10.29).

Covering all forms of land use

25   Because town and country are interdependent, the area covered by an integrated spatial strategy should normally include both significant urban areas and significant rural areas. The strategy must cover agriculture and forestry, as the largest uses of land.

26   **Production subsidies to agriculture should be phased out as soon as possible. While they remain part of the Common Agricultural Policy (CAP), farmers receiving such subsidies should be required to maintain a defined level of environmental protection on the land they manage. We urge the government to take full advantage of the existing scope for cross-compliance under the CAP to support the protection and enhancement of the environment, and to seek to widen the scope for cross-compliance as part of the reform of the CAP** (9.32).

27   **There is justification for the state to continue payments to rural land managers, including arable and livestock farmers, for achieving well defined, measurable environmental and social objectives** (9.34).

28   **We recommend that in future each agricultural holding in the UK receiving public subsidy should be required to prepare a farm plan containing actions to improve the environment which can readily be monitored; and that, to simplify the existing arrangements, all bodies giving grants, exercising regulatory functions or requiring certification of environmental performance should accept the plan as meeting their requirements for information** (9.54). **The Rural Payments Agency and its counterparts should have responsibility for all grant payments made pursuant to the plan, including payments made in respect of management of sites of special scientific interest or for farm woodland or afforestation schemes** (9.55). In this way the bureaucratic burden on farmers and landowners could be considerably eased.

29   The substantial benefits of an urban renaissance will not be realised unless there are more concerted efforts to tackle outstanding problems of environmental degradation in urban areas. As well as more effective action to reduce air pollution **we recommend that the government and the devolved administrations include in their guidance to planning authorities targets for the maximum distance any urban household should be from a green space of specified size open to the public** (9.23). **Once a clearer picture emerges of the extent of the problem posed by contaminated land and the possible uses for remediated sites, the government and the devolved administrations should set targets for the total area to be brought back into beneficial use over ten years and should plan to provide the necessary finance. They should also report on the feasibility of the 2030 goal for dealing with contaminated land proposed by the Urban Task Force** (9.14).

Improved availability of information

30   The preparation, monitoring and revision of integrated spatial strategies will be dependent on an efficient supply of up-to-date information, quantitative and qualitative, about all aspects of the environment. An improved supply of information will facilitate the production of environmental statements for projects, and will be essential to carry out the strategic environmental assessments of plans and programmes which will be required under EC legislation. Effective public involvement in environmental planning requires that all relevant information should be readily available.

31   **We recommend that data which have been gathered in the public name and for the public good should be available electronically at no cost for public use** (6.20).

32   **We recommend the creation of a virtual centre for environmental data to overcome the barriers to presenting coherent and consistent environmental information in electronic form** (6.36). A virtual centre could make full use, not only of geographical information systems, but also of the Grid software technology now emerging as a way of exchanging large amounts of data between different databases. It could be linked to the Planning Inspectorate's new Planning Portal. That project will focus on planning policies and administrative procedures, and allow appellants and objectors to communicate with the Inspectorate electronically. The virtual centre we envisage will enable people to find out about the state of the environment and the pressures on it. It will also allow assessments to be made of the overall effects of planning decisions and the likely impact of proposals under consideration, including any effects on other areas if materials or energy would have to be imported from them, of if wastes and emissions would be exported to them.

Engaging the public

33   Basic mechanisms of democratic accountability are not sufficient in themselves to ensure that the planning system will enjoy public confidence. There is much scope for eliminating unnecessary delays in the handling of cases. But, however fast and predictable a system is, it will not win and retain public support if it is regarded as unfair or biased. Nor will it retain public confidence if it is found to lead to unacceptable outcomes. Streamlining of the system must not be at the expense of full and proper consideration of environmental impacts, or of opportunities for public scrutiny of policy assumptions. **The demonstrable capacity of public participation to improve plans and policies should be fostered by improving existing procedures and developing new deliberative processes** (5.17).

34   Other environmental regimes have grown up piecemeal, and exhibit a bewildering variety of procedures. **Environmental Tribunals should be established to handle appeals in such cases** (5.36) and other regimes should extend opportunities for public participation, using the town and country planning system as a model. **We recommend that pollution control authorisation and planning permission for industrial plants should be obtained through a single open process involving a common environmental statement and, where appropriate, a joint public inquiry** (5.23).

35   The public need to be engaged with the system for setting and achieving environmental goals, not only as objectors to or supporters of particular proposals, but also at the stage of drawing up and reviewing plans. Integrated spatial strategies of the kind we have recommended will focus attention more effectively and constructively. There should be full participation by stakeholders and the wider public in the preparation of such strategies, beginning with the identification of problems, and full public scrutiny of the drafts put forward. Approaches already in use for structure plans and regional planning guidance can be further developed for this purpose.

36   **Proposals for major infrastructure projects should always be put forward within the framework of carefully considered national policies, which should always be adopted after wide public consultation, and take full account of environmental considerations** (8.49). **The national need for additional infrastructure should be probed in an open and participatory process, which where practicable should engage local communities which may be affected** (8.50). **If the inspector conducing the local inquiry concludes that the local impacts of a proposed project would be unacceptable, he should be permitted to recommend that the approval in principle should be reconsidered** (8.58).

Funding and skills

37 There is widespread agreement that resources, particularly human resources, are a key issue for effective planning. Bodies with otherwise differing perspectives told us that present resource levels do not match the requirements placed on the town and country planning system, and that it is slower and less effective than it should be.[6] One consequence is that many plans have taken so long to produce that they are out of date by the time they are adopted. There are also consequences for the time taken to decide planning applications, an issue which has preoccupied this and previous governments. The specialist environmental agencies have also had difficulty in obtaining funding to carry out some of their key functions.

38 The resources available are only one side of the equation. The tasks set must be examined to see whether they are appropriate. We have made a number of recommendations in this report for simplifying procedures, and these should help reduce the pressures on resources. Even so, present levels of resources may well be insufficient for the tasks faced in the future. Rather than being driven by a belief that resources cannot be increased, however, we consider that changes to the environmental planning system should be discussed and justified in terms of their implications for the system's effectiveness in fulfilling its purpose. **Planning authorities must be properly resourced for their tasks** (5.58). So must the specialist environmental agencies.

Part I

The need for change

Chapter 1

THE CASE FOR ENVIRONMENTAL PLANNING

How can we best shape our future environment? Does the UK have satisfactory institutions for this task?

1.1 Safeguarding the environment is fundamental to sustainable development. Much has been achieved over the last half century, notably in reducing more obvious forms of pollution. But recent assessments in Europe and in the UK have shown the quality of the environment deteriorating in many respects.[1] The pressures on the environment are severe, and we must find sustainable ways of managing them. Few of the trends are new. There is a danger they may be overlooked or underestimated because their causes and effects are widely scattered and not readily apparent. A new approach is needed.

1.2 Achieving environmental sustainability requires a strategic approach. The underlying forces creating pressures on the environment have to be identified and extrapolated, and appropriate policies adopted towards them. Sometimes the objective will be to resist or reverse established trends. But it will also be crucial to promote innovative solutions which, as far as possible, simultaneously meet environmental, economic and social objectives.

1.3 Devising and implementing sustainable solutions is going to involve all sectors of society. Success will depend on using a full range of policy instruments, deployed at different levels of government. Economic instruments will be important, as will support for research and development. Legal regulation has a vital contribution to make, not only in limiting damage from human activities, but in encouraging and facilitating innovative approaches.

1.4 Responsibility for safeguarding the environment is spread across many different public bodies. Each of the four parts of the UK can now have its own policies. Specialist agencies (responsible, for example, for pollution control or nature conservation) have the highest profile and the clearest remit. But a key role is played by the regulation and planning of land use, in the form of town and country planning.

1.5 For over 50 years, the function of town and country planning in protecting and improving the environment has been largely implicit. Planning policies have also pursued economic and social objectives, and at times have placed relatively little emphasis on environmental considerations. Nevertheless, town and country planning has been a major force protecting the UK environment. Without it, urban and rural areas would now be much less attractive. It has provided the traditional forum for thinking strategically about the future of particular areas. It is the arena in which many environmental controversies have been fought out.

1.6 The regulation and planning of land use is not something that can be considered in isolation. The ways in which land is used are linked to environmental change on many different scales. Air quality, the water cycle, biological diversity, transport, and energy production and use are also spatially related, and to significant extents policies in those fields depend for their success on decisions about land use. Equally, the management and condition of land are much influenced by other policies, and by other statutory and non-statutory regimes, as well as by town and country planning.

1.7 A quarter of a century ago, the Commission devoted part of one of its reports to the relationship between pollution control and town and country planning.[2] Since then a great deal has changed. In belated responses to that report's recommendations, the legislation and organisation for controlling pollution in Britain have been transformed.[3] The nature of environmental concerns has changed radically.[4] There is now a much better understanding of the complexity of the environment and the interconnections between its different aspects. It has been realised that objectives to protect or improve particular aspects of the environment may sometimes come into conflict with each other,[5] as well as with economic and social objectives.

1.8 Adopting sustainable development as a formal aim has created a new context for environmental policy and regulation. Major challenges lie ahead in achieving environmental sustainability. The question is, whether meeting those challenges requires radical reform or progressive adaptation of existing institutions.

1.9 A survey we commissioned of other developed countries[6] found significant common trends in the organisation of environmental responsibilities. The importance of clear strategic direction has been increasingly recognised. There is also a general concern to establish more integrated systems of administration, often with an emphasis on making these simpler and clearer in order to facilitate a greater degree of public participation. Those findings confirmed us in the view that it was time to look again at the roles and relationships of key public bodies with environmental responsibilities, and to do so on a broader basis than the Commission's 1976 report, which was primarily concerned with air pollution.

PURPOSE OF OUR STUDY

1.10 In inviting evidence for this study (see appendix A) we said our purpose was to assess whether the various regimes now existing at different levels for setting and achieving environmental goals provide an effective, accountable and transparent way of protecting the environment. A central concern has been to assess the contribution made by the regulation and planning of land use. We have also looked at such areas of policy as pollution control, air quality, waste, water and biological diversity.

1.11 The key issues we identified were:

- The extent to which current institutions promote or prejudice environmental sustainability

- Whether administrative boundaries and divisions of responsibilities are hindering the pursuit of environmental sustainability

- How well current arrangements work as a whole, given that the various regimes have been established at different times to serve different objectives

- The inherent tensions between delivering national policy targets and ensuring adequate local accountability

- Which approaches to assessment can safeguard environmental sustainability while maintaining the efficiency of planning systems.

1.12 We are very appreciative of all those who submitted written or oral evidence, produced papers, made presentations or helped us in other ways. They are listed in appendix B, which also gives other information about the way this study was conducted. A seminar in February 2000 assisted us in identifying the most significant issues, and we are grateful to everyone who participated (see appendix C). Some specific contributions and expressions of view are acknowledged in that context or in endnotes to the report, but it would be impracticable to record in detail the ways in which so many people extended our understanding of the subject and influenced our thinking.

1.13 We are aware that the government has been concerned about the effectiveness and efficiency of town and country planning. In this report we have been able to take account of the Green Paper on the planning system in England published by the Department for Transport, Local Government and the Regions in December 2001 and the accompanying consultation papers. We set out in appropriate contexts in later chapters our views on some of the key proposals put forward.

STRUCTURE OF THE REPORT

1.14 This first part of our report explains why we consider changes are needed in the present institutions. **Chapter 2** provides an overview of the present organisation for protecting and improving the environment in each part of the UK. In view of the critical role of local authorities, we consider, as well as the specialist agencies and the town and country planning system, the wider local government picture. We also outline the recent evolution of organisations at regional level in England. We identify the duties that have been placed on various bodies for promoting sustainable development.

1.15 **Chapter 3** traces the history of the concept of 'sustainable development' and discusses how it ought to be interpreted, and what are the requirements for ensuring environmental sustainability.

1.16 **Chapter 4** explains why we consider a spatial and strategic approach is necessary in environmental planning. We examine present planning procedures, and conclude that they do not amount to an integrated or coherent system for identifying and promoting the actions needed at regional or local level to safeguard environmental sustainability.

1.17 The second part of the report identifies what we believe are certain essential prerequisites for any effective system of environmental planning. **Chapter 5** considers how confidence in the system might be strengthened by preserving and extending opportunities for public involvement, making regulation more coherent and comprehensible, extending rights of appeal, and more effective safeguards for propriety.

1.18 **Chapter 6** examines the sources of information about the environment; and how data can be made more accessible to planners, developers and the public.

1.19 **Chapter 7** considers how information about the environment can be used most effectively in assessing projects, and more particularly in assessing plans and programmes. It discusses strategic environmental assessment and what role should be accorded to sustainability appraisal.

1.20 In the third part of the report we draw on the analysis in earlier chapters to reach conclusions and make recommendations about the changes needed to give the UK more effective institutions for setting and achieving environmental goals.

1.21 **Chapter 8** looks at the national level, and recommends that there should be both clearer objectives for environmental policies and properly worked-out programmes for achieving them. It highlights the potential role of town and country planning, but concludes that its role needs clarification, and that planning authorities must be given prompter and more concise guidance on national policies. We discuss the government's proposals to reform the procedures for authorising major projects put forward in pursuit of national policies. We consider the difficulties that have arisen where national policies for achieving environmental objectives require the construction of numerous plants of kinds that are likely to encounter local opposition, and suggest an approach that would help to overcome those difficulties.

1.22 **Chapter 9** reviews planning policies towards rural and urban areas, and emphasises the need for them to be compatible. It identifies some environmental problems that have to be solved if an urban renaissance is to be achieved and rural areas protected. It considers the effects climate change is likely to have on the environment in rural, urban and coastal areas, and what measures ought now to be taken in anticipation of that.

1.23 **Chapter 10** puts the case for new procedures for integrated spatial planning in order to achieve effective coverage at strategic level of a much wider range of factors than town and country planning legislation covers at present, and in particular to ensure that environmental sustainability will be safeguarded. We review the three levels of plans in the present town and country planning system in England, and the government's proposals for them, in order to determine which level can provide the most suitable basis for a system of integrated spatial planning. We discuss the new planning system being implemented in London. We review the prospects for establishing integrated spatial planning in Scotland, Wales and Northern Ireland.

1.24 Following chapter 10, there is a complete list of our recommendations.

The European and global framework

1.25 Increasingly, environmental problems are being addressed at levels beyond the nation state. A list of key environmental targets for the next 20 years compiled by the Environment Agency provides striking evidence of that.[7] Of 19 targets listed, 14 are European or international in origin; 11 the outcome of European Community (EC) legislation and three the result of agreements in wider international fora (themselves negotiated at European level, rather than by Member States individually, and being implemented through EC legislation).

1.26 Apart from Directives on environmental assessment, there has not been EC legislation on the regulation and planning of land use. However, as we show later in this report, many European policies and programmes of expenditure either depend for their success on land use decisions taken within Member States, or have significant implications for land use (for example, the Common Agricultural Policy). Our concerns about the adequacy of European institutions have been pursued through the network of European Environmental Advisory Councils (EEACs). We contributed to the preparation of a Sustainable Development Strategy for the European Union through the statement adopted at a conference held by EEACs at Stockholm in February 2001;[8] the executive summary is reproduced as appendix D.

1.27 Sustainable development will have to be achieved ultimately on a global basis. We have not addressed issues which are receiving increasing attention elsewhere[9] about the forms of global governance needed to ensure sustainability. The contribution the UK must make to achieving global sustainability, and the specific obligations created by international environmental agreements, are things we had very much in mind in undertaking this study. The UK government is responsible for fulfilling existing obligations of this nature, and the more demanding obligations it may well be necessary to accept in future. In this report we have treated such obligations as national policies, and examined how they and other national policies can best be implemented.

Chapter 2

THE PRESENT SYSTEM

How are responsibilities for protecting and improving the environment divided? How does the role of local authorities as planning authorities relate to their wider role? What duties do various bodies have to promote sustainable development? What is the likely impact of the current growth of regional organisation in England?

2.1   As the purpose of this report is to assess the adequacy of present institutions for setting and achieving environmental goals, we need to have a clear picture of those institutions. The description in this chapter is arranged as follows. We first look briefly at the UK government and the devolved administrations (2.2-2.6). We then describe the main features of the town and country planning system operated mainly by local authorities (2.7-2.15); and review the role of local authorities more generally and some current policy developments affecting them (2.16-2.28). We describe the roles of the specialist agencies which have responsibilities for particular aspects of the environment (2.29-2.48). Finally, we outline the complex organisation which has recently emerged at regional level in England (2.49-2.54).

ORGANISATION AT NATIONAL LEVEL

2.2   Until June 2001, environmental protection and town and country planning in England were handled by the same Department: latterly the Department of the Environment, Transport and the Regions (DETR).[1] Responsibility for town and country planning now lies with the Department for Transport, Local Government and the Regions (DTLR). Responsibility for environmental and countryside policies, and for sustainable development, now lies with the Department for Environment, Food and Rural Affairs (DEFRA). Protection of the built heritage is responsibility of the Department for Culture, Media and Sport (DCMS).

2.3   DEFRA has adopted as its formal aim:

Sustainable development, which means a better quality of life for everyone, now and for generations to come, including

- a better environment, at home and internationally, and sustainable use of natural resources

- economic prosperity through sustainable farming, fishing, food, water and other industries that meet consumers' requirements

- thriving economies and communities in rural areas and a countryside for all to enjoy.[2]

17

Within this aim, the first objective listed by DEFRA is 'to protect and improve the rural, urban, marine and global environment and conserve and enhance biodiversity, and to lead to integration of these with other policies across Government and internationally'. This meets concerns we expressed in consultation on a draft document.[3] We welcome DTLR's decision to prepare a sustainable development strategy for its activities.

2.4 Responsibility for environmental protection and town and country planning in Scotland, Wales and Northern Ireland, previously exercised by separate UK Departments, has been devolved to the Scottish Parliament, the National Assembly for Wales and the Northern Ireland Assembly. Scotland and Northern Ireland already had separate legislation on these subjects, and are now able to adopt their own primary legislation. Responsibility for both environmental protection and town and country planning lies with the Department of the Environment in Northern Ireland (DOENI); and in Wales with the same Minister and group of officials. In the Scottish Executive there is a split corresponding to that which now exists in England, between the Development Department and the Environment and Rural Affairs Department. Ministerial portfolios have not always coincided with this administrative division. Responsibility for town and country planning now lies with the Social Justice Minister.

2.5 The National Assembly for Wales is required to make a scheme 'setting out how it proposes, in the exercise of its functions, to promote sustainable development'; and in the year following each ordinary election to publish an assessment of how effective the proposals in the scheme have been in promoting sustainable development, and consider whether it should be remade or revised.[4] The initial scheme was adopted in November 2000.[5] The Scottish Executive has set up a Ministerial Group on Sustainable Scotland.[6]

INTERNATIONAL AND EUROPEAN OBLIGATIONS

2.6 As already noted, environmental policies in the UK are determined to a considerable extent by obligations under international agreements and by European Community (EC) legislation. The UK government is responsible for negotiating, and complying with, international agreements; and has a reserve power to require the devolved administrations to take the action necessary to implement them.[7] UK Departments take the lead in negotiations on EC Directives, with inputs from the devolved administrations; it is the responsibility of the devolved administrations to implement any new EU obligation in Northern Ireland, Scotland and Wales.[8] The town and country planning system has been much less affected than other environmental regimes by international agreements and EC legislation, but two significant factors are the EC Directives on environmental impact assessment and strategic environmental assessment discussed in chapter 7, and conventions on human rights, touched on in chapter 5.

TOWN AND COUNTRY PLANNING

2.7 The present structure of local government in the UK is described in box 2A. Town and country planning, which is a central focus of this report, is largely delivered by local authorities, except in Northern Ireland.

England outside London

Much of England now has a single tier of local government, but many areas have two tiers. In the six metropolitan areas (Tyne and Wear, West Midlands, Merseyside, Greater Manchester, West Yorkshire and South Yorkshire), county councils were abolished in 1974 and local government takes the form of 36 *metropolitan district councils*, most of which have a population of over 200,000. Elsewhere in England there are 45 *unitary authorities* established between 1995 and 1998, most of which have a population between 100,000 and 300,000. In the remainder of the country, local government takes the form of 34 *county councils*; and, within those counties, 238 *district councils*, most of which have a population in the range 60,000 to 100,000. There is no current intention to carry out any further reorganisation of local government in England.

In some of the metropolitan districts and most of the non-metropolitan districts, there are elected *parish councils* (about 8,000 in total) with limited functions.

London

The *Greater London Authority*, comprising a directly elected Mayor and an elected Assembly, assumed its responsibilities in July 2000. The 32 *London boroughs* retain their responsibilities. The Corporation of London is the local authority for the City of London.

Scotland

As a result of a reorganisation in 1996, there is a single tier of local government in Scotland. The structure of 9 regional councils and 53 district councils established on the mainland in 1975 has been replaced by 29 *unitary authorities*. The three islands councils remain.

There are over 1,000 *community councils* in Scotland. They are not local authorities, but have the statutory functions of ascertaining and expressing the views of their communities and taking such action as appears to be expedient and practicable in the interests of those communities.

Wales

As a result of a reorganisation in 1996, the structure of 8 county councils and 37 district councils established in 1974 has been replaced by 22 *unitary authorities*.

There are over 700 *community councils*, with a status and functions broadly equivalent to those of a parish council in England.

Northern Ireland

There are 26 *district councils* in Northern Ireland. They have more limited functions than local authorities elsewhere in the UK. Some services are provided by regional boards, to which the district councils nominate representatives. Other services, including planning and roads, are provided by government Departments.

2.8 The present system was created by the Town and Country Planning Act 1947 and the parallel Scottish Act. The Town and Country Planning Act 1990 consolidated the legislation for England and Wales, and further amendments were made in the Planning and Compensation Act 1991. The current Scottish legislation is the Town and Country Planning (Scotland) Act 1997. The purpose of the system is not defined in legislation, and has been stated in administrative guidance in different terms at different times. It has been seen, at both national and local levels, as a means of advancing a wide range of environmental and other policies. This is evident from the subjects, listed in box 2B, on which policy guidance is issued. Town and country planning is now seen as a major instrument for promoting sustainable development.[9]

BOX 2B   POLICY GUIDANCE TO PLANNING AUTHORITIES

Planning Policy Guidance in England

PPG1	General Policy and Principles
PPG2	Green Belts
PPG3	Housing
PPG4	Industrial and Commercial Development and Small Firms
PPG5	Simplified Planning Zone(s)
PPG6	Town Centres and Retail Development
PPG7	The Countryside: Environmental Quality and Economic and Social Development
PPG8	Telecommunications
PPG9	Nature Conservation
PPG10	Planning and Waste Management
PPG11	Regional Planning
PPG12	Development Plans
PPG13	Transport
PPG14	Development on Unstable Land
PPG14A	Annex 1: Landslides and Planning
PPG15	Planning and the Historic Environment
PPG16	Archaeology and Planning
PPG17	Sport and Recreation
PPG18	Enforcing Planning Control
PPG19	Outdoor Advertisement Control
PPG20	Coastal Planning
PPG21	Tourism
PPG22	Renewable Energy
PPG23	Planning and Pollution Control
PPG24	Planning and Noise
PPG25	Development and Flood Risk
PPG26	Contaminated Land *(in draft)*

A series of Minerals Planning Guidance Notes is issued for England

Policy guidance for Wales has been issued as a single document,[10] supplemented by Technical Advice Notes and Minerals Planning Policy Wales[11]

In Scotland, National Planning Policy Guidance is supplemented by more detailed Planning Advice Notes

National Planning Policy Guidance in Scotland

NPPG1	The Planning System
NPPG3	Land for Housing
NPPG2	Business and Industry
NPPG8	Town Centres and Retailing
NPPG15	Rural Development
NPPG19	Radio Telecommunications
NPPG14	Natural Heritage
NPPG10	Planning and Waste Management
NPPG17	Transport and Planning
NPPG18	Planning and the Historic Environment
NPPG5	Archaeology and Planning
NPPG11	Sport, Physical Recreation and Open Space
NPPG13	Coastal Planning
NPPG6	Renewable Energy Developments
NPPG7	Planning and Flooding

Other Subjects Covered in Scottish Guidance

NPPG4	Land for Mineral Working
NPPG9	The Provision of Roadside Facilities on Motorways and Other Trunk Roads in Scotland.
NPPG12	Skiing Developments
NPPG16	Opencast Coal and Related Minerals

2.9 It is widely agreed that the way the sustainable development agenda is applied to land use needs to be examined.[12] Many environmental bodies contend that planning must be assessed in the context of its contribution to strategies for sustainable development.[13] It is widely held that a much more comprehensive approach is needed, and that new environmental objectives must be integrated into the planning process.[14]

BOX 2C   **DEVELOPMENT PLANS**

In the town and country planning system the development plan for an area has two core components, a strategic plan and a more detailed plan; and (in most areas) two specialised components. The more strategic element takes various forms:

- in parts of England with two tiers of local government a *structure plan* is produced by the county council, and each district in the county then produces its own *local plan*, which by law must conform with the structure plan

- local authorities in Scotland produce a structure plan and a local plan

- some authorities in England and Scotland have been required by national government to produce a joint structure plan with one or more neighbouring authorities (see 10.54 below)

- the remaining unitary authorities in England and local authorities in Wales produce a unitary development plan, in which part I is broadly equivalent to a structure plan

- in national parks in England and Wales the national park authority is the planning authority and produces the development plan.

The specialised components of the development plan are a *waste plan* and a *minerals plan*. These are produced by county councils in England, and where appropriate by unitary authorities. There is not a requirement to produce such plans in Scotland at present, but the Scottish Executive has proposed that all local authorities should be required to produce waste plans.

All the components of the development plan are subjected to extensive consultation and scrutiny. Objectors to a proposed plan may be individuals and bodies with an interest in a particular plot of land, or those with a more general interest in policies (for example, amenity groups or business groups), or a statutory environmental agency or government Department. If objections to a *local plan* are pressed, there is a public inquiry conducted by an inspector (England and Wales) or an inquiry reporter (Scotland). A *structure plan* is considered at an examination in public conducted by a panel chaired by someone appointed by the Minister. The local authority considers whether to modify the plan in the light of the report by the inspector, reporter or panel; Ministers have powers to intervene at any stage and direct changes to any aspect of the plan prior to its adoption by the local authority. In Scotland structure plans require the Minister's approval.

In Northern Ireland the Planning Service (2.48) prepares area plans covering one or more districts.

2.10 The two complementary aspects of town and country planning are development control (the regulation of building, engineering and mining operations and material changes in land use) and development plans. Box 2C describes the components of the development plan. Legislation now requires primacy to be given to the policies in the development plan for the area, although the planning authority must also take into account any other 'material considerations'. Material considerations may include policies which appear in the supporting documentation to the development plan but are not formally part of the plan because they do not relate directly to land use; an environmental statement (if the applicant has been required to submit one); national planning policies (which may have changed since the plan for that area was adopted); but also many other things. We discuss in chapter 8 how we think the interpretation of 'material consideration' should be modified for the future.

2.11 The development plan states the policies the local authority intends to follow in determining planning applications and indicates the locations considered appropriate or inappropriate for specific kinds of development.[15] The development plan must by statute contain policies for improving the physical environment and managing traffic. On other aspects of its content there is only administrative guidance.[16]

2.12 The first round of structure plans of the present type in England were adopted between 1992 and 1998, and the process of revision has started in some areas. The original target was to achieve complete coverage of England by local plans of the present type by 1996. However, 13% of local planning authorities have still to adopt a district-wide plan. And 214 of the plans which have been adopted are now out of date.[17] Only 21% of current local plans in Scotland were adopted within the last five years.[18] In an area where an up-to-date local plan has not been adopted, the development plan previously adopted remains in force. We found one case in England in which the development plan in force had been adopted in 1958.[19]

MODERNISING PLANNING

2.13 In recent years there has been criticism of the town and country planning system from many quarters. At the 2001 UK election, the manifestos of the three main parties undertook to reform the system, but without specifying how. Criticisms have been directed both at the complexities and delays in producing development plans and at the time taken to decide planning applications. The emphasis has been on the efficiency of the service provided by the local planning authority to its immediate customer, an applicant for planning permission, rather than on its responsibilities to society as a whole. There have been particular criticisms of the time and expense incurred in considering and reaching decisions on the planning applications for 'major projects' such as Terminal Five at Heathrow. There are few projects in that category, however, and they raise distinctive issues which we discuss in chapter 8. The current controversy about the planning system goes wider.

2.14 The Conservative government started, and the Labour government continued, an initiative called 'Modernising planning'. A government statement in January 1998[20] was trailed in the press as 'the most far-reaching reform of planning regulations in more than 50 years'.[21] There has been a strong emphasis on measuring how quickly planning applications are handled. Although it is important planning authorities should be efficient, performance measures of that kind provide no indication of their success in achieving desired outcomes.

2.15 The government has now published a Green Paper on the planning system in England,[22] which claims to be promoting fundamental change. It proposes that regional spatial strategies should replace regional planning guidance; that structure plans should be abolished; and that local plans should be replaced by local development frameworks, which would be updated annually and supplemented by action plans (to provide detailed coverage, but possibly only for selected areas) and a 'statement of community involvement'. There are numerous other proposals, mainly relating to the operation of development control. Wherever specific proposals in the Green Paper are relevant to issues discussed in this report, we have taken them into account and commented on them. In the final chapter of the report we comment more generally on the approach the government is adopting towards town and country planning. There is an underlying concern in the planning profession that, instead of being central to a local authority's activities, town and country planning is becoming marginalised, out of touch both with the local community and with other local authority functions which are having a greater influence on the course of events.[23] We now therefore look at that wider local government picture.

THE WIDER LOCAL GOVERNMENT PICTURE

2.16 Two other aspects of local government are directly relevant to the theme of this report.[24] First, local authorities have other statutory functions which have the specific aim of protecting or improving the environment. Second, they also have responsibilities for economic and social development, and the way they discharge those responsibilities may have major implications for the environment, for good or ill. The overall health and viability of local government is also relevant, as are the policies adopted by national government for reinvigorating it.

OTHER RELEVANT FUNCTIONS OF LOCAL AUTHORITIES

2.17 Local authorities are creatures of statute and have the functions conferred on them by national legislation. They have a wide range of regulatory responsibilities for the environment, including some of the aspects which are of most direct concern to people, such as noise, vehicle emissions and nuisances. They are responsible for improving air quality where necessary; and in England and Wales they regulate emissions to air from smaller and less complex industrial processes. They are responsible for dealing with contaminated land. Among the services they provide are the collection and disposal of wastes.

2.18 Local authorities also have responsibilities for energy efficiency. These include a statutory duty to draw up and submit to the Minister strategies for cost-effective improvements in the energy efficiency of housing in their area; the reduction in household energy use by 2011 for which they were encouraged to aim was 30%.[25]

2.19 Local authorities have an extensive involvement in the economic and social development of their areas. A recent study[26] identified 32 types of zone or area-based initiative in England sponsored by central government, and most local authorities are involved in one or other of these. Their purposes range from coalfields regeneration to healthier schools. The same study identified 45 types of plan which local authorities themselves are required by statute to produce.

2.20 The list of plans local authorities are required to draw up includes some with a directly environmental purpose, such as air quality management plans. The great majority of the initiatives and plans listed, however, have no explicit environmental component. Nevertheless, they often have major implications for the use of land, and for the environment more generally. For example, the aims of local neighbourhood renewal strategies drawn up by local authorities include more jobs, better education, improved health, reduced crime, and better housing; and, more generally, closing the gap between deprived neighbourhoods and the rest of the authority's area and contributing to national targets for tackling deprivation.

2.21 Local authorities also have extensive responsibilities for transport. County councils and metropolitan and unitary authorities now prepare integrated local transport plans. The way they exercise those functions can contribute significantly both to improving local air quality and to reducing carbon dioxide emissions. Transport policies, for example the encouragement of cycling, walking and public transport, are inextricably linked to land use. Local authorities have a statutory duty to consider whether to set a target for road traffic in their area, in the form of either a reduction in the present level of traffic or a reduction in its expected growth.[27]

FUTURE PROSPECTS FOR LOCAL GOVERNMENT

2.22 In principle, the role of elected local authorities provides the means by which people in a given area can influence a wide range of decisions about their immediate environment and the strategies adopted towards future land use. It also provides a means of establishing clear accountability for such decisions and strategies. However, there is a worryingly low level of public interest in local government, and voting rates in elections to local authorities have fallen to very low levels. The situation has been described by a Select Committee as 'a civic crisis'.[28]

2.23 For a number of years, the main emphasis in central government policies towards local government was on improving the efficiency with which services are provided to the public. Key measures were the introduction of compulsory competitive tendering, the Best Value regime and league tables. In the interests of increased efficiency, local authorities were encouraged to enter into agreements with other organisations rather than provide services themselves. One initiative is the trialling of local public service agreements, under which a local authority enters into a formal agreement with central government to achieve a quantified target or targets for a specific service.

2.24 The present government has taken initiatives to try to improve the general health of local government and encourage local authorities to develop overall strategies. These initiatives have included experiments with novel procedures for elections, new committee structures, including the option of a cabinet system, and the possibility for the electorate to decide in a referendum that they want a directly elected mayor. The most relevant initiatives in the context of this report are the community strategies provided for in the Local Government Act 2000.

2.25 Each local authority in England is now required to produce a *community strategy* in order to promote or improve the economic, social and environmental well-being of its area, both for existing residents and for future generations. Guidance from central government[29] says that these strategies should contribute to the achievement of sustainable development locally and globally; and explains how social, economic and environmental issues must be tackled in an integrated way. The intention is that community strategies should define and clarify overall priorities by establishing a small number of key policy objectives for the area.

2.26 DTLR is encouraging local authorities to fulfil their duty to prepare and implement a community strategy by creating and working with a *local strategic partnership*. The aim is to bring together the different parts of the public sector, as well as the private, business, community and voluntary sectors. The intention is that such partnerships should operate at a high enough level to enable strategic decisions to be taken and yet be close enough to individual neighbourhoods to allow actions to be determined at community level. Where a local authority's area includes one of the most deprived electoral wards in England, funding has been made available from the Neighbourhood Renewal Fund to support the partnership.[30]

2.27 In principle, local strategic partnerships should provide a forum through which mainstream public service providers (local authorities, the police, health services, central government agencies and others) can work together to find the most effective ways of meeting local needs, and can co-ordinate their plans and initiatives (including, for example, local neighbourhood renewal strategies, local transport programmes and local public service agreements), and indeed the plethora of partnerships and joint planning procedures previously established for more specific purposes. However, such partnerships are not executive bodies and have no statutory status; so in practical terms the local authority will remain the key player. If they are accepted as establishing overarching objectives for other, more focused plans, community strategies have the potential to become powerful mechanisms for enhancing sustainability. It is too early to judge how effective they will be in practice, or how closely they will follow guidance from central government about their content and approach. There has been particular scepticism about how influential they will be in areas where the local authority is not eligible to receive additional funding for a local strategic partnership.

2.28 In Scotland, a similar initiative is being taken forward under the title of *community planning*. An initial focus of activity for partners has been to map existing policies, strategies and activities; identify key linkages; and rationalise partnership arrangements around a clear vision provided by five or six key cross-cutting themes. The timescale for plans has ranged from 5 to 20 years. One feature has been the efforts made to consult publicly during the preparation of plans and take on board input received from respondents. Some localities have also moved towards joint resourcing of key partnership activities such as funding for surveys, citizens' panels and community planning manager posts.[31] There is no additional funding available to local authorities to support this initiative.

SPECIALIST AGENCIES

2.29 Alongside the town and country planning system, statutory agencies take the lead in protecting the environment. They fall into three groups:

- agencies which control *pollution*: the Environment Agency in England and Wales[32] and the Scottish Environment Protection Agency (the Environment Agency, in particular, also has other functions, including flood defence)

- agencies which protect *wildlife and habitats and/or landscape*: English Nature and the Countryside Agency in England, Scottish Natural Heritage, and Cyngor Cefn Gwlad Cymru/the Countryside Council for Wales

- agencies which protect the *built heritage*: English Heritage, Historic Scotland and Cadw.

In Northern Ireland, the Environment and Heritage Service combines all three roles.

ENVIRONMENT AGENCY

2.30 By far the largest of the agencies is the Environment Agency in England and Wales. It was established in 1996 to bring together functions previously exercised by the National Rivers Authority (created in 1989 to take over the regulatory and river management functions of the Regional Water Authorities established in 1974) and Her Majesty's Inspectorate of Pollution (which had previously absorbed the Alkali and Clean Air Inspectorate and some smaller inspectorates), together with the responsibility for regulating waste disposal previously held by county councils and metropolitan districts. The Agency therefore has a wide range of functions, including integrated pollution prevention and control (now superseding integrated pollution control), regulation of radioactive substances, waste management, land quality, water quality, water resources, flood defence, navigation, recreation and fisheries.[33]

2.31 The environmental purpose of the specific functions the Agency exercises is more or less clear from the relevant Acts. Section 4 of the Environment Act 1995 says:

(1) It shall be the principal aim of the Agency (subject to and in accordance with the provisions of this Act or any other enactment and taking into account any likely costs) in discharging its functions so to protect or enhance the environment, taken as a whole, as to make the contribution towards attaining the objective of achieving sustainable development mentioned in sub-section (3)

(2) The Ministers shall from time to time give guidance to the Agency with respect to objectives which they consider it appropriate for the Agency to pursue in the discharge of its functions

(3) The guidance given under sub-section (2) above must include guidance with respect to the contribution which, having regard to the Agency's responsibilities and resources, the Ministers consider it appropriate for the Agency to make, by the discharge of its functions, towards attaining the objective of achieving sustainable development.

Whatever the good intentions behind this provision, it is expressed in such a convoluted way as to be almost meaningless. The Environment Agency nevertheless attaches great importance to its role in advancing sustainable development. It has been urged by a House of Commons Select Committee to do considerably more in that direction.[34] There is likewise provision for the Scottish Environment Protection Agency to receive ministerial guidance about the contribution it should make to sustainable development.[35]

2.32 The Environment Agency has identified the need to produce a long-term vision for 'a healthy, rich and diverse environment in England and Wales, for present and future generations', extending beyond the timescale of its corporate plan, and beyond its own functions. It has set out long-term objectives, and overall outcomes it will help to achieve, under nine themes:

- a better quality of life

- an enhanced environment for wildlife

- cleaner air for everyone

- improved and protected inland and coastal waters

- restored, protected land with healthier soils

- a 'greener' business world

- wiser, sustainable use of natural resources

- limiting and adapting to climate change

- reducing flood risk.[36]

To support this vision, the Agency has produced a comprehensive state of the environment report for England and Wales which, as well as describing the present situation, projects into the future the current pressures on the environment from natural forces and human activities and identifies sets of priority issues and key challenges.[37]

2.33 Like other statutory agencies, the Environment Agency is run by a Chairman and Board appointed by Ministers. In its case however there is an important proviso. Its biggest function in terms of expenditure is flood defence. This is largely financed by levies on local authorities, which represent the Agency's largest single source of income.[38] In consequence, decisions about the flood defence programme are taken, not by the Agency, but by statutory regional flood defence committees, on which the majority of members are appointed by local authorities; the Agency acts as an adviser and carries out those schemes which the committee has approved.

2.34 As a government-appointed body, the Agency has sometimes been regarded as having a 'democratic deficit'. It has therefore sought ways of engaging the public more directly in its work. Its board meetings are held in public, and the papers are available in advance on its website. Some of its initiatives have related to decisions on the more contentious individual cases. At a more strategic level, it has drawn up Local Environment Agency Plans (LEAPs) for each of its operational areas, based on wide consultation.

2.35 A Financial, Management and Policy Review (FMPR) of the Agency has just been completed. As in the case of local authorities, government thinking has tended to emphasise the Agency's responsibilities to the firms it regulates, and other readily identifiable stakeholders, rather than the wider community. One reason for this is that the Agency's activities, other than flood defence, are financed, to a large and increasing extent, by charges levied for various forms of application and authorisation. Funding from the government has been progressively reduced. But the result could well be a damaging narrowing of focus. The consultation document issued by DETR as part of the FMPR dealt at length with this aspect of the Agency, and devoted almost no space to its relationship with the public generally, or with local authorities.[39]

2.36 The Agency, on the other hand, has now recognised the need to devote a high priority to its relations with local authorities, especially in the context of preparation of development plans. However, it found great difficulty in establishing any dialogue with the Planning Directorate of what was then DETR about relevant features of national planning policies.[40]

2.37 The ministerial guidance initially given to the Environment Agency under the 1995 Act (2.31) was in very general terms, and was not found helpful in practice.[41] Nor has the Agency received guidance from central government about the contribution it should itself make to the broader environmental targets identified in its 'environmental vision' as against the contributions that might be made in some cases, for example, by local authorities. As this report was being finalised, DEFRA published proposals for new guidance to the Agency.[42] The National Assembly for Wales will be consulting separately on statutory guidance in respect of the Agency's activities in Wales.

SCOTTISH ENVIRONMENT PROTECTION AGENCY

2.38 The Scottish Environment Protection Agency (SEPA) was established in 1996 by the same Act as established the Environment Agency in England and Wales. Although both were designed to provide a holistic approach to the environment, they do not have identical responsibilities. SEPA is not responsible for flood defence or water resources (publicly owned water authorities still exist in Scotland). It is responsible for the protection of 50,000 km of rivers and lochs, 800 sq km of estuaries and over 7,000 km of coastal waters. There are some 40,000 consents for discharges to these waters. It regulates 1,200 industrial processes, 800 licensed waste disposal sites, and disposals of radioactive wastes from ten nuclear sites.

2.39 SEPA has recognised that the town and country planning system is a key tool for change, with an influence on a wide range of environmental issues from meeting carbon dioxide emission targets to the provision of waste disposal facilities. SEPA makes inputs to the system at the three levels of national policy, preparation of development plans and development control, helped by the statutory requirements for local authorities to consult it. The National Waste Strategy for Scotland has set up 11 waste strategy areas, for which plans are being prepared primarily by groups of local authorities. To ensure those plans have a spatial representation, SEPA has given support to the proposal that all Scottish local authorities should be required to prepare waste plans as part of their development plans (see box 2C).[43]

2.40 **English Nature** is a statutory agency with a board appointed by the Secretary of State for Environment, Food and Rural Affairs. Its three main areas of external work are:

- protecting and enhancing the wildlife value of designated sites

- improving the wider environment and the sea for wildlife

- influencing people's hearts, minds, policies and actions in support of nature conservation.

English Nature has considered the implications of sustainable development for its work, but does not use that concept in its corporate plan.[44]

2.41 The **Countryside Agency** was formed in 1999 by a merger of the Countryside Commission and parts of the Rural Development Commission, and is concerned with the environmental, social and economic aspects of the countryside in England. It advises the government, local authorities and regional development agencies (see 2.52 below) on countryside matters, and is responsible for designating National Parks, Areas of Outstanding Natural Beauty and Heritage Coasts, and for establishing National Trails.

2.42 **Cyngor Cefn Gwlad Cymru**/the **Countryside Council for Wales** is an agency reporting to the National Assembly for Wales, and carrying out in Wales functions performed in England by English Nature and the Countryside Agency. It provides advices on conservation issues and works with local authorities, voluntary organisations and other partners to protect and enhance the landscape, conserve wildlife and habitats, and promote public enjoyment and understanding of the countryside.

2.43 **Scottish Natural Heritage** reports to the Scottish Parliament and Executive, and was established by the Natural Heritage (Scotland) Act 1991. It aims to safeguard and enhance Scotland's natural heritage and diversity; to encourage awareness, understanding and enjoyment; and to promote sustainability. In order to respond to local needs and circumstances, it operates through three area boards, and in partnership with all relevant interests.

PROTECTING THE BUILT HERITAGE

2.44 **English Heritage** was established in 1984 with a duty to secure and promote the preservation and enhancement of ancient monuments, historic buildings and conservation areas in England. It is sponsored by DCMS. It acts as statutory adviser to the government on conservation matters; and to the Secretary of State on the listing of historic buildings and the scheduling of ancient monuments. English Heritage provides grants for repairs to buildings and monuments, archaeological excavations and improvements to conservation area, operating through regional offices. It maintains properties in its guardianship and opens them to the public.

2.45 As an Agency of the Scottish Executive, **Historic Scotland** has responsibility for conservation of the built heritage in Scotland. It schedules monuments of national importance, deals with applications for their alteration and manages over 300 monuments open to the public. It also lists buildings of architectural and historic merit and monitors applications to alter or demolish them. Historic Scotland provides grants for the repair of ancient monuments and historic buildings and runs a programme of rescue archaeology. It provides the secretariat for two independent statutory bodies which advise Scottish Ministers: the Ancient Monuments Board for Scotland and the Historic Buildings Council for Scotland.

2.46 **Cadw**, a Welsh executive agency, was established in 1984 and undertakes duties in respect of the built heritage on behalf of the National Assembly for Wales. It advises on policy issues and is responsible for listing buildings of special historical or architectural importance as well as scheduling ancient monuments. Cadw administers repair grants for historic buildings, and maintains sites in state care and presents them to the public. It also provides the secretariat for the Historic Buildings Council for Wales and the Ancient Monuments Board for Wales.

NORTHERN IRELAND

2.47 The Environment and Heritage Service is an executive agency established in 1996 within the Department of the Environment for Northern Ireland. It is the lead body in implementing environmental policies, and advises the core Department on the development of those policies. Its main activities include the control of air, water and land pollution; the identification and management of sites of nature conservation value; the management of country parks, countryside centres and historic monuments; and the protection and recording of historic monuments and buildings. Its main aims are 'to protect and conserve the natural and built environment and to promote its appreciation for the benefit of present and future generations'.[45]

2.48 Executive responsibility for development planning and development control in Northern Ireland is also in the hands of an executive agency of DOENI established in 1996, the **Planning Service**. Its main aim is 'to plan and manage development in ways which will contribute to a quality environment and seek to meet the economic and social aspirations of present and future generations'. Its operational objectives are to:

- ensure that development planning and development control promote the orderly and consistent use of land

- provide a planning framework for and support the implementation of physical regeneration projects.[46]

ORGANISATION IN THE ENGLISH REGIONS

2.49 In 1994 an integrated Government Office was created in each of the nine regions of England by merging the offices of four government Departments: Environment, Transport, Employment, and Trade and Industry. A review of these Government Offices by the Performance and Innovation Unit concluded that they should be regarded as the leading element of central government in the regions in relation to issues with 'a cross-cutting dimension'.[47] Government Offices now bring together the regional operations of six government Departments, and are at the centre of the complex network of activity summarised in table 2.1.

Table 2.1

Key regional planning documents in England (outside London)

	regional planning guidance	regional economic strategy	regional sustainability framework
prepared by	*draft prepared by local authorities in the region, acting collectively* regional planning conferences/new regional chambers (local authority members and at least 30% representatives of businesses and the voluntary sector)	*regional development agency* 8-15 members appointed by Ministers; chair and majority of members with business experience; 4 members from local government; funded by the Government Office	*Government Office or regional round table*
form of scrutiny	public examination, arranged by Government Office, which then consults on any proposed modifications	none	public examination no formal process of assessment or approval
adopted by	Secretary of State	regional development agency	regional chamber
timescale	15-20 years	5-10 years	none specified?
guidance on preparation issued by	DETR in PPG 11, revised 2000 now DTLR	DETR (until June 2001) DTI (since June 2001)	DETR 2000
consultation procedures	formal consultation stages: public conference on draft; draft RPG submitted to Secretary of State; proposed changes to draft RPG. Community participation is encouraged, especially of Local Agenda 21 groups	RDA must have regard to views of, and be willing to give an account of its activities to, *regional chamber*	none specified
date produced	new style RPG began in 1999	April-October 1999	2000 and 2001
date revision due	continual review and annual monitoring of implementation and impacts, where possible	statutory requirement is to keep under review	discretionary
statutory basis	non-statutory	statutory	non-statutory

REGIONAL PLANNING GUIDANCE

2.50 Between 1991 and 1996 the Secretary of State for the Environment issued regional planning guidance for each region, to provide a framework for the preparation of development plans. The guidance was drafted by conferences formed by the local authorities themselves, in consultation with bodies representing interests such as business, conservation and agriculture.[48] A further round of regional planning guidance covering the period to 2016 is now nearing completion.[49]

2.51 The constitutions and roles of the regional groupings of local authorities have evolved, although to varying extents. In four regions responsibility now lies with a *regional chamber* comprising the local authorities in the region and other stakeholders.[50] In other regions the responsibility lies either with a regional planning conference formed by the local authorities in the region or with a local authority association, although other stakeholders will again be involved. Regional planning guidance is published as a draft, and then considered at a public examination by a panel appointed by the Government Office for the region. The regional planning body reviews the guidance in the light of the panel's report and submits a final draft to the Government Office. The Secretary of State for Transport, Local Government and the Regions may propose changes, on which there is also consultation. The Secretary of State determines the final form of the guidance, and it is then issued by the Government Office. The regional planning body remains responsible for monitoring implementation of the guidance and reviewing it.

OTHER FORMS OF REGIONAL PLANNING

2.52 The main thrust of government policy towards the English regions over the last few years has been the setting up of business-led regional development agencies (RDAs) to promote economic growth.[51] They took over responsibility for implementing a wide range of government programmes[52] and have five statutory purposes:

- to further economic development and regeneration of their region

- to promote business efficiency, investment and competitiveness

- to promote employment

- to enhance the development and application of skills relevant to employment

- to contribute to the achievement of sustainable development in the UK where applicable.[53]

RDAs were encouraged to take an integrated and sustainable approach to regional economic issues and develop links between improvements in productivity and business competitiveness and measures to deal with the underlying problems of unemployment, skill shortages, inequalities, social exclusion and physical decay. RDAs were formally established (outside London) in April 1999 and moved rapidly to fulfil the statutory requirement to produce a regional economic strategy. All the strategies were in place by October 1999.

2.53 Other kinds of strategic planning document are also produced for the English regions. They do not have an explicit environmental purpose or dimension, but they sometimes have considerable implications for the sustainability of development, and in particular for land use within the region. They include regional housing statements, regional rural development plans, regional cultural strategies and (in regions containing areas qualifying for assistance from the EU Structural Funds under Objective 1 or Objective 2) single programming documents.

2.54 The third key document shown in table 2.1 is the sustainability framework which the government encouraged each region to produce.[54] Although much of the initial work was undertaken by Government Offices, some regions set up round tables which carried out the task: the aim in all cases was to obtain wide commitment and ownership across the region, and in particular to ensure that the framework was endorsed and adopted by the regional grouping of local authorities.[55] In some regions the sustainability framework has only recently been produced.[56] In theory, regional sustainability frameworks provide a common vision and context for RDA strategies and regional planning guidance by joining up social, economic, environmental and resource considerations and identifying the sustainable development challenges for the region. Regional sustainability frameworks are also supposed to provide the sustainable development objectives by which regional planning guidance is to be assessed (sustainability appraisal). Government has been at pains to make it clear however that they 'will not be in a hierarchy with other plans'. We discuss in chapters 7 (for sustainability appraisals) and 10 how these complex procedures at regional level are working in practice.

CONCLUSION

2.55 'Sustainable development' is now widely accepted as an objective for public bodies which have functions directed to, or important for, the protection and improvement of the environment. It is a difficult and complex concept, however, and has been given many different meanings. We regard some common interpretations as unsatisfactory. In the next chapter we trace the origins of the term 'sustainable development', and explain how we believe it must now be interpreted and applied.

2.56 Then in chapter 4 we consider whether the wider planning system is working effectively, and whether it is capable of handling the new tasks now being placed upon it by the pursuit of sustainable development.

Chapter 3

THE NEW CONTEXT

The general commitment to 'sustainable development' creates a new context for policy and regulation. How should that term be interpreted? What sort of approaches have to be adopted to ensure that the environment will be safeguarded?

3.1 In the previous chapter we noted the extent to which the concept of sustainable development has been embedded in legislation and policy: in the Act under which the National Assembly for Wales operates, in the town and country planning system, in institutions at regional level in England, and in the statutory duties of the Environment Agencies. 'Sustainable development' is not a term that can be defined in any simple way. It is often used loosely, and there is much confusion about its meaning and implications.

3.2 In this chapter we outline the character of the UK's commitment to sustainable development (3.3-3.12). We discuss what is involved in safeguarding environmental sustainability (3.13-3.23). We draw attention to the central importance of land in this context (3.24-3.31). We consider what lessons can be learned from the approach now adopted in New Zealand (3.32-3.35). We then discuss the kinds of policy instrument that need to be used in the UK in order to safeguard environmental sustainability (3.36-3.44).

THE COMMITMENT TO SUSTAINABLE DEVELOPMENT

3.3 The global concept of sustainable development was first expounded in the World Conservation Strategy of 1980.[1] The definition most often quoted, however, comes from the report of the World Commission on Environment and Development (the Brundtland Commission), published in 1987: 'development that meets the needs of the present without compromising the ability of future generations to meet their own needs'.[2]

3.4 The Brundtland Commission regarded the urgent needs of the world's poor as having overriding priority. By 'development', it meant actions taken to enhance the ability of the environment to support human populations, particularly by removing limitations imposed on that ability by the state of technology and by social organisation. What are classed as 'needs', however, varies from country to country, and between communities. So does the meaning of 'development'.

3.5 For several decades there has been keen debate over the extent to which the environment imposes limits on development and on human numbers.[3] The Brundtland Commission accepted there were ultimate limits, but believed the environment had the capacity to meet present and foreseeable future needs if social and technological obstacles could be overcome. The second World Conservation Strategy, published in 1991,[4] argued that development should be people-centred and conservation-based, and defined 'sustainable development' as the process of improving the quality of human life while living within the carrying capacity of supporting ecosystems. These and later analyses confronted the problem that, while there must, in theory, be finite limits on the capacity of the environment to support human and other users, it is extremely difficult to define them in practice.

3.6   The Brundtland Commission's call for sustainable development had a major influence on the United Nations Conference on Environment and Development held at Rio de Janeiro in June 1992. Agenda 21, the principal international agreement to emerge from that conference, consists of 40 chapters grouped in four sections, dealing respectively with social and economic processes to advance sustainability; the conservation and management of resources for sustainable development; strengthening the role of major groups within national communities, and the enhancement of the means for action.[5]

3.7   By endorsing the Rio resolutions, all governments accepted an obligation to produce national strategies for sustainable development; and many have done so, under a variety of titles.[6] The UK strategy published in 1994 was one of the first. Citing the Brundtland Commission's definition, it described sustainable development as a way of reconciling the desire of 'most societies … to achieve economic development to secure higher standards of living, now and for future generations', with a simultaneous wish 'to protect and enhance their environment, now and for their children'.[7] It reviewed, by economic resource and by economic sector, where the UK stood, and where it was projected to stand in 20 years' time on the basis of current policies. It then reviewed the processes which existed, or could be established, for pursuing sustainable development and monitoring progress. It was flanked by a Climate Change Programme,[8] a Biodiversity Action Plan[9] and a Sustainable Forestry Programme.[10] But it did not itself contain any new policies or targets, nor contain any explicit overall goal or principles. In contrast, the Australian national strategy, for example, included objectives and guiding principles, and took as the goal 'development that improves the total quality of life now and in the future, in a way that maintains the ecological processes on which life depends'.[11]

3.8   The Labour government elected in 1997 published a Sustainable Development Strategy in May 1999.[12] This says that 'ensuring a better quality of life for everyone, now and for generations to come' is 'the simple idea … at the heart' of sustainable development. It interprets sustainable development as meaning 'meeting four objectives at the same time, in the UK and the world as a whole':

• social progress which recognises the needs of everyone

• effective protection of the environment

• prudent use of natural resources, and

• maintenance of high and stable levels of economic growth and employment.

It contains (box 3A) lists of seven future priorities (including 'working with others to achieve sustainable development internationally') and ten guiding principles (including 'taking a long-term perspective', 'respecting environmental limits' and 'using scientific knowledge').

+---+
| **BOX 3A**   **UK SUSTAINABLE DEVELOPMENT STRATEGY** |
+---+

The UK Sustainable Development Strategy published in 1999 identifies as *future priorities* for the UK:

- more investment in people and equipment for a competitive economy
- reducing the level of social exclusion
- promoting a transport system which provides choice, and also minimises environmental harm and reduces congestion
- improving the larger towns and cities to make them better places to live and work
- directing development and promoting agricultural practices to protect and enhance the countryside and wildlife
- improving energy efficiency and tackling waste
- working with others to achieve sustainable development internationally.

It identifies ten *guiding principles* for government policies:

- putting people at the centre
- taking a long-term perspective
- taking account of costs and benefits
- creating an open and supportive economic system
- combating poverty and social exclusion
- respecting environmental limits
- the precautionary principle
- using scientific knowledge
- transparency, information, participation and access to justice
- making the polluter pay.

3.9 The devolved administrations are making their own commitments to sustainable development. The National Assembly for Wales has used the Brundtland Commission's definition, and adds by way of explanation: 'We will take social, economic and environmental issues into account in everything that we do.'[13] The Northern Ireland government intends to publish a draft scheme in March 2002 and adopt a scheme formally in March 2003.[14] Regrettably, the Scottish Executive has not sought to apply an overarching approach, but it has adopted three 'sustainable priorities': waste, energy and travel (WET).[15]

3.10 The current UK strategy describes its approach as 'based on achieving overall improvements in environmental quality and, where overall standards are already relatively good, ensuring that they do not slip back'.[16]

3.11 Through the first of the four main aims quoted above (3.8) the government accepts that an essential component of sustainable development is equity, not only between generations and between nations, but also between different sections of the community within a nation. As the environmental justice movement has argued,[17] any costs incurred in moving towards sustainability should not fall disproportionately on disadvantaged sections of the community. Moreover, sustainability is now generally taken to require positive action to remove clear inequalities in satisfying basic human needs, such as health.

3.12 Ultimately, sustainable development has to be achieved on a global basis; first because it incorporates the notion of equity between nations, and also because some of the threats to sustainability (such as climate change) are global in nature. In this report we focus on what the UK should do to move towards sustainable development. But we envisage the priorities for action as anchored increasingly in obligations under conventions and agreements which are intended to contribute to achieving sustainable development worldwide.

SAFEGUARDING ENVIRONMENTAL SUSTAINABILITY

3.13 Interpretations of sustainable development like that in the current UK Sustainable Development Strategy (3.8) have been much criticised for underplaying the extent to which their aims may come into conflict with each other. There are substantial practical difficulties in achieving environmental, social and economic goals simultaneously. It is often suggested that achieving sustainable development involves 'striking a balance' between conflicting aims, the appropriate balance depending on the particular circumstances.

3.14 We believe this is too facile. Environmental, social and economic goals are different in character. In many interpretations of sustainable development, environmental considerations have been far too readily subordinated to economic and social interests. There has to be a recognition that the environment can impose constraints on human actions. Sometimes this will lead to hard choices. But, in our view, the goal of protecting and enhancing the environment must be fundamental.

3.15 The statement by European Environmental Advisory Councils (EEACs) mentioned earlier (1.26) puts the case for respecting the natural environment as follows:

> The natural environment ... offers *critical* resources and services, which can seldom be substituted by, or traded for, the economic or social products of civilisation. [It] is our home, and the living world in all its diversity is of fundamental importance to our dignity as humans. These intrinsic aspects of nature may be termed *unique values*. Together with the *critical values* of the natural environment, they constitute a heritage that a *sustainable* society has to be able to hand on to future generations.

3.16 Protection of the environment involves safeguarding, not only natural features, but highly valued features which are the products of human actions. It also embraces (consistent with the usage in previous Commission reports) protecting human health against damage from pollution and other environmental factors.

3.17 Achieving environmental sustainability means achieving legitimate economic and social goals in ways that safeguard, and wherever appropriate enhance, the quality of the environment.

3.18 In proposals for a sustainable development strategy for the European Union published in May 2001, the European Commission offered a long-term vision of a society which will be more prosperous and more just, with a cleaner, safer, healthier environment – a society which will deliver a better quality of life for our generation, our children, and our grandchildren. In such a society economic growth would support social progress and respect the environment, social policy would underpin economic performance, and environmental policy would be cost-effective.[18] Such a vision can be realised only if resource consumption and environmental degradation can be decoupled from economic and social development and there is a major reorientation of public and private investment towards less damaging technologies and lifestyles.

3.19 Environmental sustainability entails protecting valued features of the environment, but does not mean preserving every feature in its present state. Some changes enrich the environment, as when heath land is restored or native trees planted. A farming system may sometimes be replaced by another which is equally, or more sustainable. Sometimes new wild habitats can be created to replace those that have been lost; establishing new reed beds in parts of lowland England is an example.

3.20 Nor does environmental sustainability imply a ban on all releases of chemicals or energy into the environment. For example, the EC Directive on water quality for freshwater fish[19] distinguishes two states of fresh waters, one suitable for salmon and trout and the other (which may be moderately polluted) suitable for coarse fish. It accepts that either state is a legitimate objective, depending on the nature of the waters in question and the uses to be made of them. We have the power to make collective choices, in the light of values and scientific knowledge, about the states of the environment we want.

3.21 The environment has a degree of resilience, but its relationship to the stresses placed on it is complex, and generally non-linear. It is not infinitely adjustable. Freshwater ecosystems can again serve as an example. If the stresses on an ecosystem become more intense it may suddenly adopt a new configuration. This may represent a stable state; but, if the stresses continue to rise, there may be a further change of state. If waters become severely polluted, with prolonged deoxygenation or high acidity, quite different ecosystems will appear, in which diversity is low and there are no fish. Multiple stresses (for example from a cocktail of pollutants, or a combination of chemicals and physical parameters such as heat, or from a combination of pollution and fishing) can affect ecosystems in complex and at times unpredictable ways.[20]

3.22 The steady increase in the concentration of greenhouse gases in the atmosphere is one example of a long-term trend which threatens global and regional sustainability. It also creates a risk of discontinuous change. In our report on energy we documented the projections of global warming by the Intergovernmental Panel on Climate Change and drew attention to the possibility that abrupt changes in the climate system might be triggered, and have even more dramatic impacts.[21]

3.23 The purpose of environmental planning is to provide an instrument for making collective choices about the states of the environment we want, prevent breaches of environmental constraints, and make adaptations possible when such constraints have unfortunately been breached (as with the changes in climate and consequent rises in sea level that now seem inevitable).

THE IMPORTANCE OF LAND

3.24 The proper use of land is a central issue for environmental sustainability. Land is used for many purposes: most of the profound changes in the physical and social conditions of human existence, from the adoption of settled agriculture to the globalising influence of information technology, have had important land use dimensions.[22] The extent of land is finite. One critical limit on the capacity of the environment is the supply of fertile land: worldwide there is very little which has not already been brought into cultivation.

3.25 Over the centuries, agriculture has succeeded in increasing the productivity of crops, pastures and livestock. Crop yields have increased considerably as new methods have been applied. Carrying capacity (in the biological sense of the capacity of a particular area to support people) has been enhanced by technology and rendered less confining by trade. It is also common knowledge, however, that some of these gains have been at the expense of biological diversity, have demanded a massive injection of energy and fertilisers or have proved unsustainable because of soil degradation, erosion or depletion of aquifers. There are massive challenges to land use if environmental sustainability is genuinely to be attained.

3.26 Most people live in towns and cities. Decisions on land use have considerable significance for their lives. In all probability such decisions contribute to spatial variations in health. There are great inequalities in mortality rates, on a large scale (for example, between England, Scotland and Wales), but also by a factor of at least two between, for example, certain parts of London or between the richest and poorest parts of Glasgow. The causes of these differences are not well understood. Two types of explanation have been put forward. Explanations in terms of *composition* suggest that the individuals living in certain areas have characteristics that predispose them to poor health. Explanations in terms of *context* suggest that, over and above the characteristics of individual residents, there are environmental factors which determine area-level variations in health. This distinction is somewhat artificial: ill health is related to low social status, and a high degree of residential segregation may amplify that effect. For example, if a school only has children from poor families, or a neighbourhood only families in poverty, there may be an emergent geographical property of social deprivation that appears to be related to ill health over and above the socio-economic characteristics of individual residents.[23]

3.27 There are two reasons why decisions about the use of land have a special character. First, the rights of owners of land have been entrenched in legal systems. Second, maintaining land in the condition preferred on environmental grounds is likely, in many parts of the world and certainly in the UK, to require human management.

3.28 In its report on soil the Commission advocated a different view of land ownership based on the concept of stewardship.[24] To give legal expression to the concept of stewardship, every owner of land could be placed under an enforceable obligation to sustain its productivity and biological diversity and other attractive attributes. Following the report of the Policy Commission on Farming and Food[25] there is a genuine possibility that such a concept can gain general acceptance.

3.29 We have to establish procedures for planning and regulating human activities which can ensure that the capacity of land and other environmental resources to support human life is sustained, and where possible enhanced. This requires scientific understanding of the characteristics of particular components of the environment, and a means of evaluating their potential. This in turn leads to choice, for there are almost always alternative ways in which a particular compartment of the environment can be used. Those alternatives involve greater or lesser intensity of use, and greater or lesser transformations from the previously existing state.

3.30 Conversion of forest to agriculture, for example, or traditional agriculture to more intensive methods, results in changes in biological diversity and perhaps some loss of species from the area as a whole. This does not mean the new use is necessarily unsustainable, but the indirect consequences have to be taken into account.[26]

3.31 Despite the critical role of land use, the guidance given to planning authorities does not reflect adequately the fundamental importance of environmental sustainability. Thus the current guidance in England on general policy and principles was produced before the current UK Sustainable Development Strategy and gives as explanation of the principles of sustainable development that '[The planning system] needs to be positive in promoting competitiveness whilst being protective towards the environment and amenity. The policies which underpin the system … seek to balance these aims.'[27] The equivalent guidance in Scotland, produced more recently, is more satisfactory, in that it refers to the planning system as operating 'in the long-term public interest' and places emphasis on enhancing the environment and on social justice.[28]

NEW ZEALAND RESOURCE MANAGEMENT ACT

3.32 The current system of environmental regulation in New Zealand was commended to us as a novel and interesting approach to safeguarding the environment. Under the Resource Management Act 1991, anyone wishing to carry out a development which does not comply with district and regional plan rules must apply for a resource consent. The decision on the application is taken on the basis of the Act's overall objective of 'sustainable management' and an assessment by the applicant of the net environmental effects of the development (what has often been called 'the biophysical bottom line'). 'Sustainable management' is defined as:

> Managing the use, development, and protection of natural and physical resources in a way, or at a rate, which enables people and communities to provide for their social, economic, and cultural well-being and for their health and safety while –
>
> a. sustaining the potential of natural and physical resources (excluding minerals) to meet the reasonably foreseeable needs of future generations; and
>
> b. safeguarding the life-supporting capacity of air, water, soil, and ecosystems; and
>
> c. avoiding, remedying or mitigating any adverse effects of activities on the environment.

3.33 We had discussions with the Rt Hon Simon Upton, the Minister who introduced the Act, and investigated how it has worked in practice.[29] It was regarded both as a form of deregulation (it considerably simplified the regulatory system) and as putting the natural environment at the centre of decision-making. Environmentalists, however, have not always been happy about the decisions reached. There have been proposals that the reference to economic well-being should be removed from the definition of sustainable management, or even that the whole phrase 'social, economic, and cultural well-being' should be removed. Applicants have found the required assessments difficult to produce, and local authorities have found them difficult to interpret.[30]

3.34 We were impressed that the New Zealand Act has a clear explicit purpose of safeguarding sustainability. We also see attractions in the concept of 'sustainable management', which carries the implication of prudent management of a finite resource. Referring to 'management' also avoids any confusion between development to meet the urgent needs of the world's poor (the sense the Brundtland Commission had in mind) and the sense in which that word is used in town and country planning legislation (and in associated phrases such as 'presumption in favour of development').

3.35 We concluded however that the New Zealand model could not easily be transferred to a much more densely populated and highly urbanised country such as the UK. Even in New Zealand, the Resource Management Act is not regarded as dealing satisfactorily with the situations in urban and peri-urban areas. An adequate system for setting and achieving environmental goals for the UK needs to be capable of dealing effectively with much more complex interactions and cumulative effects. Moreover, a single regulatory regime covering both land use and other effects on the environment may be desirable in the long run, but it does not seem a feasible aim in the UK for the foreseeable future.

INSTRUMENTS FOR SAFEGUARDING SUSTAINABILITY

3.36 If the New Zealand model would not be practicable, what approaches need to be adopted to ensure that environmental sustainability is safeguarded in the UK? One well established approach is to recognise and protect the most valuable features of the environment by formal designations, for example as listed buildings, protected species, priority habitats, or areas specially designated for conservation under UK or European legislation. The number and range of such designations has increased very considerably in recent decades, and is continuing to increase. The existing systems of designation are reasonably robust and effective; and, where deficiencies have been identified, legislation has been brought forward to correct them.

3.37 Even where a feature has been recognised as having unique value (3.15), however, its designation as such is not, and should not be, an absolute bar to changes. The apparently rigid protection offered by European legislation such as the Habitats Directive admits exceptions 'for reasons of overriding public interest' including those of a 'social and economic nature'.[31]

3.38 Designated areas and features are only a small part of the whole environment. Statistical indicators have received increasing emphasis as a mechanism for monitoring overall trends, for example in human health or in nature, and in particular for monitoring progress towards sustainability. For such indicators to be valid, they must be based on understanding of the structure and dynamics of environmental systems. That involves constructing models of such systems and reviewing them from time to time to ensure that the chosen indicators remain valid.

3.39 The UK government has promulgated sets of indicators for sustainable development,[32] including 15 headline indicators for its economic, social and environmental components (listed in box 3B). It is publishing annual reports showing the movements in these headline indicators.[33]

BOX 3B	UK HEADLINE INDICATORS FOR SUSTAINABLE DEVELOPMENT	
Economic		
H1	economic output	GDP
H2	investment	as % of GDP
H3	employment	
Social		
H4	poverty and social exclusion	
H5	education	qualifications at age 19
H6	health	expected years of healthy life
H7	housing	
H8	crime	violent crime and vehicles/burglary
Environment		
H9	climate change	greenhouse gases
H10	air quality	days of air pollution
H11	road traffic	
H12	river water quality	
H13	wildlife	farmland birds
H14	land use	% new homes on previously developed land
H15	waste	arisings and management: household and other

3.40 Establishing sets of indicators is only a means to an end. The purpose must be to identify where there may be unsustainable situations in relation to particular environmental resources or services, to formulate policies to correct such situations, and to monitor the effectiveness of those policies. To identify unsustainable situations, something more is needed than an analysis of past trends or a traditional 'state of the environment report' (which is essentially a snapshot of the situation). The pressures on particular aspects of the environment have to be quantified and projected in order to assess the likely future situation. This provides the essential basis for setting clear objectives and quantified targets for moving towards sustainable development. The need for targets and timetables has been emphasised in the statement by EEACs on sustainable development strategies (see appendix D) and by the Organisation for Economic Co-operation and Development (OECD).[34] Up to now the UK government has set few such targets.[35]

3.41 Scientific analysis is essential in determining what are critical environmental resources or services. But it is not sufficient by itself. The procedures that ought to be followed in taking significant decisions about the environment were considered in the Commission's report on setting environmental standards.[36] The three initial stages are: recognising and defining the problem; framing the questions that need to be answered; and formulating policy aims. These stages need to be informed by the articulation of people's values, and where relevant by evaluations of the effectiveness of previous policies. The investigation and analysis which follows definition of the problem and formulation of policy aims may need to involve, as well as scientific assessment, analysis of technological options, assessment of risk and uncertainty, economic appraisal and analysis of how policies might be implemented. The final stage is one of deliberation and synthesis, again informed by people's values, and leading in this context to a clear objective, and where possible a quantified target, for an environmental parameter identified as critical. Identification of what should be regarded as meriting protection as a unique feature of the environment is equally a process that will be informed by people's values, as well as by other inputs.

3.42 In the UK, achieving objectives and targets for environmental sustainability will normally involve a combination of measures. Often these will include measures to influence or control land use, even if the finite supply of land is not in itself the critical resource. The ways in which it is used have significant effects on the sustainability of other resources and services, such as water or the climate system or biological diversity.

3.43 In moving towards sustainability we see a considerable role for economic instruments which seek to internalise the external costs of private actions. Although they are not a panacea, economic or financial incentives should be used wherever possible. There may be scope for much greater use of economic instruments to steer developments which the town and country planning system may not adequately control and encourage regeneration initiatives.[37] However, economic instruments are complementary to direct regulation, not a replacement for it. Direct regulation of land use, and of activities which may lead to pollution, remains a vital instrument for promoting sustainable development and safeguarding environmental sustainability.

3.44 Taking regulatory decisions on individual cases is not an adequate approach by itself in a part of the world as crowded and dynamic as the British Isles. It is essential to work within a broader strategy, so that the interactions between different areas and the cumulative effects of relatively small actions can be taken fully into account in decisions. Such a strategy becomes even more important in the new context created by adopting sustainable development and the safeguarding of environmental sustainability as the goals of policy. The preparation of comprehensive plans for future land use in an area is vital to facilitate the identification and implementation of the options that will be most successful in reconciling economic, environmental and social objectives. And, for environmental sustainability to be safeguarded effectively, an overall view must be taken of all the significant factors which may impinge on particular environmental features such as biological diversity or water resources.

Conclusion

3.45 From the analysis in this chapter of the requirements and instruments for environmental sustainability some key messages emerge. First, regulatory systems which play a crucial part in protecting the environment ought to have that role explicitly recognised. We are impressed by the clear purpose given to the New Zealand Resource Management Act, and by the concept of 'sustainable management' it introduced. In chapter 8 we discuss the overall purpose of the town and country planning system.

3.46 If it does not seem feasible for the foreseeable future to merge control of land use and other aspects of the environment in the UK to create a single regulatory system, this places a priority on finding ways of establishing links between the two systems which are sufficiently effective that environmental sustainability does not suffer. Because many environmental problems are complex and widespread, that means establishing procedures for identifying and resolving the relationships between different factors at a strategic and spatial level. We discuss in chapter 4 the nature of the challenges the planning system has to confront and whether existing arrangements are likely to be adequate to meet that challenge. In chapter 10 we explain what kind of system we believe is required for the future.

3.47 Another key message to emerge is the need to set clear objectives and targets for moving towards sustainable development and safeguarding environmental sustainability. We discuss this further in chapter 8. Such targets, and the implementation programmes which must accompany them, are vital in their own right. They will also make an important contribution to ensuring the necessary co-ordination between the activities of different regulatory bodies.

3.48 Success in setting and achieving challenging environmental targets will be dependent on wide public support and the existence of appropriate institutions. Agenda 21 (3.6) calls on every government to 'seek internal consensus at all levels of society on policies and programmes needed for short- and long-term capacity-building to implement its Agenda 21 programme'. An OECD report has listed a set of requirements for strengthening decision-making, including improving transparency and public participation at all levels of government.[38] The concept of 'social capital' has been used to describe deep-seated features of societies and communities that facilitate collective action and, in particular, the kinds of difficult changes that will have to be made in pursuit of sustainability.[39] We have already advocated the full participation of the public in setting environmental objectives and targets. In chapter 5 we discuss how to engage the public in decisions on environmental matters and strengthen confidence in the planning system.

Chapter 4

AN INCOHERENT SYSTEM

How well suited are present arrangements to assessing the pressures on the environment and planning the actions needed at regional and local levels to safeguard environmental sustainability? How effectively does town and country planning function in this respect? How effective are its links with the plans produced by specialist agencies?

4.1 In the last chapter we identified the purpose of environmental planning as making collective choices about the states of the environment we want, preventing breaches of environmental constraints, and making adaptations possible when such constraints have unfortunately been breached (3.23). We emphasised that the proper use of land is a critical issue for environmental sustainability, and that decisions about land use have wide-ranging social and environmental implications (3.24-3.30). There need to be strong links between the town and country planning system and other areas of environmental policy in order to ensure that decisions about land use take full account of all the environmental implications, as well as the social implications. We suggested that links at a strategic and spatial level are likely to be the most important for this purpose (3.46).

4.2 In this chapter we first explain briefly why we consider a spatial and strategic approach is necessary. We then look at present planning procedures, and in particular at the relationships between some of the main plans produced at present by the bodies described in chapter 2, in order to form a view on whether the present system is coherent and efficient and whether it has the characteristics likely to make it effective in handling the interactions we have highlighted between land use and other aspects of the environment. This assessment of the present system forms the basis for considering in the second and third parts of this report what are the key requirements for an effective system of environmental planning, and how such a system can best be established.

THE WIDER IMPLICATIONS OF LAND USE

4.3 In discussions about sustainability, the concept of an 'ecological footprint' has gained wide currency. The ecological footprint of a nation, city or other area is the total area of land and water required to supply the resources it consumes and dispose of the wastes it produces.[1] A city has a footprint many times its own size. It would be wrong to infer from this that such a city represents an inherently unsustainable form of human settlement. The size of its footprint is determined by the lifestyles of its inhabitants and the technologies used to satisfy their demands. For any given level of consumption, a compact city may place less demand on resources than more dispersed forms of settlement; for example, people living there may travel shorter distances.

4.4 The ecological footprint of an area illustrates dramatically the extent to which resources and the environmental impacts of human activities flow across the boundaries of administrative areas. It highlights the interdependence of town and country in terms of natural resources, but it gives a partial and one-sided view of their relationship. The countryside provides vital services to towns. On the other hand, towns and cities continue to be the principal areas in which ideas of all kinds are exchanged and developed and the bulk of technology evolves. They are also the places where most manufacturing is done, and most public and private services are provided. They are crucial for social and economic progress.

4.5 Urban and rural areas are inextricably linked by modern patterns of mobility. The distances people travel have greatly increased. More than half the total distance they travel is for leisure or personal business.[2] People go to the countryside for recreation, and to towns and cities for entertainment and culture. The Planning Green Paper's discussion of the town and country planning system in terms of 'places in which people can live and work'[3] is far too narrow a perspective to be realistic in the 21st century.

4.6 The original motivation for town and country planning was to integrate the planning and development of urban and rural areas by regulating suburban sprawl. For much of the second half of the 20th century the predominant trend in the UK was for people and jobs to move out of cities and into suburbs and rural areas. Many rural areas came under strong pressures for development at the same time as social and economic problems intensified in parts of major cities. Latterly, central government and the devolved administrations have made strong connections between policies for regenerating large conurbations and safeguarding the countryside. We consider the implications for both urban and rural areas in chapter 9.

4.7 Many other links between urban and rural areas have great significance for environmental planning. Air pollution by ozone or particulates is a regional phenomenon to which processes in both urban and rural areas contribute. Urban development and changes in the agricultural use of land both increase the speed with which rain water reaches water courses, thus increasing the risk of flooding. Run off from rural areas and discharges of waste water from urban areas are both factors in the growing problem of eutrophication of surface waters. Agricultural activities may contaminate the sources from which water is drawn to supply urban populations. Providing additional water supplies for new urban development may require construction of new reservoirs in rural areas or abstracting more water from rivers or underground aquifers (which, unless rigorously regulated, may damage the natural environment or other users).

4.8 Decisions about the locations and types of development may have implications for the use of natural resources over much wider areas. Aggregates for use in construction are the most important mineral covered by the separate minerals plans produced as part of the town and country planning system, which until recently have been governed by the principle of 'predict and provide'.[4] Sites from which minerals have been extracted have provided a major part of the capacity for landfilling of wastes. Increasingly they are being used to provide facilities for recreation and nature conservation. Planning for these various roles needs to be co-ordinated, and assessments and policies need to take full account of the substantial amounts of aggregates dredged offshore. It is also important that new development should not be allowed on sites before valuable minerals underlying them have been extracted. For some purposes recycled and secondary aggregates can be used.[5] Government policy is to encourage that, but the procedures needed to facilitate recycling are not always in place.[6]

4.9 Waste management is another key environmental issue which is both strategic and spatial. For many years urban areas have sent a large part of their wastes to landfill sites in rural areas. Now that the use of landfill sites is being phased out, other kinds of facility will be needed on a large scale in the form of recycling plants and incineration plants. Proposals for such plants have often proved very controversial, and progress in implementing national waste management policies has been very slow. The 'proximity principle' is an attempt to make each area take responsibility for dealing with the wastes it has produced. But waste management has to be planned over areas which are often much larger than a single local authority.

PRESENT PLANNING PROCEDURES

4.10 In studying present planning procedures for the purposes of this report we drew on written and oral evidence, as well as informal presentations and discussions covering all parts of the UK. We examined a number of plans and strategies produced by the various bodies described in chapter 2, some specifically intended to protect the environment and others having major implications for it. To gain insight into the way the present system works as a whole, we also looked more closely at the range of plans[7] currently applying to one area, Cambridge and its environs. We recognise, of course, that no one geographical area can be typical. Cambridge is subject to particular growth pressures. But the evidence we have gathered suggests that the problems of horizontal and vertical integration revealed by an analysis of the Cambridge area are also widely present in other parts of the UK.

4.11 Our overall conclusion is that the UK does not have an integrated or coherent system for identifying and promoting the actions needed at regional or local level to safeguard environmental sustainability.

A PLETHORA OF PLANS

4.12 In the town and country planning system the strategic plan for the Cambridge area is the structure plan prepared jointly by Cambridgeshire County Council and a neighbouring unitary authority, Peterborough City Council.[8] This is one of apparently very few strategic plans to draw on a state of the environment report.[9] The report includes, for example, data on air and water quality and on waste generation and sites of special scientific interest. On the next occasion it will be broadened to include economic and social data, and become a sustainability report. The first main aim in the structure plan adopted in 1995 is to 'sustain and improve the quality of the environment for the benefit of present and future generations'.[10] It contains numerous, often quantified targets covering such things as carbon dioxide emissions, waste, transport and woodland coverage.

4.13 At first sight the main components of environmental planning are present: an assessment of the current situation in the state of the environment report, a clear environmental objective, and quantified targets for key parameters, backed by appropriate policies. The state of the environment report, however, is a snapshot: it does not explore the pressures on the environment by projecting their likely effects over the period the structure plan will cover. The targets mentioned in the previous paragraph cannot form part of the policies in the structure plan because they do not relate directly to land use; instead, they appear in the lengthy explanatory memorandum which accompanies the plan.

4.14 In reality, despite its wide scope, the structure plan is only one among many plans produced by the county council and other public bodies for aspects of the environment in the Cambridge area, or for subjects such as transport which are closely related to the environment. All these plans either relate directly to land use or have substantial connections with it. Although the details vary in different parts of the UK, we have found there may be as many as 30 significant plans for a given area. Table 4.1 shows for England, some of the main plans produced, their provenance, and their geographical scale. They include plans with a very detailed and specific content, such as the one for Cambridgeshire local Environment Agency plans (LEAPs) and the biodiversity action plans (contains objectives and quantified targets for 26 habitats and 19 species).

4.15 It might be possible in theory for such a plethora of plans to add up to a coherent and effective strategy for safeguarding environmental sustainability, and in particular for handling the interactions between land use and other aspects of the environment. There are several reasons, quite apart from the sheer complexity of present procedures, why that is unlikely to happen in practice. One is that, despite their complexity, they are not comprehensive: there is no plan which addresses directly the major land use in the area surrounding Cambridge, intensive agriculture and horticulture.

4.16 Another reason is that the administrative areas used for town and country planning do not necessarily coincide either with the areas most relevant for analysing and managing environmental processes or with the areas most significant in socio-economic terms. The latter point has been acknowledged in the retention of a joint structure plan for Cambridgeshire and Peterborough. However, the economic influence of Cambridge extends across regional boundaries in several directions, and has led to proposals for ad hoc studies, including one 'to investigate what the nature, possible extent and location of future growth might be within the London-Stansted-Cambridge area'.[11] The Environment Agency, on the other hand, focuses on physical geography by organising its activities primarily by reference to hydrological boundaries; LEAPs have been prepared for river catchments.

4.17 While it may never be possible to find a set of boundaries that is equally suitable for all purposes, it is more difficult to justify the differences in timing between plans. One aspect is that different plans frequently cover different future periods. The other, more damaging aspect is the inconsistency in the timetables on which they are prepared and reviewed. The main components of the town and country planning system form a hierarchy, in which it would be logical to produce the top-tier document (regional planning guidance) first, and work downwards to local plans. It has not usually been possible to achieve that sequence in practice (largely because of delays in producing local plans), let alone satisfactory co-ordination with the preparation of other environmental plans. The resulting problems were referred to in much of the evidence we received.

Table 4.1

Current environmental or environment-related plans in England

italic type indicates a plan is not prepared on the basis of administrative boundaries

	Government Office	planning authorities/ regional planning body	other local authority plans	specialist agencies
REGIONAL	renewable energy assessment rural development programme	regional planning guidance regional transport strategy regional sustainability framework regional waste management strategy (forthcoming)		economic strategy (RDA) *regional forward look (EA)* *water resources strategy (EA)* *biodiversity audit* (English Nature)
SUB-REGIONAL		structure plan waste plan minerals plan supplementary planning guidance on specific topics such as landscape character	community strategy local transport plan Local Agenda 21 strategy municipal waste management strategy (forthcoming – joint county/district)	biodiversity action plan (Biodiversity Partnership) *shoreline management plan* (EA/LA)
LOCAL		(district-wide) local plan supplementary planning guidance on specific topics	community strategy air quality management plan Local Agenda 21 strategy	*local Environment Agency plan (EA)* *catchment management plan* (forthcoming – EA) *coastal habitat management plan* (English Nature/EA/LA) *nitrate vulnerable zones (DEFRA)*

4.18 Some striking anomalies of timing which have occurred in producing the current plans for the Cambridge area are:

- regional planning guidance for East Anglia, published in 2000, fails to take full account of significant recent changes in transport policy;

- the Cambridge local plan, adopted in 1996, is based on policies in the 1989 version of the structure plan, but the revised structure plan now current had already been adopted by then, in 1995;[12]

- a new Cambridgeshire transport plan (covering the period 2001-06) has been prepared in advance of the review of the structure plan.

In addition, the Cambridgeshire biodiversity action plan was produced in 1997, too late to be reflected in the current structure plan or the Cambridge local plan.

4.19 The Planning Green Paper proposes to resolve the problems of delays and anomalies within town and country planning by abolishing structure plans and replacing local plans with local development frameworks revised every year. We discuss those proposals in chapter 10. Even if they are implemented, however, they would not deal with the issue of horizontal co-ordination with plans produced by other bodies, or plans produced by local authorities for purposes other than town and country planning. In at least one respect, indeed, problems of co-ordination would be aggravated: although the Green Paper proposes taking away the responsibility of county councils for structure plans, it would leave them responsible for waste and minerals planning.[13] Even with the same body responsible, anomalies already occur over the timetables for producing these types of plan.[14]

ADDRESSING THE ISSUES

4.20 The fundamental dilemma for planning in the Cambridge area is whether it is possible, or desirable, to restrain growth in employment and population because of the environmental consequences such growth would have. The various plans applying to the area do not confront this issue directly.

4.21 The regional economic development strategy seeks to move East Anglia up the European league table of gross domestic product per head, and regards the Cambridge sub-region as an important engine for national economic development. The emphasis in other plans is on managing the pressures by channelling growth to suitable locations. Regional planning guidance requires that development plans should not restrain economic growth; they should make provision for 'housing needs' but 'take account of the capacity of an area to accommodate development'. The policy in the structure plan is that 'Continued growth of population, housing and jobs is to be permitted, but on a selective basis.' It seeks to encourage employment growth in the less buoyant north and east of Cambridgeshire.

4.22 Although some of the wording in plans might be taken to imply a recognition that there ought to be environmental constraints on development, that has not been prominent when decisions come to be taken. Proposals have come forward for reviewing the Cambridge Green Belt and for a new settlement on Green Belt land; the equivocal, and controversial, justification offered has been 'sustainability'. There has not been any systematic attempt to assess the implications of growth in terms of the environment and natural resources.

4.23 Although the Cambridgeshire transport plan has the aim of minimising environmental impacts, it expresses doubts about the feasibility of reducing road traffic, or even its rate of growth, despite the duty to set targets imposed by the Road Traffic Reduction Act (2.21). A comment quoted in a recent study was 'Traffic just keeps growing. Cambridgeshire keeps growing.'[15] If the structure plan policy of encouraging growth in the north and east of Cambridgeshire succeeds, the assumption in the transport plan is that traffic will be boosted because developments there will have to be road-based.[16]

4.24 In view of the low rainfall in East Anglia, and the likelihood that the resources available will be reduced by climate change, a key issue about further development in Cambridgeshire is the availability of water supplies. The structure plan and the LEAP acknowledge that groundwater resources and surface water flows in summer are fully committed. There has been concern about low flows in rivers. Any increase in demand will have to be met by constructing additional storage for winter flows or by imports from outside the area. The latter are mentioned in regional planning guidance, and the structure plan refers briefly to the future need for a new reservoir. However, the environmental implications of these possibilities are not investigated.

4.25 At all levels of town and country planning the availability of water is treated primarily as an issue, not about resources and the environment, but about phasing, given that water companies have a statutory duty to provide supplies once development takes place. Thus regional planning guidance says 'Rates of development should not exceed the capacities of existing or planned water supply systems, taking into account environmental constraints, to meet projected demand.' The Cambridge local plan, adopted in 1996, simply notes that water supply is considered adequate until 2002.

4.26 The danger with this approach is that growth in population could create a 'need' for water which will override environmental objections to new supply schemes. At the public examination of draft regional planning guidance, serious concerns were expressed about the effects of abstractions on water courses and habitats in East Anglia.[17] Following a direction from the panel which conducted the public examination,[18] the Regional Planning Board for East Anglia commissioned the Environment Agency and water companies to carry out an audit of water abstraction in conjunction with the Standing Conference of East Anglia Local Authorities and nature conservation bodies. Following that special exercise, the Environment Agency's reported view is that there will be 'no environmental problems' in making provision for planned development.[19] Some concerns must remain. A point of more general concern is that an assessment of the kind eventually carried out in East Anglia was not an integral part of the regional planning process from the beginning.

4.27 There is no adequate recognition in development plans, or in other plans, of the importance of designing new developments to make less demand on resources. In the case of water, the LEAP lists demand management under 'necessary actions', but with no indication how action is to be taken forward. Regional planning guidance refers to population growth as 'inevitably' leading to additional demands for water. The structure plan says 'all new development will be expected to make efficient use of water', but that is merely a pious hope in the explanatory memorandum, not a formal policy. Formal policies that developers will be expected to 'incorporate energy conservation into the design, siting and orientation of buildings'; and that renewable energy will be 'encouraged', are expressed only in vague terms.

4.28 Good intentions expressed in development plans, such as promoting energy or water conservation, or seeking to relate new development to public transport networks, may not be easy to implement consistently or effectively, even where they are formal policies. The small new settlement of Cambourne some eight miles outside Cambridge, for example, is unlikely to be self-contained, and is not particularly well served by public transport. Many objectives in development plans are expressed in such general terms that it would be difficult to assess how well they have been implemented. In any event, there is little systematic assessment to show whether policies in development plans are being implemented and achieving the desired results.[20]

EFFECTIVENESS OF LIAISON

4.29 A general conclusion we have drawn is that liaison between planning authorities and specialist agencies during the preparation of development plans is often not sufficiently effective to ensure that the plans take full account of environmental constraints. In a planning document for the Cambridge area, the Environment Agency described itself as having 'a key supporting role' for local authorities; and reported active involvement in shaping the regional economic development strategy, biodiversity planning, and preparing a waste management strategy for Cambridgeshire.[21] A senior planner, however, emphasised the need for the Agency to be engaged actively in the preparation of development plans but felt that did not happen at present. The local planning authority has to know 15 or more years in advance what pattern of development will be acceptable from the Agency's point of view. The Agency, on the other hand, appeared to be geared to responding to specific proposals from developers and their drainage consultants.

4.30 The Council for the Protection of Rural England suggested to us that the potential for the Agency to contribute to land use strategy and offer advice to local authorities has been underplayed or largely ignored. They claimed that the Agency has 'not seen it as its duty to offer positive advice to waste planning authorities on more sustainable waste management policies' and that it appears to be 'lamentably under-resourced as a body'.[22] English Nature also identified a 'need for greater integration of Environment Agency work with local authority planning work'.[23] The Agency acknowledged to us that its work on planning liaison was under-resourced; it had no separately identified funding for this function, and about 150 staff had to cover 400 local planning authorities.[24]

4.31 There also appear to be shortcomings in co-ordination affecting other aspects of environmental policy. It is not clear, for example, how the species and habitats targets in the Cambridgeshire biodiversity action plan (4.14) will be incorporated effectively into the development plan. Fewer than 20% of planning authorities have used biodiversity action plans to inform development plan polices.[25] Fewer than one in three local authorities employs an ecologist,[26] and a declining number employ a properly qualified conservation officer for the built heritage.[27] In Cambridgeshire, however, the Biodiversity Partnership has taken a valuable initiative by producing guidance for planners and applicants for planning permission.[28]

4.32 There is no shortage of environmental aspirations in the present planning system. The general impression, however, is one of diffuseness. The many goals formulated for the environment have not been assembled in a single document, and not all of them are spatially referenced. There is no clear sense how the numerous plans relate to each other, which other plans each plan draws upon or feeds into, or what mechanisms (if any) tie it to the wider system. Probably no single person could provide that information for a given area. The erratic connections between different kinds of plan depend too often on weak lines of communication or on initiatives by individuals. Even where there are rhetorical links between different plans, it can be difficult to make them work in practice.

4.33 The existing forms of plan do not allow a comprehensive view to be taken of environmental issues. It was suggested to us in evidence, and confirmed by our analysis of the Cambridge area, that there is 'no context that rigorously [defines] the overall shape of the environment that is actually required' in a given area.[29] Some people believed an overall vision would be provided by the Local Agenda 21 process stemming from the Rio de Janiero conference in 1992 (3.6). In 1997 the Prime Minister expressed the wish that every local authority should have a Local Agenda 21 strategy in place by 2000.[30] Most authorities produced such a strategy, usually under the leadership of staff in the environmental health or planning departments, but they varied widely in character.[31] The Local Agenda 21 process has now been superseded by community planning (2.25-2.28), which has a completely different focus and sponsorship, with much less emphasis on the environment.

4.34 Despite good intentions, there cannot be much confidence that the many environmental objectives expressed in the many plans produced by local authorities and other bodies will be realised in practice. Many are expressed vaguely, with no clear attribution of responsibility for achieving them. It is therefore possible for wide-ranging aspirations to be espoused in plans, without any requirement to demonstrate how they can be met simultaneously.

4.35 It is tempting to conclude that adding new layers of activity has become a substitute for the commitment and co-ordination that could make existing institutional arrangements work better. Indeed, devising new plans is one way of denying the contradictions in a system that seeks both to accommodate growth and to protect and enhance the environment. In such a situation crucial issues can all too easily be shelved to await consideration in another part of the planning process. There may be the temptation to evade difficult issues, especially the long-term questions that are crucial for sustainability.

4.36 Coherent planning is difficult to achieve, especially in the face of rising demands on limited human resources. To be effective, liaison has to be continuous. Planning is inevitably an iterative and cyclical process; plans are subject to repeated review as environmental and social circumstances change and policies evolve. An immense effort goes into preparing the many plans within the present system. That makes it all the more frustrating if a lack of institutional capacity prevents proper co-ordination. There is no evidence that the additional resources required to produce so many separate documents have any commensurate benefit in terms of impact. Indeed the confusion and fatigue engendered by such a large number of plans produced by different bodies at different times may in themselves make the environmental planning system less effective than it could otherwise be.

CONCLUSION

4.37 Some rationalisation and streamlining of the complex environmental planning system described in this chapter would be beneficial. However, the focus needs to be much wider than the town and country planning system. There need to be much more effective procedures for bringing together consideration of economic and social objectives and environmental constraints. Only in that way can the crucial issues be identified, and sometimes difficult choices made, on the basis of adequate information and a full review of the options. We consider in chapter 10 what form new procedures should take.

4.38 For all the proliferation of plans, there is a lack of effective mechanisms for influencing some features of land use and development which are crucial for long-term sustainability. Development plans may express admirable sentiments about issues such as energy conservation, but not in a form and context that are likely to change anything in the real world. We identify in chapter 9 some key issues on which further action is needed, including in certain cases the creation of new mechanisms.

4.39 A further weakness of the present system is the way that information about complex environmental processes is scattered between a number of different bodies. We discuss in chapter 6 how such information can be made much more readily accessible, for the benefit of both planners and the general public; and in chapter 7 how it can be deployed most effectively in assessing the overall environmental implications of projects, plans and programmes.

4.40 Any reform of the system should be designed to help bridge the gap between the planning process and public values and participation. A major shortcoming of the present arrangements is that their complexity makes it very difficult for stakeholders or the wider public to form an overall view of the environmental problems and objectives in a given area or contribute to future policy. In chapter 5 we consider the importance of engaging the public, and the conditions which have to be satisfied if they are to have confidence in the planning system. The more integrated planning we recommend in chapter 10 should provide a more effective focus for public engagement.

The present confused plethora of plans needs to be rationalised. But that must be done in a way that strengthens the capacity for strategic planning and contributes to overcoming the major long-term challenges in achieving environmental sustainability. Planning of land use changes has a major part to play in meeting those challenges, provided that plans take full account of resource requirements and environmental constraints

Part II

Prerequisites for effective planning

Chapter 5

STRENGTHENING PUBLIC CONFIDENCE

What can be done to increase public confidence in the planning system? Can direct public participation in decisions be made more effective, perhaps by extending rights of appeal? Are there ways in which the various regimes for protecting the environment can be made more comprehensible? What benefit should the community obtain when planning permission is given, and how can propriety be protected?

5.1 In part I of this report we reached the conclusion that the UK does not have an integrated or coherent system for identifying and promoting the actions needed at regional or local level to safeguard environmental sustainability. We have also concluded that there are certain essential prerequisites for any effective system of environmental planning. In part II we identify and discuss those prerequisites, before putting forward in the final part of the report our specific recommendations about what kind of system is required in the UK for the future. In chapter 5 we consider why public engagement with the planning process is important and what measures should be taken to strengthen confidence in the regulatory system. It is also essential that planners and others should be able to work on the basis of accurate and comprehensive information about the current and possible future states of the environment; in chapter 6 we consider how to ensure that the best available information is easily accessible. Equally crucial, however, is the effectiveness with which it is utilised: in chapter 7 we consider how environmental information can best be used to aid decision making.

5.2 If the system for setting and achieving environmental goals is to be effective, the general public must have confidence in it. That becomes even more essential if the goals are challenging, strategic and long-term. We do not believe the present arrangements enjoy a sufficiently high level of public confidence.[1] The government claims in the Planning Green Paper that 'what was once an innovative emphasis on consultation' in town and country planning 'has now become a set of inflexible, legalistic and bureaucratic procedures', and at the same time 'people feel they are not sufficiently involved in decisions that affect their lives.'[2] Other processes, such as neighbourhood renewal, are now regarded as 'more flexible and inclusive' ways of planning the future of an area.[3]

5.3 Any system which regulates activities in the public interest[4] must be accountable, but the lines of accountability may be complicated. In town and country planning, regulatory decisions are taken by, or on the authority of,[5] elected local authorities (except in Northern Ireland). They are subject to oversight either directly by a Minister in an elected national government answerable to a Parliament or by an executive agency acting on behalf of a Minister. Local authorities also have other regulatory functions. Many aspects of environmental regulation, however, are handled by non-departmental public bodies which are accountable only in a more indirect way, through a Minister who appoints their board.

5.4 The existence of these basic mechanisms for democratic accountability, however, is not in itself sufficient to ensure the system will enjoy public confidence. The reasons the government has advanced for a lack of confidence in town and country planning are its complexity; delays and unpredictability in giving decisions; frequent failures to engage communities; a lack of customer focus; and absence of effective enforcement.[6] There is much scope for improvement in some of these respects, including eliminating unnecessary delays in the handling of cases. We concentrate here on engaging the public, on making the system simpler and more comprehensible, and on two further factors we believe are vital: ensuring public involvement extends to strategic planning; and ensuring the operation of the system is fair and impartial, and respects the rights of those affected by its decisions. However fast and predictable a system is, it will not win and retain public support if it is regarded as unfair or biased. Nor will it retain public confidence if it is found to lead to unacceptable outcomes.

5.5 People's confidence in a system may reflect their perceptions of regulatory decisions in individual cases, as much as, or more than, the strategic dimension on which this report focuses. In this chapter we consider some current issues relating to the procedures followed in individual cases which we believe have great importance for overall public confidence. In part III of the report we present the case for improvements in strategic planning which we believe will also contribute to public confidence.

5.6 The next section reviews the case for direct public participation in decisions on environmental matters (5.7-5.19). We then identify some respects in which the division of responsibilities for protecting the environment causes complications, and consider possible solutions (5.20-5.29). We discuss rights of appeal against regulatory decisions (5.30-5.47), in particular whether a new body should be created to hear such appeals, and whether third parties should be given more extensive rights. Finally we consider how the town and country planning system treats gainers and losers, and the implications of current proposals for changes in that respect (5.48-5.55); and whether there are ways in which propriety can be more effectively safeguarded in the operation of the system (5.56-5.60).

ENGAGING THE PUBLIC

5.7 The town and country planning system has long made statutory provision for public participation, and was held up in evidence submitted to us as an exemplar in that respect.[7] Public inquiries are held on draft local plans to which there are unresolved objections, as well as on some important planning applications. Drafts of structure plans and regional planning guidance are reviewed at public examinations. Local planning authorities also carry out more or less extensive consultations at earlier stages in the preparation of plans. Some have experimented with new ways of ascertaining public views, such as visioning exercises[8] and computer simulations.[9] This tradition of public participation, however, is under attack: inquiries on development plans and successive rounds of consultation are seen by the Department for Transport, Local Government and the Regions (DTLR) as major causes of rigidity and delay in the system.

5.8 Other environmental regimes, such as those concerned with pollution control, nature conservation or water resource management, have traditionally offered fewer opportunities for public participation. For example, the setting of standards for integrated pollution control and the licensing of individual processes were seen as predominantly technical exercises, without the need for wider public input. There is now an increasing realisation, however, that direct public participation is necessary and valuable in considering any environmental issue. The Environment Agencies have taken a number of initiatives in this direction. To take another example, local biodiversity action plans seek to engage the public and stakeholders in developing local strategies to help achieve national biodiversity targets.[10]

5.9   There was a demand for more inclusive public involvement in evidence submitted during the course of our study.[11] Some doubts can be raised on the basis of experience in town and country planning, and on grounds other than the delays caused. Attempts to engage a broad spectrum of people in the preparation of plans have enjoyed only limited success.[12] Where public participation has had no very obvious effect on the outcome, questions can be asked as to whether the time, effort and cost involved were justifiable in relation to other priorities. Where, on the other hand, public participation has clearly affected the decision taken, that may be portrayed as hijacking of the process by an unrepresentative group, with results which may or may not be favourable for the environment.

5.10   The reality is that participants in planning processes are unlikely ever to be representative of the whole population in any formal or statistical sense.[13] It would be impracticable for everyone to become involved in every issue that affects them. Most people may well be right in seeing no need to concern themselves with many issues that arise. Socially disadvantaged groups are less likely to participate. The length and specialised content of many planning procedures are a deterrent for many people.

5.11   Both groups and individuals, however, have often made effective use of the traditional openings for public involvement. Over time this has brought valuable new perspectives into planning and into wider policies. It has undoubtedly helped to raise the profile of important environmental issues. Public inquiries, for all their limitations, have brought together diverse participants in a visible and relatively open forum and provided vital opportunities for argument, new ideas, and critical scrutiny. It has often taken a series of challenges to individual projects to bring about changes in general policies or underlying assumptions. It is important that this function of planning procedures is not lost as result of the government's current proposals for authorisation of major projects; we discuss that issue in chapter 8.

5.12   More extensive public involvement will not necessarily resolve conflicts, nor lead automatically to policies that are widely acceptable. There will often be problems in defining what constitutes the general good, and in reconciling conceptions of it with particular interests. Attempts to pursue the general good sometimes give rise to burdens borne disproportionately in different localities; we discuss that problem later in this chapter and in chapter 8. Nevertheless, policies, plans and programmes are more likely to be soundly based if they have been the subject of an open and accountable process of deliberation and careful judgement.

5.13   The Green Paper looks towards 'a planning system that fully engages people in shaping the future of their communities and local economies'.[14] The local development frameworks it proposes (which we discuss in chapter 10) would incorporate a 'statement of community involvement' setting out arrangements for involving the community in the continuing review of the framework and in significant development control decisions.[15] The Secretary of State would be able to amend the statement if it was inadequate.[16] Developers putting forward larger and more complex proposals would be encouraged to engage with local communities before submitting a formal application.[17] Other ideas put forward in the Green Paper, such as expanding Planning Aid,[18] are also intended to make the system more accessible and transparent and to promote public participation.

5.14 The Green Paper expects local authorities to share with the community, and obtain endorsement for, the 'long-term vision for the area' and the objectives and strategy contained in the local development framework.[19] The contention is that engagement with the whole community will be more effective because the process of preparing and adopting a local development framework will be shorter and simpler than for the present type of local plan.[20] However the main emphasis in the Green Paper is on public participation at an even more local level than the district, if not in the context of individual planning applications then in the context of action plans for neighbourhoods and villages (presented as 'a new focus for community involvement')[21] and master plans for large development sites.[22]

5.15 Desirable as it is to involve people in this kind of way in the future of their local environments, many of the issues central to this report are strategic issues which need to be considered over larger areas and longer timescales. Involving the public positively at an early stage in the setting of long-term strategic goals is a more difficult task. The Local Agenda 21 process (4.33) has been an attempt to engage local communities in a broader consideration of environmental issues, and planning departments of local authorities have often been closely involved. Because Local Agenda 21 and similar exercises have not had a well defined role within the policy process, however, they have sometimes reverted to considering only very local issues or they have been marginalised and the participants left disillusioned.[23]

5.16 Lack of public involvement in wider environmental issues may in part reflect deficiencies in the structures and opportunities available for involvement at a sufficiently early stage. The Commission's Twenty-first Report examined analogous issues about the setting of environmental standards. It recognised the importance of other inputs to decision-making, of the kind we consider in the next two chapters, such as scientific and technological analysis; but pointed out that the public, as groups and individuals, can bring a wider pool of knowledge to bear on environmental policies and decisions. It also emphasised the crucial relevance of people's values, and concluded that involving the public from the start in formulating strategies is likely to be much more fruitful than merely consulting them on already drafted proposals.[24]

5.17 If suitable structures and opportunities for public involvement can be created, the result is likely to be better policies, which are also likely to be more widely acceptable. Long established approaches for obtaining involvement (such as opinion surveys, consultation documents, public meetings, public inquiries) will continue to play an important role. But approaches also need to be developed at all levels of governance which will provide ample opportunity for deliberation and challenge in a non-adversarial framework. Engagement with the sheer difficulty of finding solutions to some problems enables people to appreciate and share the dilemmas which policy-makers often face.[25] Encountering new facts and insights contributed by others can in itself help to articulate and shape values. The Twenty-first Report illustrated how some local authorities have applied such techniques with some success in developing strategies for waste disposal.[26]

5.18 **We recommend that the demonstrable capacity of public participation to improve plans and policies should be fostered by improving existing procedures and developing new deliberative processes.**

5.19 We believe one important reason why public participation has come to be seen by government and business as a cause of delay, rather than a means of improving decision-making, is that it tends to occur at a relatively late stage, not at the stage of strategic planning. A significant issue for this report is rationalising the proliferation of plans described in chapter 4, and we pursue that in chapter 10. If well conceived and implemented, such a rationalisation will both provide a powerful stimulus to public engagement with the issues and help minimise unproductive delays when individual cases later come to be considered.

REDUCING CONFUSION

5.20 Further obstacles to public participation, and to public confidence in the system, arise at the level of individual planning applications, where what the public perceive as a single issue is often covered by several Acts of Parliament, and may involve the responsibilities of more than one regulatory body. It is important to ensure that situations of this kind do not cause frustration and disillusionment, and that the division of responsibilities does not have damaging repercussions for the environment.

5.21 There is scope for significant simplification of procedures within the functions exercised by local planning authorities. Alongside the legislation for development control there are separate statutory codes covering conservation areas, scheduled monuments, listed buildings and control of advertisements. The Planning and Environmental Law Reform Group of the Society for Advanced Legal Studies has taken the view that the resulting complexity leads to unnecessary costs and delays and alienates and confuses ordinary citizens.[27] The Planning Green Paper accepts this general point, and undertakes to standardise application and administration procedures; to encourage local authorities to provide a single point for applications under different consent regimes; and to initiate a review of the case for integrating them.[28] **We recommend that the legislation on development control, conservation areas, scheduled monuments, listed buildings and control of advertisements should be consolidated and a single consent procedure introduced, provided this can be achieved without any weakening of the present safeguards.**

5.22 A situation widely regarded as unsatisfactory arises where an industrial plant requires both planning permission and consent from another body under pollution control legislation. The latter will normally base its decision on standards for emissions and environmental quality. Pollution or damage to health, and public fears about them, are material considerations the planning authority can take into account, but conditions attached to planning permissions cannot be used in ways that duplicate the pollution control regime.

5.23 One of the main concerns of local people in such cases is likely to be the possibility of health effects as a result of emissions from the plant; and they may be reluctant to accept without further scrutiny the adequacy of the standards used by the pollution control authority. The planning authority will consult people in the area before taking a decision on the planning application, and in some cases there may be a public inquiry. But these procedures are unable to take full account of the main issue of public concern. Most cases which give rise to controversy involve more complex industrial processes which require authorisation from the Environment Agencies, but a similar situation can arise in England if responsibility for controlling pollution from a proposed waste facility lies with the district council and the responsibility for determining the planning application lies with the county council.[29]

5.24 An aggravating factor in such cases is that the application to the pollution control authority is sometimes not submitted until after planning permission has been granted. The Environment Agency has been working with the Local Government Association and the Confederation of British Industry to produce a concordat aimed at synchronising the two procedures and reducing delays and uncertainty.[30] **We recommend that pollution control authorisation and planning permission for industrial plants should be obtained through a single open process involving a common environmental statement** (see 7.27-7.28 below) **and, where appropriate, a joint public inquiry**.

5.25 While implementation of our recommendation would have a significant benefit in increasing public confidence in the regulatory system, there would still be no formal mechanism for identifying the best combination of site and process. That points to the desirability of extending the scope of strategic planning so that it covers, not only land use, but the other aspects of environmental quality which are affected by emissions.

5.26 As well as cases in which the planning authority and another body exercise parallel jurisdictions, there are many other cases under the town and country planning system in which the public may expect to have some reassurance that proper account has been taken of environmental factors. Some planning applications fall into categories for which there is a statutory requirement that one or more of the specialist agencies should be consulted before a decision is taken. Consultation is required for some relatively small developments, for example (in the case of the Environment Agency) construction of a house requiring a septic tank for drainage. For other types of application there is guidance from central government that one or other agency should be consulted. These requirements for consultation are a basic mechanism for co-ordinating the regulation of land use with other environmental factors and ensuring that development control takes sufficient account of environmental issues.[31]

5.27 This mechanism is not working satisfactorily at present. The Environment Agency has had difficulty in allocating sufficient resources to this work; and the resources it can devote may be at the expense of making the contribution that would be desirable to strategic planning.[32] From the viewpoint of the town and country planning system, delays in responding to statutory consultation are seen as a major cause of delay in determining planning applications.

5.28 The Planning Green Paper puts forward proposals for rectifying this situation, including matching any statutory obligation to consult with a statutory responsibility to respond within a specified time, encouraging applicants to carry out such consultations before a planning application is submitted, enabling statutory consultees to charge a fee (provided a substantive response is given within 21 days), and monitoring the performance of government-funded bodies in responding to such consultation.[33] Subject to practical difficulties being resolved, we believe these measures will be an effective way of rectifying the situation, but only if new expectations and responsibilities are matched with appropriate resources.

5.29 The Green Paper also proposes that in future the only statutory consultees in development control should be bodies providing advice which has health and safety implications or operating a parallel consent regime.[34] **We emphasise that there should be no reduction in the obligations on planning authorities to consult the agencies responsible for pollution control, flood defence, conservation of species and habitats, countryside and the built heritage.** Indeed we believe that the views of these agencies need greater weight in some circumstances, such as vulnerability to flooding; we suggest later in this chapter how that might achieved by giving them a right of appeal against the local planning authority's decision. In cases where a parallel consent regime does not operate, and sole reliance must therefore be placed on development control to safeguard the environment, statutory consultation is, if anything, an even more important mechanism. **There will be some types of case in certain areas where the relevant specialist agency can provide the planning authority with standing advice in advance, and so dispense with the need for consultation on individual cases, and we recommend that more effort be devoted to identifying such categories of cases.**[35] Some of the Environment Agency's regions have already adopted this approach for septic tank cases in areas where there is a low risk of groundwater pollution. The integrated spatial strategies we recommend in chapter 10 will be at the level of broad policy, but they should lead to much more effective liaison between local authorities and specialist agencies and reduce the need for consultation on individual cases.

RIGHTS OF APPEAL

5.30 An essential element in public confidence in the town and country planning system is the right of applicants for planning permission to appeal against unfavourable decisions of planning authorities. Box 5A shows the role appeals play in the overall system.[36] Normally appeals are handled by a planning inspector (England and Wales) or an inquiry reporter (Scotland), appointed by, and accountable to, the Minister, who, in the vast majority of cases, has delegated his decision-making power. In addition the Minister can call in any planning application for his own decision rather than that of the local planning authority, though the numbers called-in are a very small proportion of the total applications made each year – about 130 in England. The appeals procedures offer considerable opportunities for third parties to make representations. While local public inquiries still form an important procedure for determining more controversial appeals, a large proportion of planning appeals these days are determined by written representation.

BOX 5A	OPERATION OF THE TOWN AND COUNTRY PLANNING SYSTEM IN ENGLAND

There were around 420,000 applications for planning permission in England in 2000/01. Of these 52,000 (12%) were refused. Just over 15,000 appeals were lodged against refusal, and were reduced by withdrawals to just under 13,000, 25% of refusals. The proportion of appeals allowed was 35%.

The Planning Inspectorate determined virtually all the appeals, largely by written procedures. Only 20% of appeals involved hearings and only 6% local public inquiries. The Secretary of State considered only 0.4% of appeals (about 100). These are likely to have been the more contentious or difficult cases.

5.31 Contemporary environmental legislation involving the grant of a permit or licence has often adopted a similar model of the right of appeal by the applicant against the decision of the authority concerned. Decisions of the Environment Agency, for example, concerning water discharge consents or licences under integrated pollution prevention and control (IPPC) can be appealed to the Secretary of State; and in a number of these areas, the actual power of decision making on the appeal has since 1997 been delegated to the Planning Inspectorate.[37]

5.32 These rights of appeal are restricted to the applicant for planning permission or the relevant licence, and are concerned with the merits of the case, essentially giving the opportunity to have the application reconsidered by another decision-making authority. As such, they need to be distinguished from the right to challenge the legality of the decision in the courts by way of judicial review or by statutory appeal under town and country planning legislation. The courts have consistently emphasised in such cases that it is not their role to substitute their judgement for that of the decision-making body, even if they feel it might have been misguided. Their concerns are with whether the decision is legally correct, involving such issues as the correct interpretation of the legislation, procedural fairness, taking into account only legally relevant matters, and acting not wholly unreasonably. In practice, the boundaries between substantive review by the courts and purely legal review are not always clear-cut, and are probably becoming more blurred with the emergence of broad legal principles, such as proportionality[38] and those contained in the Human Rights Act 1998, and the growth of European Community legislation in the environmental field. Nevertheless, the distinction between a merits appeal and an appeal concerning the legality of a decision remains important.

5.33 The Human Rights Act may also have direct implications for the current system. In the first major legal challenge to present arrangements, the House of Lords held in the Alconbury case,[39] decided in 2001, that the role of the Secretary of State, as both a policy-maker and a decision-maker in individual planning cases such as call ins was, when taken together with the right of judicial review, compatible with the requirement under the European Convention on Human Rights to have civil rights determined by an independent body. That decision, however, dealt only with the position of the Secretary of State, and recognised that planning decisions in general raise questions of civil rights. It has left open the position of planning inspectors making delegated decisions; the extent to which third parties have rights; and the extent to which other areas of environmental regulation are equally subject to such principles.

5.34 The last ten years have seen a substantial increase in the number of judicial reviews on planning and environmental matters, despite the heavy costs involved. At the same time there have been calls for some form of specialised environmental court or tribunal, the most radical suggestion perhaps being that of Lord Woolf, the current Lord Chief Justice, who in 1991 proposed the setting up of a court which would act as a 'one-stop shop' handling all aspects of an environmental dispute, including criminal matters, judicial review, and civil liabilities.[40] Lord Woolf revisited the subject in a lecture in May 2001 and again suggested there was a case for some new form of environmental court or tribunal.[41] Meanwhile, a major study for the Department of the Environment, Transport and the Regions conducted by Professor Malcolm Grant and published in May 2000 examined the use of environmental courts in a number of other jurisdictions including New Zealand and New South Wales.[42] The report did not advocate a particular model for the UK, but concluded there were serious weaknesses in current structures, and recommended six possible institutional arrangements for consideration, ranging from a Planning Appeals Tribunal to an Environmental Court as a division of the High Court. The government's response, in October 2000, was that it did not consider the case for reform had been made.

5.35 Against that background we have considered the current arrangements for appeals in planning and environmental cases. We have looked in particular at the position under English law, but we believe parallel conclusions can be drawn for Scotland and Northern Ireland. What is needed is a system that commands public confidence, improves consistency, is effective at reaching decisions and is not unduly costly. Our main concern is with merits appeals. With the Administrative Court now established within the High Court, we are not convinced that there is a need for a specialist environmental court dealing with judicial review or statutory appeals on legal grounds. Criminal offences concerning planning or environmental matters are probably best left to the ordinary criminal courts, though there is a case for improved guidance on sentencing and more training, especially for magistrates.

5.36 For decisions on environmental matters taken outside the town and country planning system, however, there is a great deal of inconsistency at present, both in whether there is a right of appeal on merits and in who decides any such appeal. Some appeals are made to the Secretary of State. Others, such as those concerning contaminated land or statutory nuisances, are made to magistrates' courts, which often lack the expertise to handle the considerable technicalities involved. In many contexts, for example the granting of consents in relation to genetically modified organisms, there is no right of appeal on merits. Procedures have grown up haphazardly with no apparent underlying principle, and we consider they fail to provide a system appropriate for contemporary needs. **We recommend the establishment of Environmental Tribunals to handle appeals under environmental legislation other than the town and country planning system, including those now handled by planning inspectors.**

5.37 Establishing an Environmental Tribunal would be a significant contribution to a more coherent and effective system of environmental regulation. We envisage such a Tribunal would consist of a legal chairperson and members with appropriate specialised expertise. It would rapidly develop the authority and understanding needed to handle complex environmental cases. We envisage several tribunals would be established to cover England,

and similar tribunals for Wales, Scotland and Northern Ireland. On points of law there would be a right of appeal from the Tribunal to the High Court. Applications for judicial review on environmental matters would not be considered by the High Court unless the applicant had exhausted any remedy available from the Environmental Tribunal or from other sources. The costs of setting up such a system need not be excessive compared to the benefits that would follow in improved efficiency and effectiveness, as figures supplied to the Review on Tribunals indicate. For comparison, costs of Valuation Tribunals, established on a county basis in England, run to £10 million a year.[43]

5.38 The precise jurisdiction of the Environmental Tribunal would be a matter for government, but we have indicated in box 5B various areas that would be appropriate. We envisage civil litigation will continue to be handled by the civil courts and criminal matters by the criminal courts. The new Tribunals would take over such functions as the present jurisdiction of magistrates' courts on such subjects as contaminated land and statutory nuisance. Although in general the Tribunal should have the final right of decision on appeals submitted to it, there may be cases of acute policy sensitivity where it ought to make a recommendation to the Minister rather than the final decision, and the Alconbury decision implies that such a mechanism would be consistent with the Human Rights Act. Its role would then be similar to that of a planning inspector where a planning appeal is recovered by the Secretary of State. The Tribunal's main concern would be with appeals, but it might have some original jurisdiction, for example in deciding statutory nuisance cases currently taken by complainants to a magistrates' court.

5.39 A further development of this model would combine the Environmental Tribunal with the Planning Inspectorate to establish a Planning and Environment Tribunal (on the lines of some of the options considered by Professor Grant). This would resolve the doubts remaining about the position of planning inspectors in relation to the Human Rights Act (5.33). It would be an advantage to have a firm institutional linkage between the appeals system for land use and the procedures for more specialised environmental regulation. Such a development may come in time. But our view is that it will be preferable for a tribunal to start by taking over and consolidating the wide variety of other procedures for environmental regulation, rather than risk being swamped by the much greater volume of planning appeals.

RIGHTS OF THIRD PARTIES

5.40 A very important distinction between appeals on merits and judicial review is that appeals by way of judicial review are not restricted to the applicant. Third parties such as neighbours or amenity groups may also bring judicial reviews against, say, the decision of a local planning authority to grant planning permission, the Environment Agency to grant an IPPC licence, or the decision of the Secretary of State on a merits appeal. To do so, they have to satisfy the court that they have 'sufficient interest'. Although in the 1950s and 1960s courts would adopt a strict approach and usually accept applications only from those with local property interests affected, contemporary practice is far more liberal. Local amenity groups and national environmental organisations have frequently been granted leave to bring judicial review, particularly if they made representations concerning the original application.

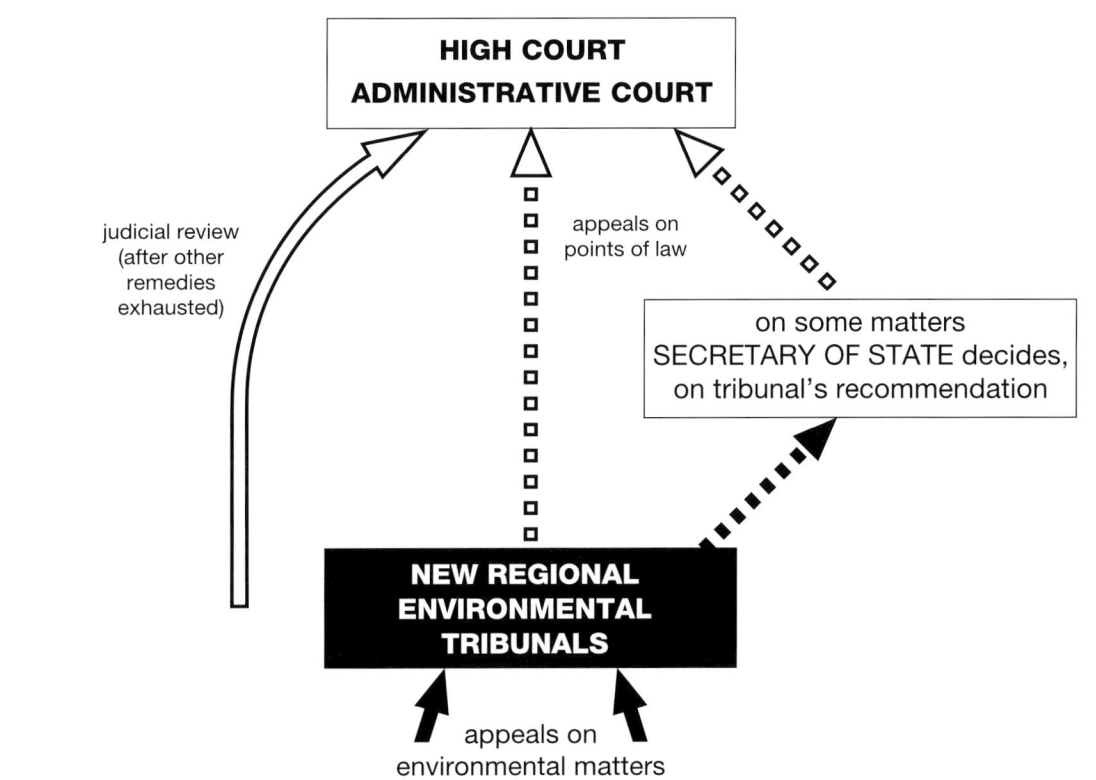

The proposed **Environmental Tribunals**, organised regionally, would hear merits or legal appeals on a range of environmental matters, including:

appeals from decisions by Environment Agency (on IPPC, discharges to watercourses, waste licences, etc)

appeals, currently heard by magistrates' courts, from notices served by local authorities in relation to contaminated land and statutory nuisances

designation of sites of special scientific interest and Habitats Regulations

decisions by Secretary of State on licences for genetically modified organisms and other government decisions where there is no right of appeal at present other than by judicial review

Access to Environmental Information Regulations.

The **criminal courts** would deal with environmental offences in the same way as at present; and, although losing some specialised work to Environmental Tribunals, magistrates would be given improved training. One court in each county might be designated to handle environmental offences.

The **civil courts** would continue to deal with environmental disputes between private parties on issues such as nuisance or negligence.

5.41 The Aarhus Convention (described later in box 6A) contains important provisions concerning rights of appeal against decisions of public authorities to permit a range of specified projects and activities. Article 9 requires that members of the public with a sufficient interest, or maintaining that a right conferred by the Convention has been impaired, shall 'have access to a review procedure before a court of law and/or another independent and impartial body established by law, to challenge the substantive and procedural legality of such decisions'. Non-governmental organisations promoting environmental interests are to be deemed to have sufficient interest in this context. Some may argue, especially since the Alconbury decision, that existing procedures in the UK, most notably the availability of judicial review, fulfil these requirements. The Aarhus Convention does not directly require a right of appeal for third parties,[44] but we have concerns that existing arrangements for the involvement of objectors in the decision-making process may not be consistent with the spirit and objectives of the Convention.

5.42 The reasoning advanced for the disparity in treatment under the town and country planning system between applicants for planning permission and other parties is that it is the applicant whose immediate rights are at stake; and that the local authority or specialist environmental agency is considered to be acting in the public interest, and has a duty to balance public interests against the private interests of the applicant. We believe this disparity reflects a pro-development bias within the system, and that the time has come for change. Logically, one way of removing the disparity would be to have no right of merits appeal, either for the applicant or for third parties. This would follow the line of arguments in the Planning Green Paper rejecting third party appeals on the ground that they would not be consistent with our democratically accountable system of planning' where 'elected councillors represent their communities.'.[45] If all rights of appeal were removed, it would remain possible to mount legal challenges in the courts, but the merits of a planning application would be handled wholly by the local authority, subject only to the possibility that it might be called in by the Secretary of State. Perhaps taking the Green Paper's arguments to this logical conclusion would be deemed too radical.

5.43 We note that third party rights of appeal exist in other jurisdictions, including Ireland and New Zealand. On the question of principle, while applicants may be considered to have specific rights in respect of the proposed development, third parties now increasingly possess legal rights which may be affected by decisions to grant permission, such as those under the Human Rights Act or inherent in European Community environmental Directives. The availability of judicial review is not an effective substitute for an appeals mechanism in this context.

5.44 We therefore favour introduction of a third party right of appeal, but we do not believe it should be an unrestricted right available to any third party under any circumstances. Subject to compliance with the Human Rights Act and the Aarhus Convention, the right of appeal should be available only in certain circumstances that would be specified in legislation. Appropriate criteria might include the size of a development and whether the applicant has been required to provide an environmental impact assessment. Despite the arguments in the Green Paper, we consider it is possible to devise a satisfactory set of clear criteria: it will be for government to put forward detailed proposals. A clear candidate is where a local planning authority takes a decision which is not in accordance with the development plan.

That presupposes the system of development plans can be improved to overcome the problems created by plans which are technically in force but manifestly out of date, an aspect we discuss in part III of this report.

5.45 We also consider that, where a decision by a local planning authority is not in accordance with the views expressed by a statutory consultee, that body should have a right of appeal on merits. A right of appeal in that type of case, which is not mentioned in the Green Paper, would be an important mechanism to secure greater integration between the planning and environmental systems. Even if statutory bodies exercised their right of appeal only on rare occasions, its existence would strengthen the weight of their views in the process, and provide an important safeguard.

5.46 **We recommend that third parties should have a right of appeal against decisions on planning applications in certain circumstances, and that similar rights of appeal for third parties should be introduced for other forms of environmental regulation.**

5.47 The introduction of such a right of appeal under these conditions should increase public confidence in the system and improve the quality of decision making. Strict time-limits for lodging appeals and provision for costs to be awarded for wholly unmerited appeals would reduce uncertainties. The government's proposals for mediation[46] and improving the performance of the Planning Inspectorate[47] may also play a constructive role. The availability of a right of appeal may also reduce the number of judicial review applications which are more in the way of merits appeals disguised as challenges on grounds of legality; such applications also involve uncertainties and delay, as well as heavy costs in judicial time. In the Green Paper, the government concludes that a third party right of appeal could add to the costs and uncertainties of planning, a prospect 'we cannot accept'. Our own view is that any costs imposed by these changes, or increases in the time taken by procedures, would be a price worth paying to ensure that environmental considerations are given their proper weight, rather than being seen as of less importance than development needs. In time, the existence of a third party right of appeal is likely to influence positively the quality of applications for development.[48]

GAINERS AND LOSERS

5.48 There is unlikely to be public confidence in a regulatory system unless the gains and losses resulting from its operation are generally perceived to be fair, and it is believed to operate impartially. The gains from the operation of the town and country planning system can be very large. In the South East of England, for example, agricultural land worth only a few thousand pounds a hectare can become worth over a million pounds a hectare if permission is given to develop it for housing. The grant of planning permission can also lead to large increases in the value of plots of land in urban areas. The more restrictive land use planning policies are, the larger such gains in land value are likely to be.

5.49 The losses that can result from decisions to grant planning permission take various forms: measurable effects on people who live near a development, costs which the development imposes on the local community collectively, or types of impacts on the environment which are of concern both to a wider group of people and in their own right. Refusals of planning permission can cause losses; but the 1947 Act effectively nationalised development rights in land and the associated development values,[49] and reductions in development values resulting from the refusal of planning permission are not therefore recognised in current legislation, except in special circumstances.[50]

5.50 In general the town and country planning system comes into operation only if and when there is a market demand to change the use of a particular plot of land, or erect buildings on it or modify the use of existing buildings.[51] However, there have long been powers available in public and private Acts to purchase land compulsorily for specified purposes. We touch briefly in chapter 9 on proposals DTLR has recently published to facilitate the use of such powers by local authorities. The principle in compulsory purchase (although it is now being reviewed) is that the price paid for land reflects its present use, rather than the use proposed by the body acquiring it.

5.51 A mechanism for preventing the grant of planning permission causing losses to the community collectively is provided by section 106 of the Planning and Compensation Act 1991, which enables a local planning authority to negotiate an agreement with a developer to whom it is granting planning permission. In this way it can obtain more from the developer than it could require unilaterally by attaching conditions to the planning permission,[52] the lever being the prospect that planning permission will otherwise be refused. A section 106 agreement may oblige a developer to contribute to the costs of infrastructure or services which the local authority considers necessary to facilitate the proposed development, for example modifications to the local road layout or a new school to serve a large housing estate. This is not fundamentally different to the practice whereby developers construct the roads and sewers within a large site at their own expense and subsequently transfer them to, respectively, the highway authority and the local water company. A developer might also provide public open space; or, where that is possible, agree to create a suitable habitat elsewhere to replace species or habitat which are being destroyed (3.19). Section 106 agreements are also a means of requiring developers to provide affordable housing.

5.52 However, such agreements are at present a major factor undermining public confidence in the town and country planning system.[53] They are negotiated in private by the local planning authority and the developer, with no public involvement. While obtaining benefits for the community out of the profits being made by developers may seem desirable, this particular mechanism can operate in an arbitrary way, in the absence of clear guidelines. The benefits received under an agreement may not necessarily go to the people adversely affected by the development. There is also a danger that, in expectation of benefits under a section 106 agreement, a local planning authority might be tempted to give permission for a development that it would not otherwise have approved.

5.53 Government policy[54] has been that such agreements should be used to offset the loss of, or impact on, any resource present on a site prior to development, but cannot be used to secure a list or range of desirable benefits from developers, even if the local planning authority considers such benefits to be related in some way to the proposed development. As the colloquial term 'planning gain' implies, that guidance is not always followed.

5.54 DTLR has put forward proposals for reform in a consultation paper issued in December 2001.[55] It proposes that the purpose of such 'planning obligations' should be 'to promote the objective of delivering sustainable development'. The options for reform discussed include a strict necessity test, full flexibility and impact fees. The proposal put forward is that local authorities should set standard tariffs for different types of development through the plan-making process. Negotiated agreements would only be allowed if they 'are clearly justified to deliver, for example, site-specific requirements'.

5.55 The proposed system is presented as a major instrument for obtaining affordable housing, allowing contributions for that purpose to be obtained from a wider range of residential developers (not only from those with sites above a prescribed threshold) and from commercial developers. It is envisaged that in some areas a large proportion of the income from the tariffs would go to fund affordable housing. Although we support the aim of increasing the supply of affordable housing, and the government's proposals would bring greater transparency (we return to that aspect below), we also have concerns about them. The link between the obligation and a site would be very much weakened. It would be much less likely that planning obligations would be used to compensate for the adverse impacts of particular developments. The standard tariffs paid by developers would be a levy on their profits (in effect, a betterment levy) with the proceeds going to local authorities to use as they wish (subject to national guidance, but the consultation paper explicitly rejects the possibility that the proceeds might go to a national fund). The financial incentive for the local authority might well be to maximise its income from the levy by granting numerous planning permissions, whether it intends to use the proceeds to provide affordable housing or for other purposes. This might be a temptation to disregard environmental and social considerations when considering both the principle of a proposed development and its design. Despite DTLR's claim, our conclusion is that this system would work against sustainable development, rather than contribute to it. It is outside the scope of our study to consider in more depth what form a new system should take, but there might be more effective safeguards if the permissible scope of conditions attached to planning permissions were widened, thus removing the need for separate arrangements.

PROTECTING PROPRIETY

5.56 The scale of the increases in land values which can follow upon the granting of planning permission, the use of section 106 agreements, and cases in which local planning authorities grant permission for development of their own land have all contributed to public distrust of the planning system.[56] New measures to re-establish public trust are needed. The system must become much more transparent, with decisions more firmly based on clear criteria known in advance. The third party right of appeal we have recommended would make a major contribution because decisions by local planning authorities which are not in accordance with the development plan would be among those which could be challenged (5.44). The planning authority would then have to demonstrate to an inspector that there is a substantial case on public policy grounds for departing from the plan.

5.57 In relation to planning obligations, we welcome the emphasis in DTLR's consultation paper on much greater transparency and effective monitoring, and the intention to apply that to the present system of section 106 agreements.[57] **We recommend that the public planning register should contain, not only all section 106 agreements entered into, but also the heads of agreement between the local planning authority and the developer which provide the basis for negotiating the detailed terms. Local authorities should also be encouraged to consult the public on the terms of such agreements.**

5.58 There have been documented cases where developers have paid for substantial local authority costs, including legal costs at a public inquiry on the local plan, where a major development has had council support.[58] In such circumstances there must be a danger that inappropriate the authority's decisions will be made because the system allows developers with a vested interest undue influence on the decision processes. **Planning authorities must be properly resourced for their tasks so that they will not have the incentive to accept forms of funding which could prejudice their decisions.**

5.59 Local authorities also regularly determine planning applications affecting council-owned land, which can raise important conflicts of interest. One example of this is school playing fields, where decisions can have a significant impact upon the local authority's finances.[59] Planning applications may relate to a development the local authority itself proposes to undertake, or may stem from some form of partnership between the local authority and the private sector or other public bodies, for economic regeneration or other purposes.

5.60 The problem is exacerbated by the vagueness of the legal duties placed on planning authorities at present. The formal safeguard is that the Minister may call in a case for his or her own decision, but there are strong pressures to limit the numbers of cases treated in that way. Nonetheless, transparency and propriety seem to us to indicate that local authorities should not lay themselves open to accusations of partiality. **We recommend that, where a local authority might have a conflict of interest in relation to a planning matter it is considering, there should be a statutory requirement for it to make a formal public declaration of the nature and extent of its interest before taking a decision. We further recommend that the decision whether to grant planning permission for any development above a specified size promoted by a local authority which is also the planning authority or affecting its land should be taken by an inspector or inquiry reporter appointed by the Minister.**

Chapter 6

ACCESS TO ENVIRONMENTAL INFORMATION

What information do we need to have about our current and future environment in order to plan effectively for a sustainable future? Who is responsible for producing that information at present? Is there a need for a more co-ordinated and focused approach that makes better use of modern technology?

6.1 Planning is inherently political in nature, and can never be a completely quantitative or technocratic process. Nevertheless, high quality information which is as comprehensive as possible on the structure and dynamics of environmental systems, the current state of the environment, the pressures on it and its likely response should be an integral part of a modern planning system. The ready availability of these data, together with qualitative information, should help planners and elected representatives enable the realisation of the community's aspirations, help potential developers put in realistic applications, and help the public interact with planning.

6.2 The planning process, and in particular its environmental component, can be thought of as being composed of a repeated sequence of steps: setting a long-term vision, describing the present state of the environment, estimating the impacts of scenarios for action, deciding on courses of action, and monitoring the impacts of the decisions. Quantitative data play a substantial role in the description and monitoring of the environment, and models can be important both in extending the range and coverage of measured data and in scenario assessments. A strong role for quantitative environmental data, however, does not undermine the need for local experiential knowledge and perspectives in identifying environmental pressures and trends.[1]

6.3 In this chapter we review the main sources of environmental information (6.7-6.11) and look briefly at the users, with an emphasis on the legal rights of access which now exist (6.12-6.14). We then explore possible ways of improving access to data (6.15-6.20) and co-ordinating their presentation (6.21-6.24). We consider the opportunities presented by modern technologies (6.25-6.34) and the best way of capitalising on them (6.35-6.41). We focus primarily on environmental data, but many of the issues raised apply equally to the socio-economic data required for planning.

6.4 In chapter 4, we considered the challenges facing planners in the coming decades if they are to contribute towards the delivery of a more environmentally sustainable society. We have concluded that, at present, insufficient weight is given to environmental considerations in decisions on the use and management of land and natural resources. Part of the reason for this is the difficulty in accessing and interpreting good quality environmental information.

6.5 It is important to recognise that improved access to and use of information is not a panacea; better information does not, in itself, guarantee better decisions. Nevertheless, in evidence to us, a number of bodies stressed the need to secure high quality information as a basis for involving communities and making sound decisions. It was also argued that information on the state of the environment should be fed more effectively into the planning system.[2] We agree. There is a strong argument that planners and decision-makers continue to contribute to environmental degradation, at least in part because they are inadequately informed about the current state of the environment, the pressures upon it, the consequences of their decisions and potential mitigation.

6.6 There are several reasons why environmental information is not used satisfactorily in the planning process at present. In some cases, may stem from a genuine lack of data or poor understanding of, or even disagreement over, cause and effect relationships underlying environmental problems; in others the data may have been misinterpreted or taken out of context. An historical example is the belief, current in the 1970s, that sewage was speedily degraded and rendered harmless when discharged to the sea. As a result, most discharges were only subjected to the primary treatment of screening and maceration. It was later realised that much fuller treatment was needed in order to safeguard the quality of bathing waters, and an urgent and hugely expensive investment programme had to be undertaken. There may even be a preference, in some cases, to remain in ignorance of environmental constraints, allowing the costs of the subsequent damage to be transferred elsewhere, often to the environment or the public purse. For instance, in the past there has been pressure for development in flood plains with the expectation that the Environment Agency in England and Wales and local authorities in Scotland would pick up any subsequent bill for flood protection. In the next chapter we consider how environmental data can be used for the purposes of decision-making, but first we broadly indicate its scope.

ENVIRONMENTAL INFORMATION: A KEY ASSET

6.7 The UK is fortunate in the range and diversity of information that is held about the state of its environment. The Environment Agency estimates that there are more than 100 national environmental monitoring programmes (generating temporal and spatial data) and several hundred national baseline environmental data sets (containing spatial data).[3] The Environment Agency not only monitors the environment directly but also carries out extensive environmental modelling such as the statutory risk assessment modelling to predict flood risk. It manages many national databases on topics such as industrial sites, landfill sites and nuclear facilities.

6.8 Public bodies such as the Natural Environment Research Council (NERC) and its subsidiary bodies, and the Ordnance Survey hold a wealth of baseline data. Much is potentially of great value in assessing environmental quality. For example, the British Geological Survey has comprehensive data on geological structures, groundwater movements,[4] soil quality, and land contamination. The Centre for Ecology and Hydrology, another body under the NERC umbrella, holds important data on surface water flows and detailed, regularly updated, maps of land use. Many of these diverse data sets are in the form of high resolution digitised maps covering the whole country.

6.9 The Environment Agencies gather a wide range of monitoring data on, for example, compliance with discharge consents, river water quality, river habitats, radioactivity, waste flows and flood risk.[5] Central government funds monitoring work on air quality, acidification, bathing water quality and compliance with a wide range of EC Directives. Biological and geological monitoring programmes are coordinated by the statutory conservation bodies and by NERC: the latter also coordinates an Environmental Change Network, which is designed to obtain comparable long-term data sets. The Department for Environment, Food and Rural Affairs (DEFRA), the Countryside Agency, the devolved administrations, local authorities and non-governmental organisations hold other important data. However, these data are rarely brought together in relation to specific locations. State of the environment reports published by some local and regional authorities are not widespread and vary greatly in quality; these reports are discussed in the next chapter.

6.10 By no means will all environmental data be of equal value in planning, particularly as they relate to land use and management. European Community and domestic legislation that sets statutory standards will often specify the location and periodicity of measurement to demonstrate compliance. Data collection may, for instance, be focused at specified locations near to recognised major point sources of pollution – an example would be monitoring of watercourses for hazardous substances downstream of factories that are known to produce them. As a result, this source of data on its own may not give the most useful insight into the state of the environment, and may be less useful for wider planning purposes. Moreover, there are some concerns that much environmental information of this kind is now gathered for purely historical reasons.

6.11 All of these useful data sets have been compiled at considerable public expense over many years. We return later in this chapter to the issue of making them available, but first we consider who needs access to them.

THE USERS OF ENVIRONMENTAL DATA

6.12 Good quality environmental information is an essential foundation for achieving environmentally sustainable use and management of land. Planners should have access to as much relevant information as possible, including the present state of the environment, and of the trends and pressures that have created that state. This picture must be informed as far as possible by measured baseline data. Decision makers are not, however, the only audience for environmental information. Developers need to have access to good data to inform their proposals, not least for those projects that require environmental impact assessments (a subject which we discuss further at 7.22-7.38).

6.13 Another key audience is the general public and groups that represent sections of the public interest. Generally available data in readily useable forms will help raise the level of debate and improve the transparency of decision-making processes. The importance of providing open access to environmental information has become firmly established in recent years. For some decades, legislation covering pollution control, waste sites and discharges to water has contained provisions requiring information on licences and monitoring data to be made available in public registers. Much broader provisions were set out in a 1990 EC Directive on access to environmental information.[6] The Directive was later augmented by the 1998 Aarhus Convention,[7] which placed public access to environmental information at the heart of achieving environmental justice and ensuring the quality and the implementation of decisions (see box 6A).

The 1990 EC Directive on the freedom of access to information on the environment has been implemented in the UK by the Environmental Information Regulations 1992.[8] The regulations cover information on the state of water, air, soil, land flora and fauna, and activities or measures which may adversely affect them or which are designed to protect them. They require government Departments, local authorities and other public bodies with responsibilities in relation to the environment to make such information available on request. The regulations set out rules for refusing to disclose information: where international relations, national defence or public security, legal proceedings, commercial confidentiality or intellectual property could be affected, or where the information relates to confidential deliberations or internal communications.

A further step forward was taken in 1998 with the completion of a new Convention on Access to Information, Public Participation in Decision Making and Access to Justice in Environmental Matters.[9] The so-called Aarhus Convention, drawn up under the auspices of the UN Economic Commission for Europe, has several wide-ranging implications for planning and decision making procedures. It recognises that 'in the field of the environment, improved access to information and public participation in decision-making enhance the quality and the implementation of decisions, contribute to public awareness of environmental issues, give the public the opportunity to express its concerns and enable public authorities to take due account of such concerns'.

The Convention gives a considerably broader definition of environmental information than that offered by the 1990 Directive: as well as information on the state of elements of the environment, it covers information on a wide range of factors which are likely to affect the environment and economic analyses and assumptions used in environmental decision-making. Grounds for refusing information are also more tightly drawn than under the Directive.

The Convention entered into force on 30 October 2001 after the sixteenth national ratification. Neither the UK nor the European Union has ratified it as yet, although the government has taken a power in the Freedom of Information Act 2000 to allow the Convention's provisions on environmental information to be transposed into law in England, Wales and Northern Ireland.[10] Comparable powers are being taken in Scotland.

In 2000, the European Commission set out plans to amend the 1990 Directive in order to bring it into line with the Aarhus Convention, and also to capitalise on developments in information technology to promote active provision of environmental information by public bodies.[11] The Commission proposed strengthening the Directive to give a formal right to information, limiting the restrictions on disclosure and making clear that bodies such as privatised utilities fall under its provisions.

Under the Commission's proposals the scope of the regime could be widened to include companies in the waste disposal, gas, telecommunications, water and electricity sectors; the transport sector, including rail operators, airlines, shipping companies, freight hauliers, road construction; and the construction industry more generally.[12] Public authorities and agencies would be required to disseminate environmental information proactively, especially by electronic means, and to make reasonable efforts to hold information electronically. Other significant changes needed to bring the existing environmental information regime into line with Aarhus include the shortening of response time under normal circumstances from two months to one month; the application of a public interest test to all exemptions from disclosure; and supplementing existing review provisions (for applicants who consider that their request has been ignored, wrongfully refused or inadequately dealt with) by a new Information Commissioner established to provide an independent and impartial review body other than a court of law.[13]

6.14 There are, however, serious barriers to widespread easy access to environmental data, which we shall now examine. These arise from perceived constraints of confidentiality, unreliable and unrepresentative data, the fragmentation of sources using varying conventions, charging for supplying data held by public bodies and the distribution methods used. We believe that government needs to act to remove these barriers.

MAKING BASIC DATA AVAILABLE

6.15 Data are often withheld for reasons of commercial confidentiality, but the fact that data apply to a commercial enterprise does not in itself justify withholding them; after all, applications under integrated pollution prevention and control (IPPC) are placed in the public domain. Prime examples are the reports which farmers submit to Agriculture Departments in order to win subsidy under the Common Agricultural Policy and agri-environment schemes. This information could give invaluable data on trends in land use at the local, regional and national levels, but is currently regarded as commercially confidential even though it relates to the distribution of public funds. To justify withholding a useful data set of this type, there must be some prospect of commercial interests being significantly injured by its release. Even where there is such a risk, this can often be minimised by removing key identifying data. **We urge the government and the devolved administrations to review all categories of data withheld on grounds on commercial confidentiality, to see which can be safely released. In particular, we recommend that Agriculture Departments place agricultural returns in the public domain.**

6.16 Many public bodies now charge, often heavily, for use of their information. The level of fees can be particularly high for access to electronic data: precisely the format that is the most powerful for planning and public dissemination, as discussed below. The decision to charge for information has its roots in the Rothschild-inspired reorganisations of government-funded research establishments in the 1970s, but largely stems from decisions in the 1980s to make these organisations generate revenue by commercialising their data sets.

6.17 As a result, important information is commonly not available to the general public. All too often, it is not used by the Environment Agencies, statutory conservation bodies or local planning authorities because it is regarded as too costly. Such an approach ignores the, often large, deferred costs of not using that information. Furthermore, effective public involvement in environmental planning requires that all relevant information should be readily available. Charging for, or allowing other barriers to access to, relevant information held by public bodies undermines that involvement.

6.18 Revenue from data sales does play a useful part in helping to fund many public bodies, such as the Ordnance Survey, the Meteorological Office, and a variety of organisations sponsored by NERC. For example, the British Geological Survey (BGS) estimates that it generates some £10 million annually (one-third of its total budget) from the sale of information and from consultancy work won on the back of its unique data sets. Making such information more widely available for free or at much lower cost would adversely affect the viability of such organisations and their data sets. However, much of this income (generally about 60-70% in the case of BGS) comes from service level agreements and contracts with other public sector bodies. The current system has created a merry-go-round of public finances with no net benefit and high transaction costs in which the full value of environmental information is not being realised.

6.19 Since only a relatively small proportion of the revenue received for environmental data by such bodies is raised from the private sector, the net cost to the public purse of providing the information free of charge would be relatively low. Indeed, a recent study for the European Commission suggested that making such public sector information freely available – as is the case in the United States – could in fact lead to an overall financial benefit for governments.[14] This is because it could be expected to provide a strong stimulus to commercial suppliers of 'added value' information, leading to an increase in employment in this sector. Developers and consultants, in particular, could be expected to be interested in such added value products, but this will only work if the government finds other ways of reimbursing the organisations collecting and holding the data sets.

6.20 We are concerned that the practice of charging for data has restricted access to information, undermining its use in planning and decision-making processes. **We recommend that data which have been gathered in the public name and for the public good should be available electronically at no cost for public use. We recommend that the government adjust the financial model for public bodies holding and developing essential data sets (such as the Natural Environment Research Council and the Ordnance Survey) and replace income from sales of environmental information with direct grants. Consideration should be given to retaining a market element by relating the level of grant to the public use made of a body's data sets.** This need not prevent public sector bodies charging commercial organisations for special interpretations of the data and specialised software for analysing it.

FRAGMENTATION AND VARYING STANDARDS

6.21 Uncertainties, gaps in knowledge or differences of interpretation will always exist. Political and institutional arrangements should be sufficiently well designed to recognise these difficulties. Nevertheless, there is considerable evidence to suggest that the current arrangements for managing environmental information in the UK are unduly fragmented and inconsistent, and as a result that information is not being drawn on sufficiently to inform planning. The proliferation of environmental databases, gathered and held by a diverse range of organisations, has grown up in a piecemeal fashion over many decades. The large number of organisations involved reflects the complex institutional arrangements for monitoring and managing different features of the environment at different levels of government. There is a clear danger that a lack of coordination between the various monitoring programmes could create data sets which are inconsistent or incoherent, and which contain significant overlaps or gaps.

6.22 A more integrated and coherent approach to the collection of environmental information is highly desirable. First, it could improve the efficiency with which data are collected, improve consistency and compatibility, avoid gaps and overlaps, and ensure that maximum value is obtained. Second, by collecting monitoring and baseline data in a more coordinated way it should be possible to present a much fuller and clearer picture of the state and dynamics of the environment. Third, a 'one-stop shop' could help planners and other decision makers make better use of environmental information.

6.23 Some steps have already been taken to try to rationalise the way in which environmental data are gathered. The need to develop a more integrated national framework for measuring the state of the environment was recognised by the Environment Agency in 1996.[15] The Agency proposed that programmes to monitor the environment should be divided into six categories or 'viewpoints':

- land use and environmental resources (including petroleum, minerals, coal, construction materials, soils and subsoils)

- the status of biological communities and populations and of biodiversity

- the quality of the environment as determined by compliance with targets and standards

- the 'health' of environmental resources and their utility

- environmental changes at long-term reference sites

- the aesthetic quality of the environment.

6.24 The Agency's initiative led to the establishment of a National Forum for Environmental Monitoring, which is intended to enable a more co-ordinated approach to environmental monitoring in England and Wales by sharing information on the purposes, aims and consequences of the existing programmes. This informal grouping is coordinated by the Agency, and includes representatives from DEFRA, the devolved administrations, local government, industry and statutory and non-statutory conservation organisations. The Forum's main output to date has been a catalogue of 70 national environmental monitoring programmes.[16] This catalogue, while useful, has several important gaps on matters such as air quality and biodiversity. The Forum has no plans to update or extend it. Overall, it seems unlikely that the Forum will be the catalyst for a comprehensive reorganisation and integration of the way in which environmental data are gathered and held though it could play a role in the new UK centre for environmental data which we discuss below.

USING MODERN TECHNOLOGIES

6.25 In recent years, the transformation in technologies for processing, manipulating, presenting and disseminating information has been remarkable. Modern technologies offer tremendous potential to extract the best value from environmental information; but, while progress has been made on many fronts, much of that potential has yet to be realised.

6.26 Modern technology could make several valuable contributions to providing a sound information base for environmental planning. Firstly, it offers a way of identifying the large quantities of environmental information and improving their accessibility: geographically referenced data sets are of particular interest in this respect. Secondly, a variety of tools, many of great sophistication, now exist to model the environment. Thirdly, good software is now available to visualise options: this has important potential benefits in facilitating public participation in planning processes.

6.27 Geographical information systems (GISs) allow large amounts of spatial data to be manipulated in virtual space. They can be used to produce tailored maps covering areas of interest, and by overlaying data sets can allow clear visualisation of environmental constraints and pressures. Numerous layers of data can be combined, and overlays can be created to help explore relationships between data sets. GISs are essentially two dimensional, and this can limit their effectiveness in cases where height or depth is an issue. Nevertheless, when combined with spatial analysis, they potentially offer a quick and effective means of interpreting complex geographical data. They can be relatively easy to use and update, and can be expanded to include new data sets, provided they are digitised and grid-referenced.

6.28 GISs are already well-established tools and are used in a wide variety of organisations, such as the NERC institutes, to hold large quantities of environmental data. The Environment Agency is making considerable use of GIS to support production of its state of the environment reports.[17] It also uses GIS software to improve public access to information: its website offers map-based information on emissions from major industrial processes, groundwater protection zones, water quality and flood risk.[18] However, the Agency has yet to use its GIS widely to inform its own environmental planning decisions.

6.29 Local authorities are also making widespread use of GIS. A survey by the Royal Town Planning Institute (RTPI) found that in early 2000, nearly 90% of local authorities had a GIS in operation or under development – up from 64% in 1995.[19] Few of the key data sets captured in local authority GISs concerned the natural environment; more usual subjects were listed buildings, ancient monuments, social and demographic data, and electoral boundaries. Several councils included contaminated land and statutory designations in their GIS, but few incorporated information on wider environmental quality. An exception is the London Borough of Newham, which has developed a system able to access a wide range of local and national data sets, and use them for an increasing range of environmental policy issues, including planning.[20] In Scotland, Dumfries and Galloway council has digitised all habitat types for its Community Biodiversity Action Plan from aerial photographs.[21] But in general the RTPI found that the main applications developed by local planning authorities were for map production or processing of planning applications: the use of GISs to map development plan policies and proposals was less established.

6.30 Several bodies told us that GIS could be an invaluable tool in environmental planning.[22] However, some warned that GISs can absorb resources without delivering commensurate benefits unless a careful assessment is made of what information should be captured, and for what purposes. Others pointed to the need for standardisation of databases and new systems for information transfer, and the need to ensure integrity of data and allocate clear responsibility for their maintenance, use and ownership.

6.31 There are, of course, technical and practical barriers to the development of GISs. Organisations may face a significant initial investment and considerable demands on staff time to prepare and regularly update data. It is vital to understand the desired end uses of a GIS before the system is built. In principle, however, once data are digitised and grid-referenced it should be possible to manipulate them in most GIS systems. For this to happen efficiently, there is a need for the training of more staff in the relevant computer skills.

6.32 The new Ordnance Survey digital Mastermap provides a large-scale information source covering the whole country with uniquely identified polygons corresponding to topographic features (houses, roads, waterways, fields etc.). Each feature has a unique digital Topographic Object Identifier (TOID) and associated attribute information. The TOID, and its associated polygon, can be regarded as a two-dimensional, attributed analogue of the National Grid coordinates.

6.33 Other technologies offer great potential to explore the potential impacts of new developments. Visualisation software is now becoming very advanced, and could be used more widely to allow members of the public to judge the likely impact of a proposed development. Interactive techniques can also be used to solicit views and inform public debate over the preferred options for siting new developments.

6.34 At present, speed of data transfer and access to sufficient computing power can limit the applicability of technologies. However, new infrastructure being developed to support e-science will be much more powerful than the World Wide Web. Besides information stored in web pages, users will be able to share very large computing resources and enormous data collections and gain remote access to specialised facilities. The Government Spending Review in 2000 announced a total of nearly £120 million for a new e-science initiative managed by Engineering and Physical Sciences Research Council (EPSRC), part of a global initiative to develop the underpinning 'Grid' system. The Grid can be defined as an enabler of virtual organisations; an infrastructure that enables flexible, secure, coordinated resource sharing among dynamic collections of individuals, institutions and resources. It is a federation - the owners of the individual resources maintain ultimate authority over their use. At present, grid developments are focused on 'big science' communities such as particle physics, astrophysics, genomics, and climate modelling. But their needs – access to very large data collections, very large scale computing resources and high performance visualisation back to the individual users – are similar to those of the planning tools and techniques mentioned above, and it is reasonable to suppose that such technology will become available in the planning field in the medium term. **We recommend that the government fund a feasibility study on the use of Grid technology in planning.**

A VIRTUAL CENTRE FOR ENVIRONMENTAL DATA

6.35 We see a need for a much stronger drive to create coherent environmental monitoring programmes and to bring data together in formats that will maximise their relevance for planning. This should be done by establishing a low-cost virtual centre for environmental information to generate a Portal on the Internet. This will save resources overall by avoiding the duplication of data. The virtual centre could possibly be modelled on the Digital Energy Atlas and Library run by the UK Offshore Operators Association.[23]

6.36 **We recommend the establishment of a virtual centre for environmental data, in order to overcome the barriers to presenting coherent and consistent environmental information in electronic form.** The centre would not be responsible for gathering raw data, nor would it be a repository of information. Such a conventional model of data management would prove cumbersome, and would fail to exploit the potential for new technologies to enhance greatly the value of data for planning. The virtual centre would act as a gatekeeper and portal for data sets held in electronic form by a wide range of other bodies, and as a result would require only a small staff. It would hold only metadata showing what is in the data set, how it was gathered, its coverage and quality, and how it may be accessed.

6.37 The Environmental Information Portal thus created would also stimulate debate on the way in which information is gathered. There will be a need for such a debate to be managed and this may require the establishment of a group of users and suppliers of environmental information. Such a group would take the lead in agreeing monitoring protocols, recommend appropriate standards for data set formats, and exercise quality control to ensure that data sets meet the recommended standards. Its role would be supportive of the virtual centre. The group would also help ensure that databases held by individual bodies are mutually compatible and are capable of being integrated with other data sets. As envisaged, this group would pool expertise in monitoring techniques and provide a centre of expertise in the integration of diverse environmental data sets. An initial focus could be to co-ordinate reporting of UK-wide compliance with EC legislation.

6.38 The virtual centre for environmental data would be a powerful tool for a range of environmental planning purposes at different levels, from drawing up national and regional policies to identifying the least damaging sites for major developments. It could also be a powerful contribution to efforts to bring the environment to the fore in spatial plans.

6.39 Our earlier proposals for improving access to information would greatly increase the effectiveness and value of such a virtual centre. **All relevant public sector bodies should be under a statutory obligation to give the new virtual data centre free access to their information.** This presumes an increase in public funding for these bodies (6.20). Guidance on the representativeness and the uncertainties of data would be available free from the data holders, but they would be able to charge for interpretation of the data.

6.40 The government has already embarked on an initiative that could be regarded as the first step towards a UK-wide spatially referenced metadata centre following a report by the Social Exclusion Unit on strategies for neighbourhood renewal. This concluded that it was essential to provide improved information at the local level, preferably free of charge.[24] The Office for National Statistics (ONS) is now taking this concept forward in a three-year, £35 million project that aims to offer a range of data for electoral wards via a full-scale GIS.

6.41 Initially, most of the indicators in the ONS system are likely to be social and economic. Nevertheless, the project shows that the government accepts the potential for improved information to influence debates in the community. By making provision for economic, social and environmental data to be accessed through consistent metadata gateways, there may be scope to shed light on wider issues of sustainable development.

6.42 In this chapter we have considered how access to environmental information can be made less expensive and more comprehensive. As we have described, modern technology has a big role to play. In the next chapter we look at how the data can be used.

Chapter 7

ENVIRONMENTAL ASSESSMENT

How can information about the environment be used most effectively to inform decisions and safeguard sustainability? What are the implications of the EC Directive on Strategic Environmental Assessment?

7.1   In chapters 5 and 6 we have discussed two prerequisites for an effective planning system, building public confidence and improving access to environmental information. The availability of information is unlikely to lead to better decisions by planners, or knowledgeable public engagement with the issues, unless suitable techniques are used to focus and harness that information. Robust procedures employing appropriate methods of assessment are therefore a further prerequisite for an effective planning system.

7.2   We have defined the primary purposes of environmental planning as preventing breaches of environmental constraints and making collective choices about the states of the environment we want (3.23). Achieving these purposes requires that accepted standards for environmental quality are not exceeded. In fact, the whole point of some forms of plan, for example local air quality management plans, is to deliver cost-effective compliance with specified quality standards; monitoring and modelling are vital components of such a planning process. At the same time, there are many aspects of the environment for which there is no formal standard; and, where there is a formal standard, the effects of a decision or plan may be important even if they do not affect compliance with that standard. Deciding on the weight to be given to effects, and the extent to which mitigation may be required, is a process involving dialogue and judgement.

7.3   Environmental information, whether quantitative or qualitative, can therefore have several functions in the planning process. These include:

- *assessing the current state of the environment*: this involves defining a baseline against which the impacts of plans and individual projects can be measured. It can identify parameters for which standards are exceeded or threatened and areas where important natural resources are being eroded. This process may also involve identifying areas which have particular characteristics that render them either suitable or unsuitable on environmental grounds for developments of particular kinds;

- *projecting the impact of pressures on the environment*: providing that the environmental systems are adequately understood, environmental data can be fed into models to show cumulative effects or extrapolate current trends;

- *assessing options*: assessing the effects on the environment of proposed plans or projects, and preferably making comparisons with the effects of alternative options;

- *setting targets or objectives and monitoring progress towards these*: it is often more sensible to focus on measuring indicators for priority objectives, rather than seeking a comprehensive overview of performance towards the achievement of all environmental objectives;

- *a focus for deliberation*: a process of information collection that is open about what kinds of data are collected, and why, can stimulate debate about the attributes we value in the environment, and thus wish to measure.

7.4 In this chapter we first review the progress made in producing state of the environment reports, on a wider scale (7.5-7.7.) and at local level (7.8-7.16). We discuss the contribution of modelling (7.17-7.21). We consider the role of environmental impact assessment (EIA) in protecting the environment and improving the quality of individual developments (7.22-7.38), paying particular attention to the scoping of assessments, subsequent monitoring and auditing, and the inclusion of effects on human health. We then consider the less well established, but perhaps more directly relevant technique of strategic environmental assessment (SEA) of public policies, plans and programmes (7.39-7.42), the recent European Community (EC) Directive (box 7D), and the relationship between strategic environmental assessment and sustainability appraisal (7.43-7.48).

THE STATE OF THE WIDER ENVIRONMENT

7.5 There has been a growing interest in using aggregated high level environmental data to inform policy making at European and national levels. The European Environment Agency produces valuable reports that bring together data from a number of countries and also offer a qualitative assessment of the state of Europe's environment.[1] The government has made considerable progress in developing and reporting sustainable development indicators for the UK.[2] In England and Wales, the Environment Agency's state of the environment reports detail the main stresses on the environment and provide a powerful mechanism for highlighting unsustainable trends. The Scottish Environment Protection Agency develops reports covering air, soil and water in Scotland.[3]

7.6 The general picture is that environmental data in aggregate form are used with increasing effectiveness to inform many national plans and policies. Presentation of aggregated data at the national level can be a powerful means of testing the overall progress towards environmental sustainability. Indicators at a national level become still more powerful when linked to targets or objectives showing the degree to which current policies and trends are unsustainable. This perspective is reinforced further when 'business as usual' forecasts of future trends are considered; trends in greenhouse gas emissions, waste production, or traffic growth show that 'business as usual' is clearly environmentally unsustainable, and have thrown the need for government action into stark relief.

7.7 The large amount of environmentally significant information compiled at national level gives a flavour of the challenge involved in ensuring that all relevant information is used in the planning process at regional and local levels. However, some of the information compiled at national level, particularly socio-economic data, may be difficult to disaggregate to smaller administrative areas. Moreover, some national environmental data sets are based largely on extrapolation and modelling from a few measuring sites, with the result that meaningful data are not available for smaller areas.

THE STATE OF THE LOCAL ENVIRONMENT

7.8   Some local authorities are already producing useful overviews of the state of their environments (see box 7A). In some cases, at least, these exercises appear to have had some impact on local planning decisions and in general awareness of environmental issues among council officers and the wider community. However, the picture is extremely patchy: there is no requirement for local authorities to produce state of the environment reports, and no guidance has been issued. There is not, therefore, any common approach to format or content. State of the environment reports at the local level tend to take one of two forms: a report that feeds directly into a policy exercise such as the structure plan (Suffolk and Lancashire)[4, 5] or an annual monitoring report on a small number of selected environmental indicators (Hertfordshire).[6]

BOX 7A   **A LOCAL STATE OF THE ENVIRONMENT REPORT**

Cambridgeshire County Council has produced two reports on the state of the environment – the first in 1994 and the second in 1998 – which are among the most comprehensive produced by local authorities.[7] The reports were compiled with the assistance of more than 20 other bodies such as local authorities, statutory agencies, environmental groups, academic institutions and utility companies. They are aimed at all bodies with an interest in the local environment, educational establishments, local policy makers and bodies preparing action plans or strategies.

The second report collects a wide range of environmental data covering energy use and production, transport, air quality, water quality and resources, waste, land use, natural and built environments, and the archaeological, cultural and physical background. It uses 42 indicators in a qualitative way to assess trends since the first report, although because of the shortage of data points it is often unclear whether the trend is real or apparent. One notable feature is that, as a result of local government reorganisation, the second report covers the administrative areas of two councils – Cambridgeshire County Council and the new unitary authority of Peterborough City Council. This suggests that changes to administrative boundaries and structures could prove a barrier to the accumulation of long-term trend data and environmental understanding at the local level.

Cambridgeshire County Council is now considering the appropriate form for its third report. This is expected to be more along the lines of a sustainable development report.

7.9   Local state of the environment reports are increasingly being turned into sustainable development reports.[8] While no central guidance has been issued on the preparation of state of the environment reports, an attempt has been made to devise indicators for local sustainability. The former Department of the Environment, Transport and the Regions (DETR) suggested 29 indicators for local use, which have been tested in 30 local authorities.[9] The environmentally relevant indicators suggested cover air quality, changes in habitats and populations of characteristic species, energy use, water use, waste arisings, recycling of household waste, traffic volumes, new homes built on previously developed land and concern about noise. While some local authorities use additional indicators to those listed by DETR, coverage of certain topics such as agricultural and industrial emissions and groundwater quality tends to be weak in comparison to noise pollution, traffic, and bird populations. The kind of state of the environment reports that we consider necessary for strategic spatial planning should have a broader range of environmental data. Analyses of environmental pressures and the economic and social trends at the root of these pressures are not strong features of the reports surveyed, although in the Suffolk example a thorough effort is made to analyse the effect of the structure plan in promoting sustainable development across over one hundred indicators.

7.10 If environmental information is to be used effectively in setting and achieving environmental goals, the concept of a state of the environment report needs to be extended to include the pressures on the environment, as in the reports produced by the Environment Agency.[10] By including scenarios showing the future impact on environmental quality of possible development paths, a state of the environment report could improve the scope for local communities to influence their future. The scenarios should cover a range of alternatives for economic and social development in the area and be open about the assumptions and uncertainties involved in generating scenarios. Local state of the environment reports should also explicitly spell out the possible consequences for the area of national or global environmental pressures, such as climate change. Predictions based on 'business as usual' should not be used unthinkingly as the basis for development decisions: such an approach underlies the failures of past policies based on 'predict and provide'. Instead, predictions should be seen as indicators of whether particular policies are liable to lead to environmental conditions that are unacceptable to the relevant community and, if so, what adjustments are needed in order to meet environmental objectives. In sum the state of the environment report should become the basis for strategic environmental assessment (see 7.41).

7.11 Earlier chapters recognised that both urban and rural areas draw resources from and export waste to other areas; this interrelationship is embodied in the metaphor of 'ecological footprint' (4.3). As communities become more affluent and more concerned with their immediate environment, there is a danger that they may improve the environment locally through importing resources and manufactured goods and exporting waste for disposal elsewhere, in effect exporting unsustainability. At a national level, these resource and waste flows raise profound questions over global sustainability. At the local level, they could be exacerbated by devolving environmental responsibilities to local communities. Data on imports and exports of key materials and wastes, obtained by systematic analytical approaches such as life cycle assessment (LCA), and material flow accounting (MFA), need to be available to ensure that communities and planners do not act in ignorance of the full implications of their decision. An example of such a tool is the WISARD LCA package, developed for the Environment Agency for use by local authorities in developing waste management strategies.

7.12 The cost of producing even sophisticated state of the environment reports need not be excessive. The virtual centre for environmental information we recommended in chapter 6 will greatly ease the task. Free access to the data available through the national Environmental Information Portal should also prevent lower quality data being gathered in place of those already in high quality national data sets – a practice that the current high cost of access to such data sets can encourage. Moreover, the portal would provide the means for disseminating local environmental data over the Internet.

7.13 In considering how often state of the environment reports should be produced, the need for up-to-date information has to be balanced against the cost and effort involved in their production; but the availability of a comprehensive range of constantly updated data from a central point in electronic form should simplify the task of updating whenever that is required.

7.14 Local authorities would generally need to improve their environmental and computer expertise in order to produce state of the environment reports of the kind described here and make full use of them. They may incur additional costs in the form of training and possibly recruitment of new staff. In our view, such costs incurred are likely to be amply repaid by the benefits derived from better informed planning and decision making.

7.15 Local authorities are now preparing community strategies designed to promote the social, economic and environmental well-being of their areas. Local sustainability indicators and state of the environment reports should constitute important inputs to the preparation of community strategies. They could also provide valuable inputs to planning exercises at a more local level, such as a neighbourhood or country town.

7.16 However, we see the major instrument for setting and achieving environmental goals in future as the modified form of spatial planning we discuss in chapter 10. We discuss there the areas for which integrated spatial strategies should be prepared and the role that the enhanced state of the environment reports discussed here should play in their preparation.

MODELLING

7.17 Modelling can be used to extend the range and coverage of measured data, thus contributing to an understanding of the present state of the environment. This understanding is important, but not sufficient: the main purpose of planning is to influence the future. It is therefore vital to understand the dynamic mechanisms which can affect environmental quality, and, if possible, to be able to model their impacts. Decision-makers need to understand the nature and the scale of pressures upon the environment, and be able to assess future impacts under a range of different scenarios or policy options – indeed, in this broader context, modelling must underpin any efforts to plan and shape our future environment. It may be particularly important in predicting the cumulative impacts of numerous distributed sources of pollution or other factors causing environmental damage.

7.18 Modelling of environmental impacts is nothing new; relatively crude mathematical formulae have informed policies on air pollution from industrial sources for many decades. However, our increasing understanding of the complex interactions and mechanisms at work, combined with ready access to powerful computers, means that modelling is reaching new levels of sophistication. A large range of models is now available to assess matters such as impacts on air quality, traffic flows, noise, and water quality.

7.19 Uncertainties are inherent in environmental modelling. In addition to natural variability, errors can arise in the input data – including errors or inaccuracies in the results of environmental monitoring programmes. Further uncertainties arise because of lack of full knowledge of the environmental system that is being modelled, and the inevitable need to make approximations of complex real-world behaviour. This means that different modelling packages can produce quite different results. A good example is the local forecasts used in the local air quality management regime, as described in box 7B. It is also vital to recognise that models invariably embody important assumptions and value judgements, not always acknowledged.

BOX 7B   **MODELLING EXCEEDANCES OF AIR QUALITY STANDARDS**

Local authorities are required to review and assess air quality; predict whether air quality objectives will be met by a specified date; and, if not, declare an air quality management area and introduce policies to secure compliance. The air quality management regime has been compromised by methodological difficulties arising from the use of different, and often incompatible, measuring, modelling and forecasting techniques. The government has been reluctant to specify techniques because this could stifle innovation and damage competition between the suppliers of modelling software. Nevertheless, the different approaches adopted by local authorities – even neighbouring authorities within a single conurbation – have produced perverse results. For example, councils in the West Midlands – an area notorious for traffic congestion – used an unusual forecasting technique that predicted no exceedances of air quality objectives by the compliance dates, even though many small market towns are declaring air quality management areas on the basis of different modelling techniques.[11, 12]

7.20 **Where compliance with a numerical standard is the goal, the body setting the standard should give clear guidance on the appropriate methodologies for modelling and measurement.** England and Wales lag somewhat behind Scotland in this respect.[13] In other cases, it may be appropriate to use a more qualitative approach to modelling and forecasting which aims to identify unsustainable outcomes.

7.21 The uncertainties inherent in modelling should be set out in a transparent way in a state of the environment report together with all assumptions and judgements made. It is important to recognise these uncertainties and make allowance for them in the decision-making and deliberative process. Forecasts should be offered showing the possible impact of existing trends and policies, and the potential consequences of other development paths. It should also be made clear that some impacts may be difficult to model fully, but may nevertheless be important.

ENVIRONMENTAL IMPACT ASSESSMENT

7.22 We now turn to the main use of environmental data and modelling in planning: the environmental assessment of projects, programmes, plans and policies. Environmental assessment is the evaluation of the effects likely to arise from a project (or other action) significantly affecting the natural and human-made environment. The environmental assessment of projects is generally referred to as environmental impact assessment and that of programmes, plans and policies as strategic environmental assessment. Ideally, though rarely in practice, environmental assessment is a systematic, integrative and iterative process in which consultation and participation are integral to the evaluation.[14]

7.23 EC legislation[15] first established the requirement for environmental impact assessment (EIA) to be carried out in the UK for development projects with the potential to cause large-scale environmental disruption. Project-based EIA is a process intended to ensure that the likely significant effects of development projects are assessed and taken into account in deciding whether the projects may proceed. It is integrated into planning consent procedures.[16] In addition, there are EIA regulations for forestry and other sectors not regulated by the town and country planning system.[17]

7.24 The main product of environmental impact assessment, the environmental statement, must contain a description of the development, a description of mitigation measures, the data necessary to identify and assess the main effects, an outline of the main alternatives considered and a non-technical summary.[18]

7.25 EIA requirements have been recently extended and tightened by an amendment to the original Directive.[19] EIA is now required for a wider range of development projects than before. Projects are categorised as either for example, (Annex I power stations, chemical plants, airports, railways, major roads, waste disposal or processing plants) or for example, (Annex II intensive agriculture and aquaculture, land reclamation, extractive mining, energy production installations, mineral production).[20]

7.26 The amended Directive makes a new requirement for a formal decision by the planning authority[21] about the need for EIA for all development projects classified as Annex II. The significance of this change is that all Annex II projects must now be subjected to a preliminary environmental screening process. Government guidance on the issue of preliminary screening contains thresholds and criteria (not specified in the EC Directive) for each category of development.[22]

7.27 Under separate procedures and legal arrangements, a more limited assessment of environmental impacts is required for the most potentially polluting industrial installations seeking a permit under the integrated pollution prevention and control (IPPC) regime. IPPC environmental assessments cover emissions to air, water and ground and set targets for fuel efficiency and noise levels.[23] We have recommended that IPPC authorisation and planning permission for industrial plants should be brought within a single process (5.24). To achieve this, it will be necessary to use modelling techniques which relate desired environmental quality to scientifically measurable parameters and limits on emissions (8.13). Making this direct connection between environmental quality and quantified emission limits will require some modification to the process of IPPC consents, to include a way of allocating permitted emissions to ensure that the quality objective is met.

7.28 If a single process is to be introduced, an essential element is that there should be a common environmental statement. The 1997 EC EIA amendment legislation[24] lends practicality to our recommendation by making explicit provision for the use of a single procedure for the implementation of EC EIA and IPPC requirements.

SCOPING

7.29 There is no requirement in the UK for the applicant to consult the local planning authority prior to submission of the environmental statement, or to undertake any form of scoping. However, as a result of amendments to the original Directive, a developer may request a formal 'scoping opinion' from the local planning authority or, where the local planning authority fails to provide one, a 'scoping direction' from the Minister, regarding the information to be included in an environmental statement. It has been found that scoping and/or early discussions lead to noticeable benefits in the accuracy of predictions in environmental statements.[25]

7.30 Where the planning authority or the Minister rules that EIA is required, certain public bodies with statutory environmental responsibilities must be notified. These bodies[26] (such as the Environment Agency in England and Wales and the Scottish Environment Protection Agency in Scotland) are required to provide the developer with information should it be requested but no requirements as to consultation are laid down.[27] The planning authority is obliged to consult with these bodies before a Schedule 1 or a Schedule 2 planning application is determined.

7.31 Studies have concluded that the current informal scoping arrangements between a developer/consultant and the local planning authority, and to a lesser extent with consultees, are working reasonably well but that public involvement in scoping is less satisfactory.[28] A review of environmental statements in 1998 found that the public (mainly in the form of major public interest groups and local action groups) was involved in scoping in only about 40% of cases and influenced the environmental statement content in only a proportion of these.[29] **We recommend that consideration be given to introducing a mandatory preliminary stage in environmental impact assessment in which the planning authority will prescribe the scope of a particular assessment after public consultation.**

7.32 While the EIA Directive and UK Regulations do not expressly require the developer to study alternatives, the environmental statement must record any alternatives that are considered. Proponents have long been urged to consider strategic alternatives (for example, alternative processes and locations) early enough for them to be considered as feasible options.[30] The lack of regulatory weight given to the treatment of the environmental impact of alternatives has been reflected in practice. A review of 100 environmental statements found that in 20 cases, no alternative sites, routes or processes were presented and that in a further 13 cases, alternatives were considered, but without any environmental criteria being applied.[31]

7.33 Neither the EC Directive nor UK Regulations require monitoring of the actual effects of a development by the developer or the planning authority. In general, environmental statements contain only limited undertakings to monitor environmental impacts and monitoring is rarely part of planning conditions. That environmental statements are produced for the planning decision and do not thereafter form the basis for monitoring and enforcement is a major weakness of the EIA system.[32] Very little monitoring of environmental impacts occurs in practice, except for monitoring required under pollution control regulation, such as IPPC. Limited resources mean that monitoring of implementation and impacts is frequently only carried out by the local authority if a problem arises.

7.34 Auditing of environmental statements after the event can help EIA practitioners to learn from experience. This should lead to improved targeting, prediction accuracy, mitigation and environmental protection for future developments. However, problems such as lack of monitoring data for actual environmental impacts, and vague predictions and the absence of regulatory requirements have severely limited the practice of auditing. The Institute for Environmental Management and Assessment offers a review service to councils that are members but not an auditing service. This lack of monitoring and auditing creates two problems: it allows sub-standard predictions to go unchecked in environmental statements and militates against the improvement of EIA practice through feedback and learning. In a recent study[33] of 28 projects granted planning permissions, half of the 865 predictions were found to be unauditable because they lacked data or were too vague or ambiguous for auditing to take place. There is clearly a need for predictions of the effects of projects to be much more specific.

7.35 The Dutch government has set up a Commission (see box 7C) devoted to monitoring the quality of environmental statements, checking the scoping and adequacy of information, and disseminating good practice. **We recommend that a counterpart of the Dutch Environmental Impact Assessment Commission should be established in the UK to provide a rigorous independent check on the assessment process. The commission could also carry out evaluations of a sample of statements and issue guidance on best practice.**

BOX 7C	THE DUTCH EIA COMMISSION

Main functions

The Dutch Environmental Impact Assessment Commission fulfils an important role as an *independent adviser*. The Dutch procedure includes fixed points at which the Commission provides advice; these points are governed by strict deadlines. The Commission's main task consists of:

- providing advice on scoping guidelines for the content of the environmental statement (advisory guidelines);
- reviewing the environmental statement drawn up by the applicant (advisory review).

In addition, the Commission advises on requests for exemption from the duty to carry out an EIA and, when requested by the relevant Ministries, reviews statements prepared in neighbouring countries for environmental consequences in the Netherlands.

Constitution

The Commission consists of about 200 experts (members) appointed by Royal Decree. These experts mainly hold posts at universities, research institutes, consultancies and government organisations. They are invited to take part in working groups on a project-by-project basis, depending on the expertise required. Commission members are appointed for a five-year period and are eligible for re-appointment. If no Commission members are available, or if there is a lack of specific expertise required for a project, other experts may be invited to take part.[34]

Post-decision evaluation

According to Dutch legislation, the competent authority granting consent for projects requiring EIA must

- specify how it intends to carry out the mandatory post-decision evaluation
- monitor and evaluate the consequences of the implemented action
- prepare an evaluation report, publish it and send it to the EIA Commission and to the statutory consultees
- take such remedial action as it sees fit (for example tightening licence conditions) if impacts are much more severe than anticipated when consent was given.[35]

HEALTH IMPACTS

7.36 A basic intention of the 1997 EIA Directive, as stated in the preamble, is to assess the effects of development projects on the environment in order 'to take account of concerns to protect human health'.[36] DETR guidance on the EIA procedure specifies that the 'effects of pollutants on water and air quality' and the 'secondary effects' resulting from the interaction of these physical spheres must be assessed, but there is no specific reference to the need to consider the potential implications of pollution on human health.[37] As a result environmental statements do not, in general, contain an explicit discussion about human health issues although many environmental effects they list, such as emissions to air, water and soil, can have implications for health.

7.37 In a recent survey of environmental statements for which health effects were relevant, the British Medical Association found that in the majority of cases the information provided was insufficient to predict actual health effects, chiefly because the 'receiving population had not been analysed in terms of their likely vulnerability and exposure to potential health risks'.[38] Environmental statements focus almost exclusively on the issue of compliance with environmental quality standards or emissions limits[39] and not directly on the health effects of the proposed project. The omission of explicit analyses of health impacts diminishes the quality of deliberation and debate that is possible during public consultation on the environmental statement after its submission to the local planning authority. This feature is certainly inconsistent with the open and transparent procedure that we have advocated for the granting of planning consent for IPPC/EIA developments.

7.38 An integrated approach is urgently needed. It makes sense for health impact assessment to be made a routine and integral part of EIA for those projects with potentially significant health effects. Since the machinery necessary for assessments has already evolved it would be inefficient to attempt to duplicate or replace it. **We recommend that human health issues be incorporated explicitly in the environmental impact assessment process.** This could be done by amending EIA Regulations and guidance to include formal requirements for an assessment of the potential effects on human health of proposed development requiring EIA, where these are deemed significant.

STRATEGIC ENVIRONMENTAL ASSESSMENT

7.39 Assessing individual projects helps to identify and mitigate environmental damage but the full value of environmental assessment is not realised until it is also applied to proposed policies, plans or programmes. Project-level assessment does not directly challenge the policies in fields such as transport and housing, which generate public sector projects and set the framework for planning consent to private sector projects.

7.40 Environmental assessment at project level is generally limited to the direct impacts on a small site. It cannot consider the cumulative effects of many small projects or management schemes that do not require EIA, such as agricultural management schemes. Nor does it deal adequately with induced impacts, where a project stimulates further development, as for example when the construction of a new road stimulates out-of-town shopping centres or even new settlements. Further limitations of EIA relate to difficulties in dealing with synergistic effects and environmental impacts that are global in nature, such as biodiversity loss and greenhouse gas emissions. Local authorities are expected to judge for themselves the possible cumulative effects of a proposed development with any existing or approved development.[40]

7.41 EIA takes place after many strategic decisions (affecting more than one activity) have already been made and therefore addresses only a limited range of alternatives and mitigation measures. There is a widely acknowledged need for a process for assessing the environmental consequences of a policy, plan or programme. Strategic environmental assessment (SEA) represents the extension of the principles of environmental assessment to strategic action. In principle, SEA can deal with many of the difficulties of EIA: it can inject environmental issues into project planning by influencing the context within which decisions are made and it allows for the consideration of alternatives or environmental/mitigation measures that go beyond the confines of individual projects.

BOX 7D   EC STRATEGIC ENVIRONMENTAL ASSESSMENT DIRECTIVE.[41]

The Strategic Environmental Assessment (SEA) Directive is now in effect. Member States have until 21 July 2004 to enact laws, regulations and other administrative provisions necessary to implement the requirements of the Directive. Most Member States, including the UK, have not yet done so.

It will require a formal environmental assessment by UK central, regional and local authorities of a range of public plans and programmes with significant effects on the environment. SEAs will be mandatory for all plans and programmes which:

* set the framework for development consents for individual projects listed in Annex I and II of the EIA Directive or Schedule 1 and Schedule 2 developments;

* are in the fields of agriculture, forestry, fisheries, energy, transport, waste, water management, telecommunications, tourism, town and country planning or land use; or

* have been determined to require assessment under the Habitats Directive (92/43), in view of likely effects on Natura 2000 sites.

For other plans and programmes, assessments will be required only if, on the basis of detailed criteria, they are considered likely to have significant environmental effects. The Commission is required to produce a report by July 2006 describing how the Directive will be applied to Structural Funds and Rural Development Programmes during the post-2006 programming period.

The Directive is modelled closely on the EIA Directive, in that the requirements are primarily procedural: 'identifying, describing and evaluating the likely significant environmental effects of implementing the plan or programme, and reasonable alternatives' etc.[42] The assessment required is broad: an analysis of the likely significant effects of implementing a plan or programme, including secondary and cumulative effects. This analysis must be made available for public inspection in addition to arrangements that must be made for substantial consultation during the assessment process.

7.42 Strategic environmental assessment will in future be required in the UK under a further EC Directive (box 7D). This does not apply to policies, there is no requirement for scoping or to establish indicators. Ideally however, strategic environmental assessment is applied throughout the multiple stages of plan and programme making: identification of alternative plan and programme objectives, scoping, establishing environmental indicators, describing the baseline environment, predicting impacts, evaluating impacts and comparing alternatives, mitigation and monitoring.[43] The ideal outcome is for strategic environmental assessment, combined with strong and specific environmental objectives, to adjust public decision-making towards an objectives-led, proactive process of strategic environmental management.

SUSTAINABILITY APPRAISAL

7.43 At present planning guidance in England recommends sustainability appraisal for the various tiers of land use plans rather than strategic environmental assessment.[44] Sustainability appraisal extends appraisal to include social and economic criteria as being of equal concern to environmental criteria. The appraisal process, outlined in detail for regional planning guidance,[45] requires that plans are assessed against a range of criteria representing the four objectives of sustainable development in national policy (3.8): maintenance of high and stable levels of economic growth and employment; social progress which recognises the needs of everyone; effective protection of the environment and prudent use of natural resources.

7.44 A good practice guide on sustainability appraisal[46] suggests that appraisal needs to be integrated with the whole plan making process from the very earliest preparatory stages through the setting of objectives, development and selection of options, public consultations and final implementation and review. In practice, most of the current round of regional planning guidance did not have the benefit of the good practice guide at the time their appraisals were carried out. Despite the emphasis on appraising different development options in national guidance, few appraisals actually did this.[47]

7.45 In many cases of regional planning guidance, where sustainability appraisals are mandatory, they have been undertaken at such a late stage that they are in fact appraisals of draft proposals rather than appraisals of various policy and strategic options.[48] An independent review of the draft regional planning guidance for the South East concluded that the appraisal could not determine whether there was a spatial strategy that would be more sustainable because there was no basis for considering the implications of growth in different locations.[49] While there is evidence that more recent sustainability appraisals have begun the process at an earlier stage,[50] we emphasise that more emphasis must be placed on the strategic function of sustainability appraisal though the rigorous assessment of different development options against environmental objectives.

7.46 The practice of sustainability appraisals has been criticised for its lack of quantification and for the 'poor science' involved in its environmental analyses. Of particular concern is the fact that the sustainability appraisal process does not need 'base-line' environmental studies as strategic environmental assessment does.[51] In addition, very few appraisals have addressed cumulative or secondary impacts as advised in national guidance.[52] More advice is evidently needed on the function of 'base-line' environmental study and how exactly to analyse indirect and cumulative effects of development options over a large scale.

7.47 Concern has been expressed that sustainability appraisal can in fact marginalise the very environmental and social appraisals that it is supposed to bolster as a counterpoint to dominant financial and economic assessments. Clearly, where the driver or imperative for a policy, plan or programme is an economic one, as it often is, appraising the effects of the policy, plan or programme in terms of economic criteria and subsequently justifying it on that basis renders the appraisal meaningless. The purpose of environmental appraisal must be to integrate environmental concerns into primarily non-environmental areas of decision-making. We believe that the environmental component of sustainability appraisal must be strengthened, as a condition for its retention.

7.48 **We recommend that the government, if it wishes to retain sustainability appraisal, strengthen the environmental component so that it will satisfy the legal requirements of the European Directive on strategic environmental assessment. We do not consider that sustainability appraisal as currently undertaken is adequate for this purpose.** The alternative is to recognise strategic environmental assessment as the central requirement with a non-statutory supplementary exercise to take account of the economic and social dimension.

Part III

The way forward

Chapter 8

PROVIDING THE RIGHT FRAMEWORK

Is there a sound framework to facilitate environmental planning? Are policy objectives for the environment, and the purpose of the town and country planning system, sufficiently clear? Are national policies communicated effectively to planning authorities? Where putting national policies into effect involves possibly controversial construction projects, can procedures protect all aspects of environmental quality?

8.1 In the final part of this report we consider how environmental planning can be made more transparent, more effective, and more accountable. In chapter 8 we recommend improvements in the legislation and policies which provide the overall framework for environmental planning. In chapter 9 we review some important respects in which more attention has to be given to the environmental implications of key policies affecting land use, and the implications for land use of likely long-term changes in the environment. In chapter 10 we consider how the environment can be protected and improved by bringing together at strategic level plans for land use and other spatially related aspects of the environment, and integrating them with economic and social planning.

8.2 The actions needed to achieve environmental goals must often be taken at local level, perhaps even by individual households or firms. There are strong arguments that environmental goals should also be set at the lowest practicable level.[1] Many environmental problems have to be addressed at national level, however. And, as we recognised at the beginning of this report, environmental problems are also increasingly being addressed at levels beyond the nation state (1.25), with governments carrying responsibility for implementing European legislation and complying with international agreements. Moreover, even when environmental goals are set locally, they are established and pursued in the framework set by national legislation.

8.3 In this chapter we look at the national level, and at some of the links between national and local levels. We consider first how national policies and priorities for the environment should be expressed (8.5-8.11) and implemented (8.12-8.18), then at the overall focus of the legislation under which the town and country planning system and the Environment Agencies operate (8.19-8.37), and how national policies are communicated to planning authorities (8.38-8.42).

8.4 We consider the government's proposals for changes in the procedures for approval of major infrastructure projects for which it is argued there is a national need (8.43-8.58). Then we consider the problem of deciding on the location of, and authorisation for, more widespread and common types of development for which there would appear to be a strong environmental or sustainable development case, but which are nonetheless likely to encounter forceful resistance, sometimes indeed on environmental grounds, often though by no means exclusively from local people. We take the case of the projected rapid growth in renewable energy installations as the example (8.59-8.74).

A CLEAR STATEMENT OF ENVIRONMENTAL OBJECTIVES

8.5 The government and the devolved administrations have an extensive range of policies for the environment, including many policies which stem from European legislation or international agreements. No part of the UK, however, has a single document in which all the environmental policies affecting it are brought together and related to each other. The Environment White Papers in the first half of the 1990s provided a comprehensive summary of policies, but were so lengthy and detailed that it was difficult to discern the overall picture.[2] The Sustainable Development Strategy for the UK published in 1999 (3.8 and box 3A) was a briefer document with a much wider scope;[3] several of the future priorities it lists are environmental, but expressed in very general terms (for example, 'improving the larger towns and cities to make them better places to live and work'). There are seven environmental indicators among the headline indicators for sustainable development established for the UK as part of that strategy (3.39 and box 3B); but, although some of them relate to targets set previously, they do not in themselves represent policy commitments, and they do not cover all aspects of the environment. When the Environment Agency wanted a list of environmental targets for the next 20 years as a basis for establishing priorities and programmes for its own work, it had to compile the list itself. The Agency told us in evidence that it thought such a list ought to have been readily available from government.[4] We agree.

8.6 The position is very different in some other European countries. The Netherlands has a firmly established system for setting environmental objectives at national level, and has recently adopted its Fourth National Environmental Policy Plan, based on the desired situation in 2030.[5] In 1999 Sweden adopted 15 national environmental quality objectives to be achieved within one generation; the government appointed a Committee on Environmental Objectives to develop comprehensive proposals on intermediate targets, strategies and policy instruments for that purpose, in co-operation with government agencies and the county administrative boards.[6]

8.7 **We recommend that a comprehensive and definitive statement of priority objectives for the environment be produced now for each part of the UK, and widely publicised.** This should be a short document of not more than a couple of pages, with cross-references to more detailed documents available on specific issues. In box 8A we have listed aspects of the environment which we think such a statement should cover. The list is not intended to be exhaustive or definitive; for example, it might well be there should be a separate objective for noise. **Wherever possible, this statement must include a quantified target or targets for movement towards the objective by a specified date.** To be comprehensive, however, it must also include objectives for aspects of the environment for which it has not so far been possible to produce accepted indicators, for example the quality of urban areas (see 9.27 below).

BOX 8A	POSSIBLE ENVIRONMENTAL OBJECTIVES FOR THE UK

Reduce emissions of persistent or bioaccumulative chemicals, to limit or reduce
   concentrations in the environment

Maintain or enhance terrestrial and freshwater biodiversity

Maintain or enhance marine biodiversity

Maintain or enhance freshwater quality and resources

Maintain or enhance groundwater quality and resources

Maintain or enhance inshore and estuarine water quality

Maintain or enhance air quality

Maintain or enhance soil quality and resources

Reduce rate and extent of climate change by reducing emissions of greenhouse gases,
   thereby reducing increase in concentrations

Reduce levels of ultraviolet B radiation in sunshine by reducing emissions of ozone-depleting
   chemicals

Enhance quality of the local/residential environment

Maintain or enhance landscapes/perceived quality of rural environment

Reduce volumes of waste

Reduce energy intensity of the economy

8.8   To avoid delay in preparing them, the initial statements should be seen as essentially compilations of existing policies in order to present them in a much more accessible and effective form. **We recommend that the initial statements of priority environmental objectives should be reviewed at an early date through a process of extensive consultation and debate about environmental priorities.** As well as engaging industry, environmental groups and other stakeholders, central aims should be to articulate people's values and aspirations about the environment, using approaches of the kind described in the Commission's report on standards (3.41) and to identify key environmental constraints. This process will produce a set of priority objectives for the environment which are robust and widely supported.

8.9   In view of the extent to which environmental policy is determined at European and international levels (1.25), on the basis of negotiations conducted by the UK government, **it will be necessary to produce a statement of priority environmental objectives for the UK as a whole, as well as for each component part**.

8.10 We accept that environmental policies should be based on 'acting proportionately; recognising that not every environmental improvement will be justifiable when all sustainable development objectives are taken into account'.[7] At the same time there is considerable potential for achieving legitimate environmental objectives simultaneously with economic and social objectives by reducing wastage and improving resource productivity (3.18).[8] **We recommend the statements of priority objectives should be prepared on the basis that sustainable development is achievable only if the environment is safeguarded and enhanced** (as we argued in chapter 3). These seem inescapable responsibilities for the UK in particular, given its wealth and the scale of environmental damage it has suffered.[9] The objectives and targets in the statements must also incorporate appropriate contributions to protecting and improving the environment outside the UK's own boundaries.

8.11 Although the UK Sustainable Development Strategy (3.8) refers to overall improvements in environmental quality, its 'main aims' refer less ambitiously to 'effective protection of the environment' and 'prudent use of natural resources'. The tone contrasts with the references under other headings to social *progress* and economic *growth*. The contrast could be taken to imply that further degradation of the environment would be an acceptable price to pay for economic growth and/or social progress. That is a widely prevalent interpretation of 'sustainable development'. We have concluded this interpretation is wholly misconceived. The statement of priority objectives and the associated targets will change the context for decision-making by raising awareness of environmental concerns. It will help ensure they are not overshadowed by the economic and social dimensions of sustainable development, which are more immediate and familiar for most people, and already the subject of many high-profile policy targets.

GIVING EFFECT TO THE OBJECTIVES

8.12 The statements of priority objectives must be collective commitments by, respectively, the UK government and the devolved administrations. One of their main purposes will be to contribute to integration of policies across government. In some cases, for example, it may be appropriate to incorporate a target in a public service agreement between the Treasury and a government Department, as has happened already for the number of farmland birds.[10]

8.13 **It is essential that each objective is underpinned by a soundly based programme for achieving it.** Modelling techniques (7.17-7.21) have to be used to translate the end-point of a desired environmental quality into the mid-points of scientifically measurable parameters, and in turn to translate those into the required policy measures (for example, limits on emissions or restraints on activities leading to emissions). In drawing up the statements of priority objectives the government and the devolved administrations must also take responsibility for co-ordinating their effective implementation. Clear and comprehensive programmes for implementation do not always exist at present.

8.14 Although there are quantified targets under international agreements for reducing the UK's emissions of nitrogen oxides, for example, the contributions that different sectors should make have not been properly explored and discussed. It is therefore difficult to be sure that the target will be met, and even more difficult to know whether the burden will be shared equitably and efficiently between transport, agriculture, electricity generation, other industry and the service and domestic sectors.

8.15 A good example of the kind of programme we consider necessary is that already in place for reducing emissions of greenhouse gases to comply with the Kyoto protocol and move towards the government's own more ambitious target for 2010.[11] Although we have criticised some elements in it as not being adequately defined,[12] it has the great merit of bringing together contributions from all sectors, from all levels of government, and from a full range of policy instruments. In this case the programme is UK-wide, incorporating contributions from the devolved administrations. It includes fiscal measures designed to influence energy use by industry, and some measures taken at European level such as the voluntary agreement with car manufacturers and energy efficiency standards for products. It also includes changes in the building regulations and measures local planning authorities will be encouraged to take with the aim of reducing energy demand.

8.16 An important theme of all the programmes must be to identify and put into effect measures which will simultaneously contribute to economic, environmental and social objectives. We pointed out in our report on energy, for example, that developing renewable sources contributes to a diversity of UK energy supplies, and that energy efficiency programmes for houses help reduce fuel poverty. There will also be opportunities to contribute to more than one environmental objective; for example reductions in the amounts of fossil fuels used reduce emissions of other pollutants, as well as carbon dioxide. Central government and the devolved administrations can often increase the likelihood that several objectives will be achieved simultaneously, for example by introducing economic instruments or through the design of suitable programmes; but it will often be industries and local authorities which have the knowledge and insight to be innovative and imaginative in devising solutions which make the maximum contribution to sustainability within their particular circumstances. It is vital, however, that all measures are designed and assessed by reference to explicit and rigorous criteria for environmental quality and impact.

8.17 The nature of the implementation programme will vary according to the objective, in particular whether it incorporates a quantified target and the nature of that target. In the case of greenhouse gas emissions there is an overall target for the UK. Measures taken in Scotland, Wales and Northern Ireland towards achieving that target are the responsibility of the devolved administrations, and the UK programme has been produced jointly with them; they are also developing their own programmes.[13] The Department for Environment, Food and Rural Affairs (DEFRA) collates projections of emissions from different sources, calculates whether the measures being taken at all levels of government and by all sectors are sufficient in total to achieve the target, and will monitor overall progress.

8.18 In other cases, the objective set nationally will have to be interpreted and applied within local situations. This is particularly true for the objectives of improving the quality of residential and rural environments. Cultural factors and people's values are important factors determining what is considered desirable. And for at least some aspects, such as landscape, it will be difficult or impossible to define valid quantitative indicators. The adequacy of the institutions available at regional and local levels will be crucial for these objectives, but it will be important for the other objectives as well.

A CLEARER BASIS FOR TOWN AND COUNTRY PLANNING

8.19 In implementing many of those policies the town and country planning system will continue to play a central part. To do so effectively, however, it will need to undergo significant changes. In part this will be a matter of improving its credibility and ensuring it enjoys public confidence, an aspect we discussed in chapter 5. In part it will be a matter of improving the capacity for strategic planning; we deal with that in chapter 10. We have concluded it is also desirable to introduce greater clarity about the purpose of the town and country planning system, in a way which recognises its crucial importance for environmental sustainability, as well as its other purposes.

8.20 As already noted (2.8), a distinctive feature of the British town and country planning legislation is that, since the introduction of comprehensive planning controls in 1947, there has been little on the face of the legislation that provides any guidance as to the purpose of the system. As Professor Malcolm Grant has put it,

> The Act carefully avoids any definition of 'planning' or of its aims and objectives: 'planning' from a reading of the Act as a whole is to do with whatever central government and the local planning authorities decide it is to do with.[14]

8.21 Furthermore, when dealing with planning applications, authorities must have regard to the provisions of the development plan so far as it is material and to any other material considerations.[15] Since 1991 there has been a presumption in favour of applications consistent with the development plan.[16] There is no further guidance in the legislation as to what are or are not material considerations. This is left almost exclusively to the discretion of government through its policy advice and the individual judgements of local planning authorities, with the courts providing some fairly general boundaries.[17]

A STATUTORY PURPOSE

8.22 Given the extensive reach of planning controls, and the complexity of the system, the absence of a statutory purpose is somewhat surprising. Most contemporary regulatory legislation in the environmental field provides at least some degree of statutory guidance about its purpose[18] and in the case of European Community Directives and Regulations there are extensive preambles which are used by the courts and regulatory bodies as an important aid to interpretation.

8.23 Even in the case of planning, pre-1947 legislation contained a rather more precise statement of goals. For example, section 54 of the Housing, Town Planning etc. Act 1909 provided for the permissive preparation of town planning schemes 'with the general object of securing proper sanitary conditions, amenity, and convenience in connection with the laying out and use of the land'. The Town and Country Planning Act 1932 contained a similar statement of objectives for planning schemes.[19]

8.24 Modern British planning legislation is infused with discretion and implicitly acknowledges that planning is an intensely political function. It may be that in the immediate post-war period there was a greater consensus as to the purposes of planning, but it is clear that there have been significant shifts of emphasis since then with national government possessing a large degree of policy influence through the issue of circulars and policy guidance, its own institutional relationship with local government, and its specific powers, particularly in respect of appeals, under the planning system.

8.25 The courts themselves have intervened, providing rulings as to the legitimate purpose of planning, and their views have similarly developed over the years, being fairly restrictive in the 1950s, later acknowledging wider social purposes, and now handling the potential conflicts between land use planning and the dedicated environmental regulatory controls which have developed since the introduction of land use planning controls.

8.26 As we have already noted in chapter 5, the planning system has long provided opportunities for a large degree of public consultation and participation, and in this respect offers a contrast to many other areas of environmental regulation which until fairly recently were characterised by a lack of openness and public involvement.[20] The planning system has constituted an important forum for the articulation of different perspectives and the challenging of prevailing assumptions where difficult social choices are being made. This was particularly noticeable in the 1970s and 1980s, when environmental groups used the opportunities provided by planning procedures to question underlying 'predict and provide' philosophies in areas such as water reservoir development, energy facilities and highway developments.

8.27 Many would argue that the flexibility that the planning system provides, which is epitomised by the lack of statutory objectives, has been a strength. It can adapt to changing public perceptions and reflect rapidly changing policy priorities. In the 1980s, for example, government policy urged local authorities 'always to grant planning permission, having regard to all material considerations, unless there are sound and clear cut reasons for refusal'[21] and to avoid taking enforcement action against small businesses if at all possible. More recent guidance gives greater emphasis to environmental protection and sustainable development.[22]

8.28 However, as we try to lay the basis for a planning system appropriate for the 21st century, we question the wisdom of maintaining a structure infused with such a degree of discretion and so liable to oscillate between what Professor McAuslan has vividly described as the competing 'ideologies' of planning law.[23] For those charged with taking planning decisions or the construction of development plans there often remains confusion as to the purpose of planning. Professor Grant has criticised planning law as being a subject for the most part 'unsympathetically handled by Parliamentary draftsmen and their departmental advisors' and concluded that:

> It lacks any overall coherence, and comprehending and interpreting it is a difficult enough task for the professional, let alone the layman. The paradox is that this is [the] administrative system which is perhaps more than any other reliant upon general public support, yet in an era of public participation evinces every sign of slipping farther and farther away from popular intelligibility.[24]

Though written over twenty years ago, his words still ring true today.

8.29 We make other recommendations later about the consolidation and simplification of policy guidance, but we feel that the time has come to inject a clearer expression of the purposes of town and country planning into the primary legislation. Though it should be more about enabling development to take place in appropriate ways (which may often be environmentally beneficial) than about preventing development, town and country planning remains at heart a powerful regulatory system. In terms of the relationship between government and citizens, it is both appropriate and consistent with contemporary developments in administrative and constitutional law that the underlying legal structure provides a more explicit statement of the basis and purpose of this relationship. The European Convention on Human Rights, for example, now incorporated into the UK by the Human Rights Act 1998, provides a general right for the peaceful enjoyment of possession, but this right is not to prevent the state from enforcing laws deemed necessary 'in accordance with the general interest'.[25]

8.30 We have given some thought to how such a statement of purposes should be constructed. There are four ways in which the purposes of legislation can be expressed: (a) a statement of its general or overriding purpose (b) a statement of principles (c) the specification of criteria against which decisions must be taken and (d) a set of binding rules for taking decision.

8.31 In the field of town and country planning an example of binding rules might be a zoning system which grants development rights in designated areas. The British system of planning controls, however, has rested (even in designated areas such a Green Belts) on policy presumptions rather than binding rules in this sense; we accept that this is a valuable feature which should remain. Nor do we believe it would be easy to construct a comprehensive statement of principles for inclusion in primary legislation, and giving any statement of principles such a form would in any case be too inflexible.

8.32 Our conclusion is that the town and country planning legislation should be amended to include both a statement of its general purpose and a set of criteria to be taken into account in decision-making. Except in cases of blatant non-observance, we recognise that it is unlikely that such a general objective would be directly enforceable by the courts; it would be more akin to what is described in written constitutions as a directory duty. It would act as a gravitational rule, providing a context and guidance for subsequent policy development and decision-making. As such, the drafting needs to provide sufficient flexibility, but avoid such blandness or vagueness as to have little longer-term effect.

8.33 For these reasons, we do not feel it would advance matters greatly to state in the legislation that the purpose of town and country planning is simply to 'promote sustainable development'. We recognise that planning is not simply concerned with environmental protection, but we look for a form of legislative wording which does not merely restate a set of potentially conflicting interests but expresses appropriate relationships. An interesting model is the wording of the environment section of the South African Constitution which refers to 'securing sustainable development and use of natural resources while promoting justifiable economic and social development'. The references to 'justifiable' development implies that such development must be consistent with environmental goals. We also emphasise that the policy aim should be, not merely protection of the environment, but its enhancement; the wording of a purpose clause should reflect that. **We recommend that the town and country planning system should be given a statutory purpose, and that, rather than use the term 'sustainable development', an appropriate purpose would be 'to facilitate the achievement of legitimate economic and social goals whilst ensuring that the quality of the environment is safeguarded and, wherever appropriate, enhanced'.**

8.34 Such a statutory statement of purposes for town and country planning would flesh out what is meant by the 'general interest' (8.29) and would provide a greater degree of stability and a clearer focus for the more detailed development of policies and guidance, as well as providing the courts with a firmer set of principles on which to construct the legitimate boundaries of the system. Such a statutory statement will not in itself resolve the difficult and complex decisions that are inherent in planning. But it would provide more certainty to the legislative structure, and an expression of key principles within which individual decisions can be made. We also believe that it will attract greater public understanding and support as to the underlying purpose of the system.

8.35 The legislation under which the Environment Agencies operate is also unsatisfactory. The Environment Agency has a principal aim referring to sustainable development (2.31) which is so convoluted as to be almost incomprehensible, and certainly is of no practical value. Their specific functions are exercised under a number of different Acts. When they were established, the government of the day decided the rationalisation and consolidation of that legislation was too large and difficult a task to be undertaken immediately and should be left to a later date. We are disappointed that six years later a start has not yet been made. **We repeat the recommendation made by the Commission in 1996 that the diverse legislation the Environment Agencies inherited should be reviewed to give it coherence and relate it to consistent general principles, and the necessary changes should be enacted at the earliest practicable opportunity.**[26]

MATERIAL CONSIDERATIONS

8.36 To complement the general purpose clause we have recommended for town and country planning legislation, there needs to be a clearer specification of the criteria against which decisions on planning applications should be made. At present, legislation refers to the development plan and to 'material considerations'; but it has never attempted to define what considerations are material. We have concluded the time has now come to incorporate a definition of 'material consideration' in the legislation. We do not envisage this will be elaborate or exhaustive; rather, it will ensure that some key considerations are given legislative prominence. **We recommend that town and country planning legislation should stipulate key aspects of the environment and natural resources as material considerations that should be taken into account in considering all planning applications.** This is consistent with what we have recommended should be the general purpose for the town and country planning system.

8.37 The specific considerations listed could include 'the preservation and enhancement of amenity, biological diversity and the physical environment', 'the promotion of public health and well-being' and 'the need to sustain the potential of natural and physical resources to meet the reasonably foreseeable needs of future generations' (which reflects the longer-term goals of environmental sustainability). Introducing such criteria into legislation does not detract from the general principle that in the final analysis 'matters of planning judgment are within the exclusive province of the local planning authority or the Secretary of State'.[27] However, if both a general purpose clause and criteria for material considerations are introduced, this would be sufficient to influence the general direction of planning in the way we consider necessary.

IMPROVED POLICY GUIDANCE

8.38 Although the policies of national government do not in themselves have any statutory force within the town and country planning system, they are a material consideration which has to be taken into account in decisions on planning applications.[28] They also indicate the kind of policies local planning authorities are expected to include in development plans. All those involved in, or affected by, the town and country planning system need to have clear and up-to-date guidance about national policies, and not least about the priority objectives for the environment (8.7) and their implications. At present guidance is provided through the series of Planning Policy Guidance notes (PPGs) in England, the series of National Planning Policy Guidance notes (NPPGs) in Scotland, and a single document for Wales.[29] A wide range of subjects is covered, as was shown in box 2B. This guidance is supplemented by various circulars; an expanding literature of good practice guides and research reports; and in Scotland and Wales, respectively, by series of more detailed Planning Advice Notes and Technical Advice Notes.

8.39   The Planning Green Paper acknowledges a widespread concern in England that the present PPGs are lengthy and 'often unfocused' and mix 'key planning policy principles, which must be followed, with good practice advice'.[30] Similar concerns were expressed in the evidence submitted to us. The guidance given can often be equivocal, and do little more than inform planners that they have to strike a difficult balance between competing objectives. A further shortcoming of PPGs is that they are revised individually as the government thinks fit and as resources allow, and are often out of date and inconsistent with each other and with other statements of government policy. We have already noted (3.31), for example, that PPG1, *General policy and principles*, was issued almost five years ago, and is now out of date in important respects.[31]

8.40   In the Green Paper the government proposes 'to review the whole body of national planning guidance and particularly the PPG series so that it concentrates on the key planning policies that should be determined at the national level'.[32] The aim is 'to seek much greater clarity in the expression of planning policies and to describe them much more in terms of objectives and outcomes to be achieved'.[33] There is therefore the prospect of some improvement on the present position. We are concerned, however, that the change will not be sufficiently rapid and fundamental. The intention is to review seven PPGs over the next two years,[34] but that would still leave almost three times as many requiring attention. A full review of the PPG series would therefore take a considerable time to complete, and would still leave guidance scattered between a large number of separate documents. In contrast, the intention with the parallel series of Minerals Planning Guidance Notes is to concentrate policy guidance in one key document, supplemented if necessary by technical or system notes,[35] and we welcome that.

8.41   **We recommend that planning policy guidance for England (the PPG series) should be condensed into a single document updated at frequent intervals, both on the Internet and in paper form; that consideration be given to a similar rationalisation of planning policy guidance for Scotland; and that the National Assembly ensure that the guidance document for Wales sets out clear policies and is regularly updated.** In each case, the guidance document should set out clearly the overall objectives of national policy, including the environmental objectives, and follow that with chapters specifying objectives in relation to particular aspects of land use. The Internet version of the document could be amended as often as necessary, with the changes publicised and notified to all planning authorities. The paper version should be reissued not less frequently than every two years. There would be extensive references to good practice guides and other, more detailed documents published separately.

8.42 To promote sustainable development, the guidance document should aim to help planners find ways of reconciling economic, social and environmental objectives wherever possible and bringing about environmental improvements. In cases where objectives are in conflict, it should indicate clearly how planners should interpret environmental constraints. The guidance should be in sufficiently clear terms to produce changes in land use trends which the UK government and the devolved administrations judge are at odds with sustainable development.

A CLEARER CONTEXT FOR MAJOR PROJECTS

8.43 The Green Paper also refers to the government's intention to 'issue national statements about our major infrastructure needs so that we set a clear policy framework for investment decisions which have national significance'.[36] A recurrent criticism of the town and country planning system has been the length of public inquiries. The Heathrow Terminal Five inquiry set a new record by sitting for 524 days over four years; previously the longest public inquiry had been that for Sizewell B nuclear power station in the early 1980s, which sat for 340 days. There have been less than a dozen national-scale projects since 1984 for which the public inquiry lasted more than three months. Although such cases are relatively infrequent, however, the government considers the present planning system is 'unwieldy and expensive for all concerned' and 'takes too long to process major infrastructure projects [which] are essential to our economic future and bring benefits through better services'.[37]

8.44 As well as airports and large power stations, major projects might include ports, reservoirs, major roads and railways, major oil and gas installations and chemical works, and quarries and mines. Not all these types of project require authorisation under the town and country planning system.[38] They are all likely at present to require approval from a Minister or from Parliament before they can proceed; but they would not include all the cases considered by Ministers under the town and country planning system (5.30 and box 5A).

8.45 A consultation paper on reform was issued in May 1999.[39] In July 2001 the Secretary of State for Transport, Local Government and the Regions announced[40] that the government would be proceeding with a package of measures which would 'help to get projects in place more quickly by streamlining the procedures and cutting unnecessary delay whilst ensuring the process remains open and fair and democratically accountable'. This package consists of:

'up-to-date statements of Government policy which would normally have involved public consultation, to be in place before major projects are considered in the planning system'

'an improved regional framework which will assist consideration of individual projects'

'new Parliamentary procedures to enable the Secretary of State to put a project of national significance to Parliament for agreement and debate on the broad principles ahead of a more detailed inquiry'

'more clearly focused terms of reference' for the public inquiry, a strict timetable, and stronger powers for inspectors to ensure the timetable and terms of reference are adhered to

reform of the arrangements for compulsory purchase and compensation.

These proposals apply only to England. Consultation papers have subsequently been issued on the parliamentary procedures envisaged[41] and on compulsory purchase and compensation.[42]

8.46 The proposal is that the Secretary of State should designate an individual project as a major project for the purpose of the new procedures. It is likely that he would do so on the basis of a list of project types; while projects designated would generally be 'of national significance', that is not at the moment proposed as an express requirement.[43] The Secretary of State has suggested the new procedures might apply to two or three projects a year.[44] A draft Order would be laid before both Houses of Parliament 60 sitting days after designation in order to obtain approval in principle for the project, including the need for it and its location; those issues could not then be considered at the subsequent public inquiry. Planning permission and any other consents required would be given by the Secretary of State following the public inquiry.[45]

8.47 When he designated a major project the Secretary of State would lay before both Houses of Parliament the application and environmental impact assessment submitted by the developer and the relevant national policy statement(s) and regional planning guidance. The developer would be required to submit within 21 days 'a statement of the wider economic and other benefits of the project'. There would be a further 21 days after that in which anyone could submit objections and representations to the Secretary of State, who would copy them to Parliament.[46] It is not known as yet what procedures Parliament would adopt in order to scrutinise a proposed project.[47]

8.48 There is general agreement that it is advantageous to assess a proposed major project in the light of an up-to-date statement of government policy in the relevant field, even though such a project is now more likely to be promoted by a private sector organisation than by a government Department or nationalised industry. Producing such a policy statement is likely to take a significant time, and that process would have to precede the designation of a major project. In the case of nuclear waste a House of Lords committee has called for government policy to be enshrined in an Act of Parliament and subject to regular endorsement by Parliament.[48] As the government's proposals stand, however, there would be no formal safeguard to ensure that a satisfactory policy statement was available before parliamentary procedures started; parliamentary approval would relate to the specific project, not overall policy. Although there would no doubt be strong political pressures that a general policy should be in place, the consultation paper says only that there would 'generally' be such a policy, on which there would 'normally' be prior public consultation.[49]

8.49 **We emphasise that proposals for major infrastructure projects should always be put forward within the framework of carefully considered national policies, which should always be adopted after wide public consultation, and take full account of environmental considerations including the statement of environmental objectives we have recommended** (8.7). The overall aim of policy should always be to achieve justifiable social and economic goals whilst safeguarding and enhancing the environment. Government may well think it prudent to seek parliamentary endorsement for its overall policy before specific projects come forward. But there must certainly also be adequate opportunities for a wider public contribution to, and scrutiny of, the proposed policy framework. The policy put forward should be informed both by rigorous analysis and by articulation of people's values, using procedures on the lines of those which the Commission advocated in its report on setting environmental standards.[50]

8.50 A national policy underlying major infrastructure projects should normally look at least 25 years ahead, and be reviewed every 5-10 years to take account of changes in circumstances. Major projects are often a lumpy response to a long-term trend. For example, a new airport or runway is put forward in response to the recorded and projected increases in air travel, a new road in response to increases in traffic. Those long-term trends might be damaging to the environment to the point where they could not be regarded as sustainable. **The national need for additional infrastructure should be probed in an open and participatory process, which where practicable should engage local communities which may be affected.** Government should commission research on the factors creating the apparent need, and their overall impact; consider the possibility of measures to reduce or halt increases in demand; examine whether there are alternative approaches which might have the effect of removing the need for new infrastructure; and investigate methods of mitigating, or compensating for, environmental damage. In short, the government should carry out a strategic environmental assessment of the policy options (7.42).[51]

8.51 If the government concludes there is an unavoidable need for new infrastructure, it will be difficult in most cases to frame a valid national policy unless it also covers what would be the best location or locations for that infrastructure, taking environmental, social and economic factors into account. The policy would at least have to cover the criteria for choice of locations, even if not the actual locations. Under the government's proposals the location of a proposed project is one of the issues which Parliament will be asked to endorse, and which could not then be considered at the subsequent public inquiry.

8.52 Port facilities can be taken as an example. The government may form a view on the likely growth in sea-borne freight, and its likely sources and destinations. It should reach conclusions on such issues after consultation and public debate, and after considering alternative scenarios, and should explain and justify its position. On the assumption it sees a need for significant additional infrastructure, it ought to consult on a range of options for the pattern of development. Should there be expansion at all ports? Or would the best overall solution on environmental, social and economic grounds be to expand a few ports, or one port, or to construct a new major port? The answer is likely to depend on, among other things, the location of ports relative to the main centres of demand, the availability of road and rail links, and the distances between ports. The resulting policy would provide a national framework for the sustainable development of sea-borne freight, and would have a strong spatial content in terms of which ports ought to expand and why.

8.53 There appears to be a general move towards this kind of approach. The government intends to publish a national aviation strategy, supplemented by seven regional consultation documents exploring capacity options. Environmental groups and local authorities have broadly welcomed this because, for the first time in aviation policy, there is the prospect of a shift away from the 'predict and provide' approach. Whether that will happen in practice remain to be seen. For major surface transport projects the location in broad terms is likely to be an intrinsic part of the project; but alternative routes may well be possible. Moreover, there is now an established requirement that multi-modal studies should be carried out in order to explore alternatives to building a new road.

8.54 As the national policy Parliament would be asked to accept under the government's proposals is likely to have to cover the location for the relevant type of project, the formulation of that policy ought to involve consultation procedures which are appropriate in those circumstances. Although the proposal submitted to Parliament would be accompanied by an environmental impact assessment, it is not clear to what extent that would explore alternative locations; and there would be severe limitations on the depth in which Parliament itself could investigate such issues within the kind of timescale the government is envisaging. Several bodies which have studied this topic recently have concluded that there ought to be much more extensive scrutiny of a proposed major infrastructure project than Parliament would be likely to provide. A task force containing representatives of planners and the construction industry has proposed the creation of a Major Projects Evaluation Commission to investigate the basis for individual decisions to be taken at ministerial level.[52] It envisaged this commission would define a methodology for such decisions by setting out best practice for evaluating the economic, social and environmental aspects of projects. It would also promote public participation and mediation and produce protocols for compensation to affected parties.

8.55 After considering how a nuclear waste repository should be authorised the House of Lords Science and Technology Committee recommended that a site should be selected under the aegis of an independent Nuclear Waste Management Commission.[53] The Radioactive Waste Management Advisory Commission recommended that a planning inquiry commission should be set up to produce a short-list of two or three sites for such a repository.[54] A planning inquiry commission is a two-stage public inquiry, in which the first stage would consider general issues and the second stage specific locations.[55]

8.56 As part of its proposals for expediting consideration of major infrastructure projects, the government has laid emphasis on providing a better regional planning framework (8.45, 8.47). In chapter 10 we set out the case for an improved form of planning at regional and sub-regional levels which would take much fuller account of environmental factors. If those proposals are accepted, it would facilitate the selection of the most suitable sites for major infrastructure projects. However, it would not be a complete solution to the problem of site selection. The openness and transparency of the process leading to the national policy framework and any proposed major projects presented to Parliament will affect their real, or perceived, legitimacy. **The issues involved in framing a national policy underlying major infrastructure projects may be better handled by a body which combines inquisitorial and adversarial elements, as a planning inquiry commission would.**

8.57 The final stage in authorisation under the government's proposals would be a public inquiry confined to detailed matters. Under these circumstances a public inquiry could be much shorter. Environmental groups, on the other hand, have valued the ability of public inquiries to question and debate the claimed need for a major project and associated government policies, and to consider possible alternatives. They fear the government's proposals are designed to drive through major projects without adequate opportunity for reasoned debate and scrutiny. The goal of reform, they argue, should be to reach better decisions, rather than simply to speed up the process. They consider that the possibility of questioning the location for a project is a vital part of a public inquiry.

8.58 Even with a national policy in place, and irrespective of any requirements under the Human Rights Act, **there must continue to be open hearings at which local people and others can express views about the local impacts of a proposed major infrastructure project and challenge claims by the developer**. The government has left open the possibility that, in the light of the inspector's report and recommendations following the public inquiry, the Secretary of State might decide a project should not proceed, although it says this would happen only in 'exceptional circumstances'.[56] **We recommend that, if under the government's proposals for major projects the inspector conducing the local inquiry concludes that the local impacts of a proposed project would be unacceptable, he should be permitted to recommend that the approval in principle should be reconsidered.**

A CLEARER FRAMEWORK FOR ACHIEVING NATIONAL TARGETS

8.59 Developments which do not count individually as major infrastructure projects may nevertheless be of national importance in aggregate. Several types of development are essential if the objectives for UK environmental policies are to be met, but often encounter strong opposition. They include coastal sewage works needed to comply with the requirements of European Community (EC) legislation about treatment of discharges or to improve the quality of bathing waters to meet EC standards; and plants for the recycling or incineration of wastes needed to meet targets for increasing recycling and phasing out landfilling of wastes. Our earlier recommendation that the procedure for planning applications for such plants should be co-ordinated with the procedure for authorising them under pollution control legislation (5.24) will help matters, but other measures are also likely to be necessary to overcome continuing difficulties in obtaining planning permission in such cases.

8.60 To investigate what form such measures should take we consider here another type of case, plants for generating electricity from renewable sources, and in particular wind turbines. The government's target is that 10% of UK electricity should be obtained from renewable sources in 2010, and in our report on energy we recommended that a much higher target should be adopted for the longer term.[57] Success in achieving such targets may depend to a large extent on developing wind energy, which is the most commercially competitive large-scale renewable resource at present. The expansion of renewable energy is a policy with a clear environmental justification which enjoys very wide public support.[58] In our report on energy, however, we concluded that 'Planning applications have met with so much resistance in numerous localities that the development of wind energy on land in the UK is, in effect, stalled.'[59] More recently the review of energy policy by the Performance and Innovation Unit concluded that 'The business of obtaining planning permission for renewable investments, particularly onshore wind in England and Wales, remains costly and time-consuming.... Unless success rates increase, targets will not be met.'[60]

8.61 Opposition to the types of project identified above may reflect concerns about their effects on the immediate locality. In the case of wind farms, however, such concern would be mainly about noise, which we concluded is not now a significant problem;[61] consistent with that is the finding that public support for renewable energy tends to increase in the vicinity of a plant after it has come into operation.[62] Issues of much wider concern are the visual intrusion into what are often wild and beautiful landscapes and the hazards posed to birds in flight.[63]

8.62 The government has tried to engender a more positive approach to renewable energy by promoting regional assessments through the Government Offices in the regions. The intention was that these would lead to regional targets for renewable energy provision, which would be reflected in regional planning guidance, and thus in development plans.[64] The Department of Trade and Industry (DTI) is still reviewing the results of these assessments. Emphasis has been placed on the role of regional sustainability frameworks (2.54), but these are likely to give only very general endorsements: for example, the framework for the West Midlands, produced by the regional Round Table and adopted in 2000, says merely 'Renewable energy generation must be increased in the region.'

8.63 The Performance and Innovation Unit has recommended that regional planning bodies should give greater prominence to energy issues in regional planning guidance and that Regional Development Agencies should set regional targets for renewable energy, 'initially at indicative levels' following DTI's current review of regional assessments.[65]

8.64 We have some concerns about this approach. First, there could be a misconceived tendency to expect a broadly equal contribution from each region. In reality, the resources of some types of renewable energy are very unevenly distributed. Second, there are indications that the regional assessments were not produced on a consistent basis.[66]

8.65 **We recommend that targets set for developing renewable energy at regional and local levels should have a firm and consistent basis in terms of the capacity for developing each of the main types of renewable energy without damage to the environment.** A starting-point already exists in the assessments of the potential of renewable energy made by the Energy Technology Support Unit.[67] In the case of onshore wind, average wind speeds can be mapped to identify the areas in which it is possible to generate electricity, using wind turbines, at a cost within the buy-out price set under the Renewables Obligation. A very large area of the UK's uplands and coasts fall into that category. Areas in which it is considered environmentally unacceptable to build wind farms would then be eliminated. These might be defined as National Parks, Areas of Outstanding Natural Beauty, Heritage Coasts, National Nature Reserves, and possibly most other Sites of Special Scientific Interest.

8.66 There would then be a further judgement about constraining, but not entirely ruling out, wind farms in locally designated areas of high landscape and nature conservation value. There would also be a need for carefully drawn 'buffer zones' around the most prized landscape areas, such as National Parks, in order to protect views in and out of them.

8.67 Further constraints would be introduced by way of additional buffer zones, establishing various minimum distances between wind farms and airports, housing and other noise-sensitive buildings, woodland and high tension overhead cables. A crucial judgement would also have to be made concerning the minimum acceptable distance between two wind farms. This may vary from area to area; for example, the distance might be shorter in areas of lower landscape value (where windfarms might also be allowed to be taller and larger).

8.68 A bias in favour of proximity to power consumers and to regional and national grid connections should be introduced into this extensive mapping exercise. A sequential approach might also be adopted in identifying land most suitable for wind turbines, as is now the case for retail and housing developments. Previously used land in urban landscapes would be considered first (provided the turbines could be kept the specified minimum distance from buildings), followed by land within major transport corridors, then previously used land in rural landscapes (such as unrestored mineral sites). A similar approach could be adopted for the other renewables which are likely to play a significant part in meeting the government's 10% target – including offshore wind, energy crops and energy from waste.

8.69 **We strongly support giving greater prominence to energy issues in regional planning guidance.** This would be one significant step towards developing regional planning documents into the integrated spatial strategies we advocate in chapter 10. Although regions will differ considerably in the extent to which they are able to meet their own demands for energy, or could do so in future, analysis of their demands and sources will lead to a better understanding of the environmental and resource issues affecting the region. However, the methodology for setting regional targets for renewable energy should be specified at national level, on the general lines described above, in order to ensure transparency.

8.70 Some regions are taking a very positive approach to developing renewable sources. Examples are the strategy for energy in the North East of England produced by the Northern Energy Initiative,[68] and Renewables Northwest, a joint venture by the Northwest Development Agency and United Utilities.[69]

8.71 A factor in the low success rate of wind energy schemes in England may have been that policy guidance has not been kept up-to-date.[70] In contrast, in Scotland, where new planning guidance was issued in November 2000, two-thirds of planning applications for wind energy schemes have been successful.[71] Scottish guidance sets out the following clear 'guiding principles':

The Scottish Ministers wish to see the planning system play its full part by making positive provision for [renewable energy] developments by:

  facilitating and guiding renewable energy developments in up-to-date structure and local plans;

  ensuring that development control decisions are taken efficiently, consistent with national and international climate change policy commitments and obligations; and

  preventing the unnecessary sterilisation of renewable energy resources;

while at the same time:

  meeting the international and national statutory obligations to protect designated areas, species and habitats of natural heritage interest and the historic environment from inappropriate forms of development; and

  minimising the effects on local communities.[72]

Planning authorities are encouraged to use the development plan to guide developers to locations where renewable energy developments are likely to be permitted; and, where the development plan is unlikely to be updated in the near future, to consider preparing a non-statutory statement on the subject, after consultation.[73]

8.72 **We recommend that planning policy guidance on renewable energy in England, which is now nearly nine years old, should be revised and reissued as soon as possible.** This is not among the guidance the Planning Green Paper has listed for revision in the next two years.[74] In any event, as already indicated (8.41), our preference would be to see it become a chapter of a single guidance document. We support extending the scope of planning guidance on energy to include the national case for new investment in all types of energy-related facilities for which the regulatory decisions are taken by local authorities.[75]

8.73 From our consideration of the case of renewable energy, a more general conclusion emerges. **Mechanisms are needed to ensure that legitimate societal needs can be met in the face of preferences opposing the developments implied by those needs. The town and country planning system is intended to be such a mechanism but such developments must be essential parts of comprehensive and generally accepted policies, they must stem from transparent assessments of needs and environmental capacity, and there must be more imagination in countering any adverse effects on particular areas.**

8.74 A measure that might help to gain a more ready acceptance for renewable energy plants and the other types of project mentioned at the beginning of this section is an extension of the present arrangements for compensating nearby landowners for 'injurious affection'. The Compulsory Purchase Act 1965 and the Land Compensation Act 1973 enable landowners to obtain compensation for injurious affection if the use of public works (such as airports or highways) causes a depreciation in the value of their land as a result of a specified list of physical factors, including noise and smell. These provisions generally apply where a civil claim for nuisance cannot be made because the works involved were carried out under statutory authority. This is a complex area of law which we have not examined in detail. But we understand the Law Commission is now studying the issue, and we look forward to the result of their work.

Conclusion

8.75 In this chapter we have discussed changes in the framework for environmental planning at the level of the UK government and the devolved administrations. Our aim is to provide stronger, clearer objectives for protecting the UK environment, and enabling the UK to make an appropriate contribution to global environmental protection, within the context of policies and objectives for sustainable development. Many of our proposals relate to aspects of the town and country planning system. In the next chapter we consider the outcomes of this complex, highly evolved system, focusing on the location and quality of built development and the protection given to the rural environment and coasts.

Chapter 9

SAFEGUARDING TOWN, COUNTRY AND COAST

Is there a consistent approach to the environment in town and country? What more needs to be done to facilitate an urban renaissance? respond to a crisis in the countryside? and protect the coasts?

9.1 As we emphasised in chapter 4, there are close links between town and country, and the planning system needs to take account of such interactions if it is to develop integrated strategies that will safeguard environmental sustainability (9.2-9.7). In chapter 8 we identified maintaining or enhancing urban and rural environments as among the priority objectives for environmental policy (box 8A). It is also crucial for sustainable development to maintain thriving communities in urban and rural areas. The quality of the environment is a significant factor in ensuring this can be achieved. In this chapter we identify some specific respects in which further action may be needed to protect and improve the environment. We look first at some issues in urban areas (9.8-9.27), then at the future of the countryside (9.28-9.58). We also look at what needs to be done to protect coastal environments (9.59-9.65), at sustainability issues relating to water (9.66-9.71), and at some longer-term factors with implications for planning policy (9.72-9.74).

DEVELOPING SUSTAINABLE PLANNING POLICIES FOR TOWN AND COUNTRY

9.2 For much of the second half of the 20th Century, the predominant trends in the distribution of population and employment in the UK were those of suburbanisation and counter-urbanisation.[1] These changes have been associated with development pressures in rural areas and with intensifying social and economic problems in parts of our major cities.[2] Latterly, central government and the devolved administrations have made strong connections between policies for regenerating large conurbations and protecting the rural environment. These were discussed in rural and urban White Papers for England published at the end of 2000.[3, 4]

9.3 One of the main aims of these new policies is to concentrate the bulk of new development, including house building, in existing towns and cities in order to boost urban economies and reduce the overall environmental impact of development. Planning guidance has been rewritten to favour compact, higher density, mixed use residential developments and to bring about the reuse of old buildings and the recycling of abandoned and contaminated urban land in preference to the development of green-field sites.[5] In addition, planning policy has shifted from a 'predict and provide' approach to one that 'plans, monitors and manages' the supply of new homes.[6]

9.4   As part of the effort to avoid the wasteful use of land, government has adopted targets for the recycling of land and buildings to provide new homes; in England the target is for 60% of new homes to be supplied in this way. The target appears close to being achieved with the average over the period 1989 to 2000 being 57%. However the overall figure masks considerable variation in regional numbers which, in 1997, varied from 35% in the South West to 85% in London.[7] The setting and fulfilment of regional targets seems appropriate if national targets are to be met in an effective and equitable way.

9.5   In Scotland, Wales and Northern Ireland shifts in planning policy intended to aid the regeneration of cities and change the balance between green-field and urban development have taken place later than in England.[8, 9, 10] A specific 60% target has not been implemented in Scotland because it was seen as too easy for some authorities and an impossibility for others.[11] In Northern Ireland a target for 60% of new homes to be supplied within existing urban areas rather than by building on rural green-field sites has been adopted; this is similar, but not identical to the target for new dwellings in England.[12]

9.6   The Commission's report on transport discussed the potential of larger settlements and denser urban forms to reduce the demand for travel and car dependency.[13] In our report on energy we noted that denser forms of housing also tend to achieve higher levels of energy efficiency in home heating, as well as being better suited to the use of combined heat and power and shared heating systems.[14] Reducing the demand for new infrastructure would also help to make more efficient use of resources such as aggregates.

9.7   We strongly commend the government's attempt to encourage a change in direction and to focus the bulk of new built development within existing towns and cities. Although this approach is not without risks,[15] we are persuaded that it has the potential to achieve major environmental benefits for both urban and rural areas as well benefiting the economy by reducing the wasteful use of resources. It would be impracticable, and undesirable, to attempt to locate all new building within existing urban areas. Given that gradual urban expansion will continue, a key objective is to ensure that the total urbanised area increases in a way that enhances overall environmental quality. This is likely to require different specific solutions in different areas, but we endorse the advice in the planning guidance for England that authorities 'should be prepared to justify their views fully in public'[16] and we would add that they should be able to demonstrate that environmental sustainability will be safeguarded.

REALISING THE POTENTIAL OF URBAN COMMUNITIES

9.8   We are concerned that the substantial benefits of an urban renaissance will not be realised unless there are more concerted efforts to tackle outstanding problems of environmental degradation in urban areas. Transport, traffic and associated air pollution, noise and other impacts are issues that we have discussed extensively elsewhere, and we regret the slow progress in this field. The extent of contaminated land in urban areas may also be a major obstacle to progress and we consider this important issue below. Other factors that contribute substantially to the quality of the urban environment include access to parks and open spaces and the prevalence of litter, graffiti and dilapidation.

9.9 A large proportion of the vacant and derelict land available for redevelopment has been contaminated by previous industrial or mining use. Although statistics on contaminated land exist for some areas, there has not been a detailed, UK-wide survey of the entire range of major contaminants.[17] There is no simple agreement about what constitutes contamination because this is related to land use. Most land with significant contamination as defined in legislation is located in or immediately around urban areas. Contamination of land poses a risk to health which has caused some public unease, although a Commission report found no firm evidence of adverse effects on health.[18, 19] Under some circumstances, migration of contaminants, primarily into surface and ground water, may pose a wider environmental risk.

9.10 Provided that contaminants cannot migrate, the acceptable level of contamination and the choice of technology for remediation depend on the use for which the land is to be restored. Uses which carry an intrinsically higher risk of exposing people to contamination, such as high-density family housing, require more thorough and therefore more expensive remediation. However, these are usually the higher value uses of the land. Redevelopment of contaminated sites therefore requires consideration of the value of the new use against the cost of remediation. Under some circumstances, removal of contaminated soil for *ex situ* treatment or disposal may be the most appropriate option. In line with the view expressed in the Commission's report on soil,[20] **we recommend that the overall policy objective for contaminated land should be to identify and seek to bring about the combination of remediation and subsequent use that represents the best practicable environmental option for each site**.

9.11 The Environmental Protection Act was passed in 1995 and embodied a more proactive approach to contaminated land, but the Act was not brought into force until 2000 in England and Scotland, and 2001 in Wales. Local authorities now have a duty to inspect their areas to identify contaminated land and establish on whom responsibility for remediation falls, based on the polluter pays principle. They are then obliged to ensure remediation takes place through voluntary agreement with the responsible party (for example, the landowner) or, failing that, by serving a legal notice or carrying out the work themselves. They must keep a public register showing what remediation has been agreed, been demanded or taken place, and in Scotland (but not elsewhere), all the sites they have identified. The Environment Agencies have important roles in providing site-specific advice to local authorities, regulating special sites, and monitoring and reporting on overall progress.

9.12 Local authorities were asked to produce strategies for undertaking the inspection of their area by July 2001 in England, October 2001 in Scotland and October 2002 in Wales, with extra finance made available for this task. However, there is as yet no timetable for completing either the inspections, or the remediation of all identified sites, although the Scottish Executive intends to establish targets for overall progress once more is known about the extent of contaminated land. **We recommend that the government and the devolved administrations set target dates for local authorities to complete their inspection of contaminated land, and provide the necessary finance for them to do so.**

9.13 While implementation of the new regime is an important advance, it also has major limitations. The legislation defines 'contaminated land' as land which appears to a local authority to be:

> in such a condition, by reason of substances in, on or under the land, that (a) significant harm is being caused or there is a significant possibility of such harm being caused; or (b) pollution of controlled waters is being, or is likely to be, caused.

As the Commission has previously emphasised, this does not by any means cover all the sites which require action.[21] Immediate remediation is required to the point where the risk of significant harm or pollution is contained, but full remediation cannot be carried out unless the subsequent use is defined. This regime will not on its own, therefore, lead to remediation of contaminated land that may be contributing to blight and holding back urban regeneration if it currently poses no direct environmental or public health threat.

9.14 The Urban Task Force recommended a 'Clean up our land' campaign, with a goal of bringing land defined as contaminated back into beneficial use by 2030.[22] **We recommend that, once a clearer picture emerges of the extent of the problem posed by contaminated land and the possible uses for remediated sites, the government and the devolved administrations should set targets for the total area to be brought back into beneficial use over ten years and should plan to provide the necessary finance. They should also report on the feasibility of the 2030 goal for dealing with contaminated land proposed by the Urban Task Force.** In England Departments should work with Government Offices to produce regional programmes to meet national targets.

9.15 To implement our recommendation and that of the Urban Task Force where there is no immediate commercial use, government must intervene through bodies such as England's Regional Development Agencies and the local enterprise network in Scotland, or they must work in partnership. There is a strong case for public funds to finance remediation in order to bring about environmental improvements and regeneration, including the creation of open spaces for people to enjoy.

9.16 Various European Union (EU) and UK government funding schemes exist to do this, including tax relief. One initiative was the Partnership Investment Programme to subsidise schemes that would not be commercially viable, either because the land required extensive remediation and preparation or because the local property market was weak. This scheme had to be suspended after the European Commission ruled that it did not comply with European Community (EC) law on state aids.[23] To date the government has not introduced a full replacement, although there are a number of substitute schemes which are currently under review in England.[24] **We urge the government to put in place mechanisms to replace the Partnership Investment Programme for land remediation.**

9.17 Uncertainty about the extent of contamination of a site makes developers unsure about the total costs of remediation; removing this uncertainty might considerably accelerate the rate at which contaminated land is remediated and brought back into use. **Government should inject more public finance into site investigations and remediation not covered by the statutory regime for contaminated land, and develop means of recovering at least a proportion of the cost of these investigations from any subsequent commercial scheme.**

9.18 The Urban Task Force recommended the establishment of a national framework for identifying, managing and communicating the risks that arise throughout the assessment, treatment and after care of contaminated sites.[25] This may now be emerging with the implementation of the new statutory regime, new planning guidance, and long-awaited Environment Agency publications on the state of contaminated land, guideline concentration values for key land contaminants above which remediation is required and model procedures. **There should be a single web portal that would allow local authorities, developers, their professional advisers and the public to access information on contaminated land throughout the UK, and through which all relevant public documents, including research findings, would be freely available. This should also include the public registers maintained by local authorities.** We suggest that the Environment Agencies co-operate to run a system that will provide information for the entire UK, and that the information accessed through it should be linked to the virtual centre for environmental data we have recommended (6.36). Where land changes ownership or use, the parties to the transaction should be required to pass on full information on the method of remediation employed, and on types and levels of contamination before and after remediation.

COMPULSORY PURCHASE

9.19 Achieving an urban renaissance will require effective use of as much urban land as possible. The reinstatement of contaminated land has been discussed in the preceding section, but the ability of local planning authorities to assemble parcels of land for development is also important. Some believe that the compulsory purchase system is not achieving its intended purpose of providing an efficient and fair means of assembling land.[26] In particular, there is uncertainty about the powers available to local authorities,[27] which are therefore discouraged from making use of them. The government has proposed legislation to clarify that local planning authorities can use compulsory purchase for a full range of planning and regeneration purposes, including halting the physical, economic and/or social deterioration of an area. It has also proposed other measures to make the system quicker and fairer, including encouraging use of alternative dispute resolution techniques and extending compulsory powers to the acquisition of land for mitigation purposes. Local planning authorities wishing to purchase land compulsorily would no longer have to point to detailed proposals for its future use.[28]

STANDARD OF THE BUILDING STOCK

9.20 Both town and country planning and building regulations have a role in ensuring that the quality of the country's building stock is improved so that it becomes more environmentally sustainable. But at the moment neither is making an effective contribution. In our report on energy we recommended that the regulations mandate much higher standards of energy efficiency in new homes and commercial and public sector buildings; the latest revision of the regulations for England failed, in our view, to achieve this.[29, 30]

9.21 In the long run it may be desirable to merge building regulations and development control, as has recently been suggested.[31] Pending that, **we recommend that the government and the devolved administrations review the respective roles of the town and country planning system and the building regulations in order to design and implement an effective system for achieving substantially better environmental performance in new or refurbished buildings**.

IMPROVING PARKS AND OPEN SPACES

9.22 Concern has been expressed in recent years about the loss of open green spaces within urban areas to development and about the neglect of public parks.[32] These urban and peri-urban green areas ought to be given as much protection as National Parks, National Scenic Areas, Areas of Outstanding Natural Beauty or Heritage Coasts and deserve as much attention on the part of policy makers. Among several failings identified by the House of Commons Select Committee on the Environment, Transport and the Regions in its report on town and country parks was a lack of information on the quality and quantity of parks and open spaces, and the ways in which they are used and maintained.[33] Government has said a parks revival should play an important part in the urban renaissance and has undertaken to commission research.[34] Government has also set up an Urban Green Spaces Task Force for England which is due to make its recommendations for improvements in 2002.[35]

9.23 We consider it particularly important to provide adequate areas of good quality open green land managed for public access and enjoyment and for wildlife conservation within towns and cities and at their edges. **We recommend that the government and devolved administrations include in their guidance to planning authorities targets for the maximum distance any urban household should be from a green space of specified size open to the public.**[36]

9.24 There are precedents for such activities. For example, Scottish Natural Heritage operated its 'Countryside around town' initiative for many years, while some planning authorities have adopted concepts such as green corridors and wildlife zones within urban areas. We welcome these and more recent initiatives such as the 'Millennium Greens' which comprise some 250 newly opened green spaces, and the 'Doorstep Greens' which aim to create new green spaces in particularly disadvantaged neighbourhoods. The Central Scotland Forest has been established between Edinburgh and Glasgow by a consortium led by the Central Scotland Countryside Trust. In England, twelve Community Forests are being planted close to large urban areas. Initiatives of this type are supported by a diverse range of organisations, including local communities, local authorities, the Countryside Agency, bodies that disburse National Lottery income and commercial sponsors.

MIXED COMMUNITIES

9.25 Although social factors have not been the focus of our study, we recognise that they are extremely important in determining the success of urban areas. The urban renaissance must benefit all sections of the community. The aim must be to create communities that are inherently healthy in environments of high quality, and subsidies of various kinds for homes affordable to low income households have a role to play in this. An example is the proposal from the Mayor of London's Housing Commission that there should be 50% affordable housing in all new schemes.[37] We endorse the advice in current planning guidance that, in new and redeveloped urban areas, planning authorities should create mixed and inclusive neighbourhoods that cater for a variety of household types, incomes and sizes, and avoid the creation or perpetuation of neighbourhoods dominated by low income households.[38]

CONSISTENCY IN APPLYING PLANNING POLICIES

9.26 The government, the devolved administrations, their agencies and local authorities must apply policies for sustainable planning and urban regeneration consistently across the full range of their interests. Current planning advice suggests that developed areas should be used in preference to green-field sites and that amenities that generate a large number of trips should be sited in areas well-served by public transport, such as towns rather than out-of-centre locations.[39] However major facilities such as new National Health Service hospitals are still being built on edge of town sites while more central facilities are closed. We discuss in the next chapter how adopting integrated spatial strategies can help address some of these difficult issues.

9.27 The strategy of renaissance is ambitious. It is essential that the policies designed to bring about this broad aim should be monitored and where necessary adjusted. Important in this respect will be the development and use of indicators of the quality of life and the environment in urban areas, including indicators of deprivation, crime, public health and the availability of public transport. Some indicators should take account of the quality of people's immediate surroundings (for example, the presence of litter and graffiti) and this is likely to be of more immediate concern than national and global environmental issues to them.[40] In its Urban White Paper for England,[41] the government undertook 'to develop a comprehensive set of key indicators for overall urban analysis by Summer 2001', but it is expected that this will not now be achieved until Spring 2002. We believe that such indicators will need to be linked to meaningful targets and policies if change is to occur.

SAFEGUARDING THE FUTURE OF THE COUNTRYSIDE

9.28 To assess whether enough is being done to protect and enhance the rural environment, we look first at support for agriculture and forestry, at the role of town and country planning in the countryside and the case for extending it, and at other regulatory regimes which seek to control adverse impacts from agriculture and forestry. We then discuss the implications of introducing environmental impact assessment for agriculture, and finally, whether there is a case for further measures and what form they should take.

9.29 Agriculture is still the prime user of land,[42] covering three quarters of the surface area of the UK in 2000.[43] The Policy Commission on the Future of Farming and Food recently examined the state of the industry in England and noted the sharp decline in total farm income in recent years.[44] The recent problems in agriculture have drawn attention to the changing nature of the rural economy and helped highlight the importance of service industries, tourism and leisure to the countryside, where they now employ far more people than traditional activities such as farming.[45] Rising living standards, leisure time and mobility have contributed to the growth in rural tourism and recent legislation now guarantees public access to mountain, moorland, commons, down and heath in England and Wales.[46] A wider range of society – be they country or urban dwellers, are likely to play a growing role in debates on the future of rural areas.

SUPPORT FOR AGRICULTURE AND FORESTRY

9.30 Farming has been highly successful in increasing the amount of food produced from a given area by taking advantage of advances in technology and economies of scale. In this sense it is no different from other industries that attempt to make their assets more productive and generate increased income. Agriculture is however unusual in that much of the finance needed to make these changes has come from taxpayers, in the form of subsidies for crop and livestock production and for various land management activities such as drainage. Large-scale government support dates from the second world war, and had the aim of making the UK more self-sufficient in food production. In recent decades support has been provided through the Common Agricultural Policy (CAP) of the EU, and that constrains the ability of the UK government to make its own arrangements.

9.31 The post-war process of agricultural intensification, encouraged by production subsidies, has met its objective of boosting farm output but it has also had a significant environmental impact on parts of the countryside.[47] Although agriculture manages many parts of our natural heritage responsibly, there has been rising concern over the problems that some farming practices have caused. This has stimulated changes in agricultural policy, including the establishment of a number of agri-environment schemes to encourage more environmentally friendly farming. These schemes are currently funded by arrangements under the CAP and by direct national funding. The Environmentally Sensitive Areas Scheme seeks to maintain or enhance areas of particularly high landscape, wildlife or historic value in England by compensating farmers for adopting certain management practices. Similarly, the Countryside Council for Wales operates the Tir Gofal scheme under which farmers enter into a ten-year agreement to implement a whole farm management plan for maintaining and enhancing areas of conservation and landscape value. However, the bulk of agricultural support remains linked to crop and livestock production; agri-environment schemes still accounted for less than 8% of the subsidies flowing to UK farmers in 2000.[48]

9.32 Under the current CAP rules, countries can apply their own set of conditions, including environmental ones, to the payment of production subsides; this is known as 'cross-compliance'. We have heard no persuasive arguments against this approach and, in our view, recipients of public subsidy ought as a matter of principle to accept certain obligations. **We consider production subsidies to agriculture should be phased out as soon as possible. While they remain part of the CAP, we recommend that farmers receiving such subsidies should be required to maintain a defined level of environmental protection on the land they manage. We urge the government to take full advantage of the existing scope for cross-compliance under the CAP to support the protection and enhancement of the environment, and to seek to widen the scope for cross-compliance as part of the reform of the CAP.**

9.33 We note that the recent report from the Policy Commission on Farming and Food, which was published just as we concluded our study, similarly supports a phasing out of production subsidies. Like the Commission we believe that a prosperous rural economy is essential to the future of the countryside, and we agree that the low level of farm incomes is an obstacle to the creation of a better rural environment.

9.34 **We believe there is justification for the state to continue payments to rural land managers, including arable and livestock farmers, for achieving well-defined, measurable environmental and social objectives. We recommend that the Department for Environment, Food and Rural Affairs (DEFRA) and the devolved administrations launch a wide debate on rationalising the support for owners and managers of rural land through the introduction of schemes that serve environmental and, where appropriate, other objectives.** In the first instance, those proposals will have to be drawn up within the constraints imposed by European law. In the longer run, the government should press for changes to European law that will remove obstacles to such a unified approach.

9.35 Forestry has also been heavily subsidised, also originally with the aim of national self-sufficiency, by using tax allowances as well as grants. In this case, however, policy is decided within the UK. The generous tax treatment has now been removed, and the terms and conditions of grant schemes now place a greater emphasis on protecting and improving the environment, for example through creating broadleaf or mixed woodland.[49]

ROLE OF TOWN AND COUNTRY PLANNING IN THE COUNTRYSIDE

9.36 Farming and forestry operations were expressly excluded from the definition of 'development' in the Town and Country Planning Acts. As they are very important forms of land use, and as they continue to have potential to cause significant environmental damage, we have considered whether this is an anomaly that ought to be ended. Following devolution, the Scottish Executive sought views on this possibility, but many of the responses urged caution.[50] In their evidence to us the National Farmers Union argued that protection of many features of the rural environment, such as semi-natural habitats, is more likely to be achieved through encouraging land managers to apply more environmentally sensitive management methods (either traditional ones or more modern equivalents devised to achieve the same outcomes), rather than simple prohibition.[51] Advice, financial incentives or cross-compliance may therefore be equally, or more, effective than direct regulation. A further argument is that local authority planning departments are already under heavy pressure and currently lack the expertise to deal with agriculture and forestry.

9.37 We do not regard these arguments as necessarily conclusive in the longer term. However, a new form of control over potentially damaging agricultural operations, is being introduced, and is discussed below. We have concluded that experience ought to be gained of that regime before further consideration is given to requiring planning permission for changes in agricultural land use. We recommend that in the meantime other measures are introduced to improve the protection of the rural environment; in particular, there should be action to encourage the adoption of farm plans which we discuss later in this chapter.

9.38 One aspect of agricultural land use is already controlled by the planning authority under separate legislation.[52] In England and Wales, landowners have to notify the local planning authority before removing a hedgerow; if the hedgerow has high historic, cultural or wildlife value under criteria set by Ministers, the authority may prohibit its removal. It cannot, however, ensure that the hedgerow is properly maintained, although the landowner may be able to obtain a grant under an agri-environment scheme towards the cost of doing so.

9.39 In this context, forestry is in a different position to agriculture. Felling is regulated by the Forestry Authority, and through its grant schemes it also effectively controls planting. It consults the local planning authority about any significant application and in virtually all cases an agreed solution is reached. The Forestry Commission told us that making forestry operations subject to planning permission would make little difference in practice; it had no view on whether or not the change would be desirable.[53] Given that the change would require primary legislation and cause disruption to procedures, we do not see a sufficiently strong case for making forestry operations subject to planning permission unless it were decided to make that change in respect of agricultural operations.

9.40 Even where other activities of farmers and foresters (erecting buildings, creating new roads, excavating land) fall within the definition of 'development' they are subject to only limited coverage by town and country planning legislation as there are important 'permitted development rights' for agriculture and forestry. Over the years these have allowed thousands of large, essentially industrial buildings to appear in the open countryside without the community having any influence on their appearance or location.

9.41 These permitted development rights have been reduced in recent years, in response to rising concern about the changing appearance of the countryside. In England new agricultural buildings over a certain height and/or within a certain distance of a road, dwelling or school now require planning permission. In National Parks and Areas of Outstanding Natural Beauty permitted development rights have been withdrawn; elsewhere in England, local authorities can ask the Secretary of State to withdraw permitted development rights for farming and forestry if they believe there is a real and specific threat to the rural landscape.

9.42 We were struck by the fact that the Country Landowners Association argued in favour of withdrawing permitted development rights for farming and forestry developments, although they made the proviso that this should be 'subject to appropriate policies to ensure that the needs of agriculture are met'.[54] The Performance and Innovation Unit also made this recommendation in its report on rural economies, but it did not appear in the government's Rural White Paper.[55] **We recommend the withdrawal of the permitted development rights that currently apply to building conversions, and the construction of new buildings, roads and vehicle tracks when these activities are associated with agriculture or forestry.**

9.43 There is general support for a more diverse rural economy in which tourism and leisure, on-farm food processing and retailing and other industries grow to help protect rural areas from economic decline. Diversification is increasingly being encouraged by DEFRA and the devolved administrations through advice and subsidy schemes such as the England Rural Development Plan, the proposed Rural Development Programme for Northern Ireland, the Rural Development Plan for Wales 2000-2006 and the Farm Business Development Scheme in Scotland.

9.44 The town and country planning system can influence the diversification process because some of the changes involve conversions of buildings, or construction of new buildings. There are social and economic arguments for encouraging new industry and commerce in the countryside, but it could have damaging environmental impacts, such as inappropriate development. Research commissioned by government has found that the great majority of diversification projects are related to tourism or nearby urban economies rather than adding value to land-based products or taking advantage of their rural locations in ways unrelated to tourism.[56]

9.45 The government is concerned that planning authorities may have prevented some well founded diversification projects from going ahead by refusing planning permission, and has made recent changes to policy guidance on the countryside and transport to address this.[57] In Scotland, policy guidance on rural development was published in 1999 and is currently being reviewed for its effectiveness.[58] Broadly, however, it seems that town and country planning controls have not been a major obstacle to diversification, although some farmers have complained that the process for dealing with planning applications is cumbersome.[59, 60] **We recommend that the impact of new planning guidance on rural diversification is monitored for its effectiveness in protecting the environment and to ensure that it does not block beneficial diversification projects. We also recommend that information is collected on the rate at which diversification is proceeding in rural areas, the quantity and type of employment created and maintained, and the overall environmental impact of diversification including its effect on travel patterns.**

OTHER ENVIRONMENTAL REGIMES

9.46 A number of legal controls and voluntary schemes have been introduced to prevent or limit various adverse effects on the environment from agriculture. There have been some significant recent developments. In 2001, as a result of EC legislation, integrated pollution control was extended to cover some aspects of farming: new or substantially modified intensive pig and poultry units have to adopt best available technology to reduce emissions and the production of wastes.[61] Existing units will have to comply with the regulations by 2007.

9.47 Even more far-reaching is the EC Nitrate Directive. This is an environmental measure that aims to reduce diffuse water pollution caused by nitrate released as a result of agricultural activities. In areas designated as *nitrate vulnerable zones* (NVZs) farmers must comply with action programmes to improve the management and use of manures, slurries and synthetic fertilisers by limiting the times and rate at which they are applied to land. In 2000, the European Court of Justice ruled that all waters, not just drinking waters, must be protected, either by designating the whole of a national territory as an NVZ or by adopting a targeted approach.[62] The implementation of the EC Water and Waste Framework Directives will also have implications for agriculture.[63] These will provide strategic frameworks to complement existing legislation (such as the Nitrate Directive) as well as establishing a number of new environmental objectives.

ENVIRONMENTAL IMPACT ASSESSMENT FOR AGRICULTURE

9.48 We now turn to a new piece of legislation that may help prevent further damage to the countryside. One of the provisions of the EC Environmental Impact Assessment (EIA) Directive (7.23-7.26) is that an assessment needs to be prepared before uncultivated land or semi-natural areas are converted to intensive agriculture if this is likely to cause significant environmental effects (see box 9A). The government has now belatedly accepted the need to comply with this aspect of the Directive, and in consequence to introduce a consent procedure for such conversions. The regulations will come into force by February 2002 in England and similar regulations will apply in Scotland, Wales and Northern Ireland.[64, 65, 66, 67] It will be for DEFRA, and its equivalents in the devolved administrations, to decide whether an EIA is required for a project and, if so, whether the project should be allowed, modified or refused.

BOX 9A	ENVIRONMENTAL IMPACT ASSESSMENT FOR THE USE OF UNCULTIVATED LAND OR SEMI-NATURAL AREAS

The government is introducing regulations that will require an environmental impact assessment (EIA) when a land manager wishes to bring uncultivated land or semi-natural areas into intensive agricultural use and there is a likelihood of significant environmental effects. Much of this land is already covered by agri-environment schemes, under which land managers receive subsidy for fulfilling some conservation obligations, or is designated as Sites of Special Scientific Interest and other statutory nature conservation designations thereby receiving a degree of legislative protection from environmental damage. EIA, however, offers another means of protection, in that a new consent regime will be administered by DEFRA in England and its equivalents in the devolved administrations.

There will be penalties for non-compliance but DEFRA and its devolved counterparts intend, wherever possible, to apply the regulations in co-operation with farmers. If a project raises environmental concerns, DEFRA says it will try to agree a way forward with the land manager that takes account of business needs as well as environmental factors. Land typically included:
- Meadows and grazing pastures;
- Downland or other or open enclosed upland grassland;
- Grassland with some tree cover (such as orchards, parkland and wood pasture; lowland and coastal heathland (including dry and wet heath);
- Moorland (including bog) and upland rough grazing (including intake).

This land would be considered uncultivated if it had less than 25% to 30% of ryegrass, and/or white clover, or other sown grass species indicative of cultivation. Where there are difficulties in determining whether the land is uncultivated using the above test, farmers should ask DEFRA for advice. In making their decision, DEFRA will take into account previous agricultural operations on the land over the last 15 years, including ploughing, re-seeding and draining.

- EIA procedures will apply where scrub is cleared or managed with an aim of converting to arable or stock farming including intensification of such an existing use.
- Marsh; fen; open water; water courses; saltmarsh; ditches; ponds.

Operations covered by the regulations include cultivations, spreading soil or other material including fertiliser or lime in excess of existing routine application rates, drainage works and flood defences, infilling of ditches and ponds, clearing vegetation in readiness for cultivation and the introduction of livestock grazing at intensive stocking rates, or increasing stocking to intensive levels.

The regulations do not apply to planning, land drainage improvement works carried out by Operating Authorities [such as Internal Drainage Boards or the Environment Agency] or forestry projects (covered by separate EIA regulations) or operations on land already in intensive agricultural use. For projects on land managed under Environmentally Sensitive Areas or Countryside Stewardship Scheme agreements, DEFRA believes it is unlikely that an EIA will be necessary. This is because of the environmental protection that already applies under these schemes.

The procedures involve an application by the land manager with an initial screening in which DEFRA (or its devolved administration equivalents) consider whether the project in question is likely to have significant environmental effects. Where it does – and DEFRA has to decide this within 35 days – the land manager must prepare an Environmental Statement assessing the environmental implications of the project 'which contains sufficient information to allow a reasonable decision on whether the project should proceed.' DEFRA then consults with English Nature, English Heritage, the Environment Agency and the Countryside Agency and decides whether the project should be rejected, allowed to proceed, or modified. Statements will be open to public inspection, with advertisements placed in local newspapers.

If a project is refused, or conditions are imposed on it, the applicant has the right to appeal within 21 days. The regulations allow the Secretary of State wide discretion to determine the appeals procedure. In administering the new regime, DEFRA will take account of:

- Habitats and particular species of flora and fauna covered by the UK Biodiversity Action Plan, whether the land has any environmental designation such as a Natura 2000 site, National Park, AONB, national or local nature Reserve, Heritage Coast, SSSI.
- Archaeological or other historic features
- Distinctive landscape character, taking account of the Countryside Agency's Countryside Character approach
- Other environmental considerations, such as the value of the land as a wildlife corridor
- Whether the land is recognised in local planning authority development plans as being of particular landscape or recreational importance
- Implications for public access
- Potential effects on pollution, soil erosion or flood protection arising on or beyond the site in question.

9.49   This new consent procedure will be an important backstop for preventing further loss of valued habitats and landscapes and other forms of environmental damage. **We call on DEFRA and the devolved administrations to ensure that the rural environment enjoys the best possible protection under the EIA Directive. In particular, they should not hesitate to refuse consent to schemes that would cause significant environmental damage, nor miss such schemes at the initial screening stage. Screening should be carried out by staff with appropriate environmental training using rigorous criteria.**

9.50 **We recommend that local planning authorities should be added to the list of statutory consultees for environmental impact assessment of intensive agriculture.**

9.51 To ensure the success of the EIA scheme, effective publicity should be used to bring the regulations to the attention of every farmer, rural land owner and rural land manager. The government and the devolved administrations should publish an annual report on the operation of EIA in agriculture, which could be combined with reporting on the operation of the EIA schemes for forestry projects and types of development covered by the town and country planning system. The report should show the number of applications for initial screening, the number of projects for which an assessment has been required, the decisions on those projects, the findings from independent assessment of the screening process, monitoring, the number of breaches of the regulations and the number and outcome of prosecutions. This report should also give an overall assessment of the contribution the regulations are making to conserving semi-natural habitats and curbing environmental damage.

NEED FOR FURTHER ACTION

9.52 Agri-environment schemes have succeeded in bringing about some conservation benefits; for example, greater numbers of wading birds are now found in some lowland wet grasslands and valued habitats and landscape features such as dry stone walls have been preserved.[68] The Countryside Survey 2000 indicated that several other negative trends observed during the 1980s had been halted or reversed (for example, loss of ponds and hedgerows, acidification of upland soils, worsening of the biological condition of streams).[69] However it also recorded continued deterioration in indicators such as the plant diversity of some grasslands.[70] Agriculture remains the major cause of unfavourable condition in Sites of Special Scientific Interest (SSSIs).[71]

9.53 It is essential that agricultural operations that can cause significant air, water and soil pollution are adequately regulated. **We recommend that there should be a thorough review of controls on environmental impacts of agriculture. This should include measures for protecting the conservation value of the countryside and for controlling agricultural pollution. We further recommend that the specialist environmental agencies should co-operate to conduct an independent assessment of the efficacy of the new EIA regulations and the other measures mentioned above in five years' time.** If this review indicates that the arrangements have failed to prevent further deterioration of the rural environment, then we would recommend extending town and country planning control to damaging agricultural operations for the reasons given above. Commensurate with this extended remit, there would need to be a major increase in resources and training for officers working for local planning authorities.

9.54 There is now a proliferation of grant schemes, production subsidies and voluntary and mandatory measures in the agricultural sector. Considerable progress can be made towards a more coherent approach by rationalising the way they are administered. We believe that this can sensibly be achieved by bringing together all their requirements in a single farm plan. The aims should be to obtain the maximum environmental benefit in return for the expenditure involved, reduce the bureaucratic burden on farmers and landowners, and achieve outcomes that are sensitive to the characteristics of particular areas and the views of the people who live in them. **We recommend that in future each agricultural holding in the UK receiving public subsidy should be required to prepare a farm plan containing actions to improve the environment which can be readily monitored; and that, to simplify the existing arrangements, all bodies giving grants, exercising regulatory functions or requiring certification of environmental performance should accept the plan as meeting their requirements for information.**

9.55 **We recommend that DEFRA move swiftly to bring forward proposals for legislation for a farm plan scheme, following wide consultation, and produce guidance on the format and content of such plans with an emphasis on securing environmental protection and simplifying current administrative procedures. The Rural Payments Agency and its counterparts should have responsibility for all grant payments made pursuant to the plan, including payments made in respect of management of SSSIs or for farm woodland or afforestation schemes.**

9.56 We would expect all plans to indicate the broad aims of farm management; state the measures to be adopted to conserve soil, minimise erosion and prevent pollution; indicate how any scheduled sites (for example, SSSIs, ancient monuments, limestone pavements, and access land) will be safeguarded; and whether there are any plans to convert uncultivated land and semi-natural habitats to intensive agriculture (in which case the farm plan could serve as the preliminary statement required under the new measures relating to environmental impact assessment). Should there be proposals to establish farm woodlands, or apply for membership of an agri-environment scheme, details would be given in the farm plan.

9.57 Farm plans, despite their broad coverage, should not be voluminous. They must simplify, not complicate, life for farmers and landowners. They should indicate the limits within which the farm will be managed but leave the farmer as much flexibility as possible to operate within those limits. They will need to be updated at suitable intervals. To keep costs down, farm plans could be based on a standard template available electronically, for example via the Internet.

9.58 The Commission's report on soil emphasised the importance of advice to farmers on pollution prevention, conservation and the sustainable use of soils and recommended that at least the initial visit from advisers should be free. The first visit to explain the format, content and process for preparing the farm plan and its use in securing grants should likewise be free. If subsequent visits and assistance are required, the costs could be recouped against future grants and spread over several years.

PROTECTING COASTAL ENVIRONMENTS

9.59 The coast is a heterogeneous environment, often the site of major industries, large residential areas and highly valued natural habitats. It is perhaps not surprising that coastal development is regulated by a complex web of policies and subject to many competing interests, some of which are outlined in the table 9.1. This was identified as a matter of concern by the House of Commons Environment Committee in its 1992 report on coastal zone protection, which suggested that as many as 240 public organisations had responsibilities in the coastal zone. In their evidence to us, a number of bodies were concerned that the arrangements continued to be fragmentary, allowing gaps to emerge (for example, planning controls do not extend below the high water mark)[72,73] and, on occasion, resulting in insufficient integration, for example, between environmental protection and flood defence measures.[74,75,76]

9.60 Moves have already been made to take a more integrated approach to the management of coasts. At the national level, DEFRA, the devolved administrations, the specialist agencies, local authorities and a variety of other bodies are involved in drawing up shoreline management plans (SMPs) which aim to provide a strategic and co-ordinated approach to coastal defence. English Nature is leading the development of Coastal Habitat Management Plans (CHAMPs) that will help implement the EC Habitats and Birds Directives. At a higher level of integration, the European Parliament and Council have developed a Recommendation for Integrated Coastal Zone Management that aims to promote sustainable development of coasts.

9.61 We believe that, as in urban and rural areas, developing soundly based and integrated policies for the coast requires access to good quality information. Data are often gathered for specific purposes, such as the compilation of shoreline management plans, but not made widely available. We make the point in chapter 6 that work funded from the public purse should be used to benefit other equally valuable initiatives, for example, in research and planning. **We therefore recommend that DEFRA and the devolved administrations take the lead in ensuring that sponsor bodies co-operate to make data from the second round of shoreline management plans for the UK publicly available in their entirety through a central point.**

9.62 The Crown Estate owns parts of the foreshore, the majority of land below the low water mark out to the 12 mile territorial limit and the mineral rights in this zone. These areas do not fall under the planning system but are nevertheless subject to strong development pressures such as the extraction of aggregates, laying of pipelines and requests to establish offshore energy schemes. Currently these pressures are regulated and managed by the Crown Estate Commissioners and their agents, although forthcoming regulations will make the Secretary of State for Transport, Local Government and the Regions and the devolved administration equivalents the competent authorities for minerals extraction.[77] The Crown Estate Commissioners nevertheless still face a potential conflict of interest because they are required to maintain and enhance the return from the estate while at the same time having due regard to its good management. We believe regulation of marine development should have a strong presumption in favour of environmental protection and that extending the town and country planning system could provide an appropriate solution. **We recommend that planning protection is extended below the high water mark and to the sea-bed.**

9.63 All policy on coastal issues needs to take account of the significant sea-level rise likely over coming decades. This is partly a natural phenomenon resulting from the readjustment of the Earth's crust following the last Ice Age (the southern and eastern parts of Great Britain are slowly sinking while Scotland is rising), but the effects are likely to be reinforced by climate change, as higher temperatures lead to thermal expansion of the sea and the melting of glaciers and ice. The threat from flooding due to sea-level rise may be exacerbated by a number of accompanying trends such as increased wave height, storminess, tidal surges and interaction with river flooding and coastal erosion, although it is currently difficult to be precise about the scale of these effects.[78]

9.64 In England, 8% of the land area is already at risk of river flooding, while some 1.5% of the land area is at risk of flooding from the sea.[79] Some 10% of the population live in such areas and over £200 billion of assets are at risk.[80] In its 1998 report on flood and coastal defence, the House of Commons Agriculture Select Committee expressed the opinion 'that flood and coastal defence policy cannot be sustained in the long term if it continues to be founded on the practice of substantial human intervention in the natural processes of flooding and erosion'. In particular, investing in 'hard' defences to defend the existing coastline in perpetuity is likely to be extremely expensive in some areas. Instead, options such as managed realignment (a process that allows some loss of land but provides a degree of flood protection and new areas of wildlife habitat) may need to be employed. DEFRA believes that, while the actual areas at risk of flooding are likely to alter little with climate change, the risk of flooding events may increase.[81] The threat of climate change therefore adds to the argument that new approaches to flood and coastal management, such as managed realignment, should be investigated and adopted more widely.

Table 9.1

Regulating the marine environment and shore

Issue*	Regulation
General	Crown Estate Act 1961 *Proposed EC Integrated Coastal Zone Management Recommendation* *European Spatial Development Plans*
Marine and coastal pollution	Water Resources Act 1991 Convention for the Protection of the Marine Environment of the North East Atlantic (OSPAR) EC Nitrate Directive EC Bathing Water Directive Urban Waste Water Treatment Directive Proposed EC Water Framework Directive Proposed Marine Environmental High Risk Areas
Extraction of marine aggregates	*Government View Procedure* due to be replaced by forthcoming Environmental Impact Assessment and Habitats (extraction of aggregates by marine dredging) Regulations
Disposal at sea	Food & Environmental Protection Act 1985 London Convention Protocol 1996 Environmental Quality Standards for discharges
Operation of ports	*Guide to Good Practice on Port Marine Operations*
Renewable energy schemes	PPG22: Renewable Energy NPPG6: Renewable Energy (Scotland)
Flood and coastal defence	Coast Protection Act 1949 Land Drainage Acts 1991 and 1994 Water Resources Act 1991 Environment Act 1995 PPG25: Development and Flood Risk PPG 20: Coastal Planning NPPG13: Coastal Planning DEFRA High Level Targets for Flood & Coastal Defence *Shoreline Management Plans (SMPs)*
Conservation	UN Convention on the Law of the Seas, Statutory protection of SSSIs 1992 EC Habitats Directive (Coastal Habitat Management Plans (CHaMPS), designation of marine Special Areas of Conservation), Ramsar Convention on the protection of wetlands (need proper title) EC Birds Directive (and Special Protection Areas), SMPs Wildlife & Countryside Act 1981, Marine Nature Reserves National Parks (Scotland) Bill UN Convention on Biological Diversity, Local Agenda 21, UK Biodiversity Action Plan CITES

*Excludes regulations and initiatives relating to marine safety, navigation, fisheries and tourism.
Non-statutory policies are in italics.

9.65 Wider adoption of managed realignment will require more widespread recognition that human interventions have created an artificial coastline and that on occasion the most sustainable option may be to allow some loss of the coast to natural processes. Such a consensus will be particularly difficult to establish among property and land owners whose assets will be threatened by such an approach, and for whom only limited compensation is currently available.[82, 83] Planning guidance may also need to be tightened to prevent properties being built on sites where it is known that they will eventually become vulnerable to coastal flooding or coastal erosion. The wider environmental impact of managed realignment also needs to be investigated; for example, how can the siting and design of schemes maximise the benefits in terms of new habitats? and what will the effects be on the dynamics of other parts of the coast?

SUSTAINABLE WATER RESOURCES AND FLOODING

9.66 Water is already in short supply in southern and eastern Britain in summer.[84] Climate change may well bring hotter and drier summers over the coming decades, with a higher proportion of winter rain falling in short periods and running off more rapidly. One consequence could be diminished recharge of the aquifers on which much of South East England depends for supply, and reduced flows in rivers with damaging consequences for their ecology and value as amenities. The result may be demands for the construction of more reservoirs in wetter parts of Britain, feeding either long artificial pipelines or transfers between river basins. Superimposed on any climate-induced changes, there may well be changes in demand related to changing patterns of consumption. All of this will require careful planning.

9.67 Once planning permission is granted for urban development, water companies are under an obligation to provide supplies. In future they may not be able to do so in some areas at an environmentally acceptable cost. There is scope for substantial gains in efficiency in water use by reducing domestic demands and reducing the amounts of water required by industrial firms and domestic appliances. Dual water systems, which use surface water or recycled water from buildings ('grey water') for purposes for which high quality water is not required, also show promise. Such schemes have a higher capital cost, but would reduce the water bills paid subsequently by householders in areas where the water supply to all new houses is required to be metered. **We recommend that allocations for developments should not be made until it has been established that water supply and sewerage can be provided in an environmentally sustainable manner.**

9.68 Our current knowledge suggests that while climate change may make water shortages more common in some areas in summer, it may also increase the risk of flooding.[86] Inland flooding already has a high public profile following the autumn 2000 floods which were the most extensive since 1947. These events led to insurance claims of over £700 million[87] and were the result of the wettest autumn since records began in the 18th century. While it is not possible to determine whether the floods were caused by climate change or simply reflect natural variability, rainfall and river flows have been increasing over the last 50 years; a pattern consistent with climate change.[88] It seems likely such events may become more common in future.[89]

9.69 One particular problem highlighted by the floods was the number of houses that had been built in flood plains, sometimes without householders realising this was the case.[90] The Environment Agency opposes development in flood plains but planning permission for new homes has often been given in the face of such opposition[91] because, although the Agency is a non-statutory consultee on flood matters, it does not have the power to veto development it considers unsustainable. There has been pressure to check such development, which brings higher risks of flooding and increased insurance premia and can impose additional flood defence costs on local authorities.

9.70 Such concerns have recently led to the revision of planning guidance in England in the form of PPG25 *Development and Flood Risk*. PPG25 states the government considers that development within the flood plain should be 'wholly exceptional and limited to essential transport and utilities'. It also acknowledges that, while there are many uncertainties, climate change could exacerbate existing risks. We endorse its stated commitment to operating the precautionary principle in this area and to reviewing the guidance within three years of publication in the light of further evidence on climate change. Other relevant planning guidance contains a presumption against development in flood plains or unstable areas but either does not explicitly address climate change or makes only a limited mention of it.[92, 93] **We recommend that all relevant planning guidance contain comprehensive advice on the risks of inland and coastal flooding under current conditions and following a period of climate change. We further recommend that the Environment Agency should be made a statutory consultee on flooding issues.** Consideration could also be given to stipulating that climate change should be a material consideration in relation to planning applications (8.36-8.37).

9.71 A number of other options should be investigated for their ability to ameliorate the effects of flooding. For example, sustainable urban drainage systems, which involve ponds and wetlands, can be used to provide extra drainage and treatment capacity, sometimes at relatively low cost. They have already been promoted by the Environment Agency but resisted by water companies because of additional maintenance obligations.[85] The question of whether better agricultural land management practices could help reduce soil and water run-off from fields also needs to be explored.

LONGER TERM FACTORS INFLUENCING PLANNING POLICY

9.72 Earlier in this chapter we considered how the town and country planning system, wider government policies and socio-economic trends have influenced past and current land use patterns, and examined some of the prospects for the future. Alongside these powerful forces, it is likely that factors such as the need for better management of natural resources and the potential for climate change will help shape the medium to long-term future of parts of the UK. Despite the uncertainty associated with some of these issues we believe that taking account of them in decision-making processes could help avoid some of the disruption and cost that might otherwise be encountered.

9.73 Planning guidance and building regulations can play a role in ensuring that buildings are more energy efficient, robust in the face of extreme weather conditions and less prone to subsidence. Land use planning is also one of the factors that can help the UK cut its emissions of greenhouse gases by encouraging more sustainable development of urban areas and transport systems. DTLR currently has a research project addressing some of these issues and expects to publish a guide for planners in spring 2002. The guide will bring together information about the part that the planning system can play in adapting to the impacts of climate change and contributing towards reducing future greenhouse gas emissions.

9.74 Planning guidance needs to be reviewed to ensure that it takes sufficient account of coastal processes, changes in water availability and flood risk and explicitly acknowledges the potential for climate change. We believe however that there is a need to go further: there should be greater awareness amongst planners of these issues and they need to have access to training, tools and expert advice so that they can incorporate climate change into day-to-day planning decisions. Climate change is also an overarching issue which needs to be taken into account in strategic plans, and in the integrated spatial strategies we propose in the next chapter. There is however uncertainty about the size, direction and timescale of many of the risks associated with climate change, which means that expert help and risk-management advice are crucial. **We recommend that climate change, its effect on natural resources and the managed environment, the scope for adaptation and the scope for reducing emissions of greenhouse gases is specifically taken into account in spatial strategies, and that planning departments receive guidance and training in dealing with climate change issues.**

CONCLUSION: INTEGRATING URBAN, RURAL AND COASTAL PLANNING

9.75 The protection and enhancement of the environment is the responsibility of a complex network of authorities, agencies and voluntary bodies that operate at a variety of levels from the national to the local, through a mixture of statutory and non-statutory measures. This network tends to grow larger and more complicated as new issues arise. The result is a fragmentary approach which is unlikely to be the most effective way of protecting and enhancing the urban, rural and coastal environment. We have not, however, been able to identify a credible means of assigning all these responsibilities to one body, or type of body. There are also good reasons to believe that some organisations have more expertise than others in tailoring measures to suit local circumstances or addressing a particular environmental issue.

9.76 We therefore believe that integrated, long-term strategies for sustainability should be based on encouraging partnerships between bodies with a relevant interest, and giving organisations with responsibilities for environmental protection a clear role in the developmentof such partnerships. Strategies for sustainability should be built on the principles outlined elsewhere in this report, including extensive public debate and engagement and a clear statement of objectives and targets.

9.77 Rather than there being a single path to development, many different choices are possible and the alternative options for the future of urban and rural areas should be discussed and researched. For example, should alternative land uses such as leisure and tourism play a larger role in areas where existing economic activities such as agriculture are in decline, or where the potential environmental gains appear to be largest or most affordable? There has been a tradition of public engagement in some aspects at least of debate over urban development and planning. It is less obvious that this has been the case in past discussions over the role of the countryside, which tend to have been confined to farmers, government Departments and agencies and conservation organisations. More recently a wider round of debate has been encouraged through initiatives such as 'A Forward Strategy for Scotland', the 'Strategy for the Future of Farming in Wales' and Northern Ireland's 'Vision for the Future of the Agri-food Industry'.[94] We commend these efforts and believe that local communities, both urban and rural, and a wider range of non-governmental organisations should be encouraged to join the debate and help to shape the future of the countryside.

9.78 At the beginning of this chapter we explained our view, which we share with the government, that the fates of urban and rural areas are intimately linked. We believe that a crucial aspect of improving the protection and enhancement of the environment is that the planning system, and indeed wider policies, should recognise the interconnectedness of urban, rural and coastal areas – something which we do not believe is currently taking place. In the next chapter, we propose the introduction of integrated spatial strategies, explicitly designed to ensure that these interrelationships are recognised and acted upon.

Chapter 10

Integrated spatial strategies

What are the requirements for spatial strategies that will advance sustainable development and safeguard environmental sustainability? Does the town and country planning system, and the changes to it currently proposed, meet those requirements? If not, how can they be met more adequately? What are the implications for other plans and strategies?

10.1 The purpose of environmental planning, as we have defined it (3.23), is to provide an instrument for making collective choices about the states of the environment we want, to prevent breaches of environmental constraints, and to make adaptations possible when such constraints have unfortunately been breached. We concluded in part I of this report (4.11) that the UK does not have an integrated or coherent system for identifying and promoting the actions needed at regional or local level to safeguard environmental sustainability. In part II of the report we identified some important prerequisites for effective planning, including engaging the public from the earliest stages of identifying and framing issues.

10.2 In chapter 8 we argued that the essential basis for environmental planning is legislation with a clear and explicit purpose and clear national policies, including in particular a comprehensive set of objectives for protecting and improving the environment, expressed wherever possible in quantified targets. Environmental regulation and planning at regional and local levels will not be the only instruments needed to achieve such targets, but they will have a crucial role. At the same time we acknowledged there are many other choices about the environment which ought to be left to be made at local level. In chapter 9 we advocated changes to legislation and public expenditure programmes with the aim of achieving environmental objectives more effectively in towns and cities and in rural and coastal areas.

10.3 Two themes running though this report have been the need for a much closer relationship between land use planning and other aspects of environmental policy, and the need to recognise the interdependence of urban and rural areas. We suggested in chapters 3 and 4 that these requirements can best be met by a system of planning which is strategic and spatial.

10.4 We have concluded that such a system needs to be based on a new form of *integrated spatial strategy* which will embrace economic, social and environmental objectives. We agree with the government that a rationalisation and streamlining of present planning procedures is required. Our concept of an 'integrated spatial strategy' differs from the 'spatial strategies' proposed in the Planning Green Paper for England in that our perspective is much wider than the town and country planning system and we envisage a much more complete incorporation of environmental factors into the policy process. In referring to strategies as 'integrated' we do not imply that economic, social and environmental objectives can ever be reconciled completely. What integrated spatial strategies will provide is a much more effective mechanism for bringing together consideration of economic and social objectives and environmental constraints. Only in that way can the crucial issues be identified, and sometimes difficult choices made, on the basis of adequate information and a full review of the options.

10.5 In this chapter we explain what we mean by an integrated spatial strategy and consider how that concept can be applied most effectively in the different parts of the UK. We first review briefly what has been meant by a 'spatial plan' (10.6-10.12). We then present the case for bringing together in a single policy document for a given area all the factors which have spatial implications, and therefore ought to be taken into account in decisions about land use in that area (10.13-10.21). We set out the conditions which in our view have to be met if a system of integrated planning on these lines is to be established successfully (10.22-10.33). With those conditions in mind we review some current planning documents to see how closely they approach to the form of plan we are advocating: we look first at regional planning guidance in England (10.36-10.49); then at the spatial development strategy being prepared for London (10.50-10.53); then at structure plans (10.54-10.63) and local plans (10.64-10.71). Finally, we make specific recommendations about the introduction of integrated spatial strategies (10.72-10.93).

WHAT IS A 'SPATIAL PLAN'?

10.6 A 'spatial plan' has been defined as a plan designed to 'influence spatial structure by managing territorial development and co-ordinating the spatial impacts of sectoral policies'.[1] The concept of spatial planning acquired a special resonance at European level with growing recognition of the need to co-ordinate the operation of the Structural Funds in stimulating developments of different kinds in designated areas of Member States. The European Spatial Development Perspective, adopted in 1999, provides a broad policy framework for co-operation between Community sectoral policies with significant spatial impacts.[2]

10.7 The term 'spatial plan' is often used loosely, however, and sometimes as virtually a synonym for a land use plan.[3] Enthusiasm for spatial planning in the UK has stemmed from a view that development plans for town and country planning are too narrow in scope. One weakness is that they may not cover adequately all the activities which meet the definition of 'development' in the legislation. Large power stations, for example, are outside the control of local planning authorities and receive authorisation from the Secretary of State for Trade and Industry or the Scottish Minister. Spatial planning must certainly include energy infrastructure, and we await the government's response to our previous recommendation that it should be brought within the town and country planning system.[4] Similarly, the Commission's report on transport recommended that trunk road schemes be integrated fully into structure plans and development control.[5] Developments by or on behalf of the Crown do not generally have to obtain planning permission; the Planning Green Paper says the government will introduce legislation when an opportunity arises to remove that exemption 'subject to certain safeguards relating to the national interest'.[6] The location and nature of other major projects is dictated by national policies. Often projects in all these categories have either not been included in development plans drawn up by local authorities or have been imposed on those plans by national government. The resulting lack of coherence has been a serious deficiency.

10.8 In addition to their immediate impact, large projects may lead directly to other forms of development. We have previously pointed to the need, when considering a proposal for a power station, to include all the transmission lines and other infrastructure required for its operation. Moreover, large projects often exert more indirect, but strong influences on land use and the environment in the surrounding area.

10.9 Land use is much affected by government policies in other fields, whether or not they involve large individual projects. To be successful, therefore, spatial planning also needs to take into account, and as far as possible influence, all the significant spatial impacts of policies.

10.10 The methodology of spatial planning has recently been reviewed by consultants for the National Assembly for Wales.[7] They identified four approaches:

- *vision statements* providing an aspirational vision in selected policy areas, possibly complemented by key indicators, but not including maps or visual representations

- *strategic frameworks based on key principles,* with at most only a broad visual representation of certain topics in map form, with the result that spatial dimensions of policy are treated only 'in a relatively implicit manner'

- *strategic frameworks based on functional analysis of key themes* utilising computer simulations and geographical information systems, and including visual representation at a range of appropriate scales

- *master plans* presenting prescriptive designs for land use in the form of detailed maps.

10.11 The consultants noted that 'Wales already has numerous vision statements in key policy areas but … these are not sufficiently reconciled in terms of their spatial implications.' As they pointed out, it is also inherently difficult to monitor the implementation of vision statements. On the other hand they advised that 'A prescriptive master plan approach is now absent from all leading "best practice".'[8] The Welsh Assembly has decided to prepare a strategic framework based on a combination of functional analysis and key principles. The consultants saw this as able to be 'highly specific in its spatial focus, which greatly assists implementation, monitoring and review'.

10.12 We believe spatial planning provides an invaluable tool for identifying the most sustainable forms of development for a given region, area or location.[9] The environmental and social challenges it can address include:

- whether certain areas are reaching the environmental limits to their capacity to accommodate further growth

- whether growth can, and should, be channelled from the areas of greatest economic potential to the areas of greatest social need

- whether patterns of social change which lead to concentrations of spatial disadvantage can be effectively influenced

- how to ensure that development takes forms which will minimise the need to travel.

Integrated spatial strategies

10.13 The environmental purpose of spatial planning can be defined as bringing about a spatial distribution of activities which will safeguard sustainability by protecting and enhancing the environment. To achieve its potential in that respect, it must be carried out at a strategic level, and cover all activities and policies which have significant spatial implications for the environment. Alongside economic and social objectives, it must take full account of all aspects of the environment, and the constraints they impose. We have used the term 'integrated spatial strategy' to describe a spatial planning document which has those characteristics.

10.14 We consider below how closely planning documents produced within the town and country planning system approach what we are advocating. Clearly, integrated spatial strategies need to cover the types of development not at present included in that system (10.7), and the developments below high-water mark we have recommended should be brought within it (9.62), if in either case these are on a strategic scale. Key issues about minerals and wastes also need to be an intrinsic part of integrated spatial strategies, rather than being dealt with as at present in separate plans prepared and reviewed on different timetables.

10.15 It is also essential that integrated spatial strategies cover agriculture and forestry, as the purposes for which by far the greatest proportion of land is used. In Scotland the former regional councils, as planning authorities, prepared indicative forest strategies to show the preferred areas for afforestation and areas where it might create problems; but there have been few such strategies in England and Wales,[10] despite guidance from central government[11] and a previous Commission recommendation.[12]

10.16 Although use of land for agriculture has not been subject to control in the same way as use for forestry, a requirement for prior consent is being introduced belatedly for changes in agricultural land use which are likely to cause significant environmental effects (9.48). Moreover, land use for agriculture is heavily influenced by European and national grant schemes (9.30-9.34), and is increasingly being regulated to limit its impact on the environment, especially in the form of water pollution (9.46-9.47). It seems essential that agricultural methods, policies and regulation should be considered at a strategic level and on a spatial basis alongside other relevant factors. **We recommend that the use of land for agriculture, forestry and countryside recreation should be issues covered in all spatial planning in future.**

10.17 An integrated spatial strategy must extend beyond direct questions of land use to cover all aspects of the environment which are spatially related. These include air quality, noise, all dimensions of the water cycle (water resources, water quality and floods), contamination of land, and the capacity and vulnerability of soils.[13] Other aspects of the environment which are spatially related, even if in less obvious ways, are the amounts and kinds of energy obtained and used, the amounts and kinds of wastes produced and disposed of, and biological diversity. Safeguarding landscapes and townscapes must also feature in an integrated spatial strategy.

10.18 A key function of integrated spatial planning will be to make explicit the demands on environmental resources entailed by developments projected or proposed in the area covered by a strategy.[14] Preparation of the strategy should involve assessing whether those demands can be met in ways that are environmentally sustainable and exploring ways of meeting them that would be least damaging to the environment. In addition to the supply of land for development, the most important environmental resources to assess in most regions will be the supply of water, the resources of soil, the availability of aggregates, and the capacity for waste disposal.[15]

10.19 The starting-point in preparing an integrated spatial strategy must be a rigorous analysis of environmental, economic and social factors. As well as analysing the current state of the environment, this must assess the pressures on it, based on projections of economic and social trends and alternative assumptions about policies. The projections must extend sufficiently far into the future to identify trends which will be unsustainable in the long term. And the plan eventually adopted must cover a sufficiently long period to provide a robust basis for large investment decisions by public bodies and private companies. We believe that, especially on issues about natural resources, this points to the need for a plan period of 25 years. For analytical purposes it may well be desirable to make some projections which extend well beyond that, for example to cover the likely long-term effects of climate change.

10.20 Whatever the area selected as the basis for spatial planning, there will be flows of resources and pollution across its boundaries (7.11). Integrated spatial strategies should identify and quantify significant flows of this kind taking place currently or projected to occur in future. Examples of such flows include large demands placed on the water resources of an adjoining area, damage to the quality of its water or air, or large quantities of waste sent into it for processing or disposal. If a continuation of present trends and policies would impose significant environmental damage on an adjoining area, preparation of an integrated spatial strategy should include exploring the full range of options available for avoiding that and achieving a better overall outcome for the environment.

10.21 **We recommend the introduction of integrated spatial strategies which take account of all spatially related activities and all spatially related aspects of environmental capacity. They should be four-dimensional, covering the atmosphere and groundwater as well as the land surface, and looking at least 25 years ahead.**

Conditions for establishing integrated spatial planning

10.22 Having defined the purpose and scope of integrated spatial strategies, we now discuss how they need to be prepared and implemented. We first set out some general conditions that will have to be fulfilled if integrated spatial planning is to be effective. These provide the basis for considering what areas integrated spatial strategies can best cover, where responsibility should lie for preparing and implementing them, and the relevance of proposals for England in the Planning Green Paper.

10.23 The areas for which integrated spatial strategies are prepared must be sufficiently large and self-contained to allow an integrated view to be taken of the considerations inherent in sustainable development. That means there must be substantial linkages and interactions between environmental, economic and social factors within their boundaries. They will normally contain both significant urban areas and significant rural areas, so that the interdependencies between those two types of area can be taken fully into account.[16]

10.24 We envisage integrated spatial strategies will in future be the dominant planning documents for the areas they cover, and will supersede many existing types of plan. We see them as the key instrument for rationalising the present plethora of spatially related plans produced by public bodies which was analysed in chapter 4.

10.25 Each strategy should incorporate carefully chosen statistical indicators for sustainability, even though it may be difficult to construct quantitative indicators for all the relevant aspects of the environment. Many of those indicators are likely to be common to all areas; comparisons between areas are an important component in evaluating and reviewing policies and performance.[17] Some additional indicators may have to be defined and applied to reflect the particular circumstances of an area.

10.26 The strategy should, wherever possible, include quantified targets for protection and improvement of the environment, to be achieved by specified dates. Some of those targets will be set locally. Many will derive from a higher tier of government, reflecting the sets of priority environmental objectives we have recommended (8.7). Some of those will apply uniformly to all areas (targets for air quality might be an example). Others may be unequal contributions to a national target in order to reflect differences in circumstances between areas (for example, targets for developing renewable energy sources, for increasing waste recycling or for reducing road traffic), and may have to be the subject of negotiations with national policy makers. The implications of all targets deriving from a higher tier of government must be taken fully into account in the analytical report (10.19), whether the targets are environmental, economic or social.

10.27 Wherever the lead responsibility for an integrated spatial strategy is located, its preparation and implementation will necessarily involve a partnership between a number of public bodies. At the technical level, evidence we received emphasised the importance of co-ordinating and developing links within the existing pool of expertise, given the increasing specialisation of environmental professions.[18] At the policy level, there will have to be much clearer and stronger lines of communication than have existed hitherto between the different bodies involved.[19]

10.28 There must be a strong focus on the mechanisms for delivering the objectives and targets in the strategy. **An integrated spatial strategy must specify exactly what contributions are expected from local development plans and from the activities of other public bodies.** In order to make the expected contributions, public bodies, including government Departments and agencies, will have to include appropriate provision in their programmes.

10.29 **To ensure that all the relevant bodies contribute fully to preparation of the integrated spatial strategy, and are committed to its implementation, it should have a firm statutory basis, and the lead body should be clearly designated. All other public bodies should be placed under a duty to co-operate in its preparation and comply with it where it affects their activities.** As we consider it essential the strategy should be binding on government Departments, the process of adoption will have to involve approval by government.

10.30 Progress towards the objectives and targets set in the strategy will have to be carefully monitored, together with movements of other indicators from the baseline values recorded in the analytical report. This, together with other significant changes in circumstances, will provide the basis for reviews of the strategy at five-year intervals. The improvements in the availability of environmental information recommended in chapter 6 will facilitate considerably the preparation and monitoring of integrated spatial strategies.

10.31 The areas for which integrated spatial strategies are produced must have the technical, financial and political resources needed for an exercise of this nature. They must be areas the public recognise, and can identify with. Preparation of an integrated spatial strategy should have a high profile as an open and transparent process. Although two key documents, national policies (10.26) and the analytical report (10.19), will be available at the start of the process, there is a crucial further stage of identifying and framing the problems faced by a particular area. This must be much more than a technical exercise. The strategy should be informed from the beginning by the perceptions and values of the people in the area; several procedures have now been devised and applied for this kind of purpose.[20] The initial submissions from government Departments and statutory agencies should be made public, and submissions should be invited at the same time from a wide variety of non-governmental organisations.

10.32 The draft strategy should be considered at a public examination conducted by an independent panel. After 2004, when the new EC Directive must be applied, it will have to be accompanied by a strategic environmental assessment (7.42 and box 7D). Strategic environmental assessment will be a much more meaningful and cost-effective process if applied to integrated strategies which have sought to take environmental considerations fully into account from the earliest stage.

10.33 These are the general requirements for a system of integrated spatial strategies which will make a crucial contribution to promoting sustainable development and safeguarding environmental sustainability. They must cover large areas. They must be of a strategic nature, and not unnecessarily complex or detailed. They must be imbued with a genuine vision of the long-term choices facing the area they cover, and the ways in which those choices can best be resolved. And they must be acceptable to the populations they affect, who must have a direct involvement in their preparation and ratification.

CURRENT PLANNING DOCUMENTS

10.34 We now review some current planning documents to see how closely they approach to our concept of an integrated spatial strategy. We look first at *regional planning guidance* in England and its relationship to other plans and strategies produced at regional level, then at the *London spatial development strategy* now being prepared, and then at structure plans. The final type of planning document we discuss is *local plans* and the proposals for their replacement put forward in the Planning Green Paper for England.

10.35 As we noted earlier (2.48), town and country planning in Northern Ireland differs in being a function of a government Department, rather than local authorities. The Strategic Framework for Northern Ireland, published as a draft in 1998 and adopted in 2001,[21] has been a pioneering exercise in spatial planning, and is described in appendix G.

10.36 The organisation at regional level described at the beginning of this report (2.49-2.51 and table 2.1) produces non-statutory regional planning guidance for each of what are now nine Government Office regions outside London, and also a regional economic strategy (2.52) and a regional sustainability framework (2.54).

10.37 Current policy is that the main purpose of regional planning guidance is 'to provide a regional spatial strategy within which local authority development plans and local transport plans can be prepared'. This should identify:

> the scale and distribution of provision for new housing and priorities for the environment, transport, infrastructure, economic development, agriculture, minerals and waste treatment and disposal…. By virtue of being a spatial strategy it also informs other strategies and programmes.[22]

Academic commentators have described regional planning guidance as evolving into a spatial plan in which sectoral policies with land use implications can be co-ordinated.[23]

10.38 The most contentious issues in regional planning have been the amount and location of provision for new housing and the location of new growth areas. In the South East, decisions on housing provision were largely imposed by the Secretary of State in the face of significant opposition from local authorities and the public.

10.39 Regional renewable energy assessments have been prepared by Government Offices as a separate exercise (8.62). The case for integrating planning of land use and transport, strongly urged in the Commission's report on transport in 1994,[24] has been taken to its logical conclusion at regional level: regional planning guidance is now required to include a regional transport strategy. Local transport plans, on the other hand, have been introduced as separate documents.[25]

10.40 The list of environmental and natural resource issues regional planning guidance is expected to cover includes countryside character, biodiversity and nature conservation, the coast, minerals, waste and energy. In some cases targets set nationally may be reproduced. For example, guidance for the South East adopts the national targets for 25% of household waste to be recycled or composted by 2005, 30% by 2010 and 33% by 2015.[26] On other issues, such as biological diversity, there is less guidance nationally. Draft regional planning guidance has also covered environmental issues which were curiously absent from the list, such as water resources and flood risk.

10.41 A crucial point is that information on strategic environmental constraints and resources should be available to the regional planning body to inform the planning process. The specialist agencies have been involved in the preparation of regional planning guidance, and also undertake regional planning on their own account. In general, the various elements do not seem to be well co-ordinated. There is no formal state of the environment report underlying regional planning guidance, still less the more sophisticated kind of analytical report we identified earlier (10.19) as an essential element in integrated spatial planning.

10.42 The Environment Agency has produced state of the environment reports, but for its own regions, not Government Office regions. Its conclusions about the differences in environmental priorities between its regions are summarised in table 10.1. It has also produced regional water resource strategies to assess the environmental consequences of four hypothetical development paths over the next 25 years. It is not yet clear how such strategies will seek to manage the risks to water resource availability and existing ecosystems caused by climate change. The Agency prepares regional plans for flood defence as the basis for decisions by the regional flood defence committee (2.33). It is producing regional waste management assessments to address issues about capacity for waste disposal and treatment. English Nature drew up sustainable development indicators for biodiversity in each region as a contribution to regional planning by other bodies.[27] Regional biodiversity action plans are produced, although they were originally regarded only as an interim measure.[28]

Table 10.1

Relative pressures on the environment: the Environment Agency's assessment

Stress	Anglian	Midlands	North East	North West	Southern	South West	Thames	Wales
Sea level rise	H	N/A	M	L	H	M	H	M
Flood risk	M	M	H	M	M	L	H	L
Household density	L	M	M	M	H	L	H	L
Public water supply demands and availability	M	H	L	M	M	M	H	L
Area worked for aggregates	L	M	M	L	H	M	H	(M)
Emissions of CO2 from part A processes	M	H	H	M	M	L	L	M
Emissions of NOx from part A processes	M	H	H	M	M	L	L	M
Emissions of SOx from part A processes	M	H	H	M	M	L	L	M
Emissions from transport	M	H	M	M	L	L	H	L
Loads from sewage-treatment works	M	M	H	M	H	L	M	L
Nutrient loads to sea	L	M	M	H	L	M	H	M
Metal loads to sea	M	M	H	H	L	M	L	M
Pesticide loads to the sea	L	H	M	H	L	M	M	M
Waste arising (municipal)	M	H	M	M	M	L	H	L
Pollution incidents	M	H	M	M	L	H	L	M
Totals: high (relative)	**1**	**8**	**6**	**3**	**4**	**1**	**8**	**0**
low (relative)	**4**	**0**	**1**	**2**	**5**	**8**	**5**	**6**

The two regions with the greatest stress were denoted **H** and the regions with relatively low stress **L**. Where data were lacking, M (moderate) was assumed and placed in brackets. Where pressures are approximately equal, more than two regions might be designated **H** or **L**. **N/A** means that region does not experience the stress in question.

SOURCE: Environment Agency (2000). *Environment 2000 and beyond*. Table 3.4. Further details were given in table A4.1.

10.43 The round of regional planning guidance now emerging seems to be taking more account of environmental issues, or at least of biological diversity and water issues. A greater degree of stakeholder involvement during its preparation may have helped to achieve that. Moreover, there has been much debate on those subjects at public examinations of drafts. The panels conducting the examinations have generally looked for a more comprehensive and robust approach to the environment than was apparent in the drafts; and recent panel reports have been quite radical in some of their recommendations.[29] There are wide differences, however, in the extent to which water issues and biological diversity are covered in guidance. The fullest treatment of biological diversity is in the guidance for the South West, which sets quantified targets for maintaining or creating 20 different habitat types. These targets were based on a regional biodiversity audit co-ordinated by English Nature. Similar audits were available in two other regions (South East, and Yorkshire and the Humber), but not utilised to the same extent; and in the remaining regions information was not available to define any such targets.

10.44 Regional planning guidance is flanked by, and in some regions may be overshadowed by, the regional economic strategy produced by the regional development agency (RDA). There is great potential for RDAs to promote sustainable development through their activities in supporting industry. They have already shown enthusiasm for green industries such as renewable energy. They could ensure that approaches such as waste minimisation and efficient resource use are incorporated in plans for cluster developments. Some of them are designing sustainability criteria for inward investment decisions.[30] However, the regional economic strategies they produced were strongly criticised for not showing awareness of environmental issues.[31] The performance of RDAs is assessed by reference to nine measures, for example gross domestic product per head in the region. Absurdly, a single measure, the percentage of new homes in the region provided on previously developed land, is regarded as the sustainable development indicator.[32] There are also five activity indicators, of which the most relevant in the present context is the net area of derelict land brought into use.[33] The use of these particular parameters reflects the inheritance RDAs received from English Partnerships.

10.45 The draft regional planning guidance recently published for the West Midlands[34] is an example of what is emerging from the new round. It is presented as a spatial plan, and applies a spatial approach to environmental issues. However, its coverage of environmental issues, whilst a considerable improvement on the previous guidance, is not comprehensive. The two key diagrams on 'Quality of the environment' (covering assets and areas of enhancement) show, among other things, designated areas in the countryside, flood plains and forests, but there is only a token representation of three 'major urban environmental improvement areas'. Significant aspects of the environment which are spatially related but not mapped in this document include water resources, soil types and quality, air quality, contaminated land, areas affected by subsidence, waste production and disposal, and energy production and use. Nearly all of them are covered by policies in the guidance but the implications of these policies, and their interactions with other regional policies, would be more effectively brought out if they were discussed in spatial terms. In some respects the draft guidance reveals conflicts, for example between the environmental importance of some areas and their economic potential, but it does not contain proposals for resolving them. Nevertheless the new draft guidance for the West Midlands demonstrates a clear movement in the right direction.

10.46 The Planning Green Paper envisages that the regional spatial strategies it proposes as a replacement for regional planning guidance would have statutory status, a change we would support. It also presents them as more concise and focused, reflecting regional diversity and specific regional needs, within the national planning framework; and cross-referring to national policies, rather than repeating them.[35]

10.47 In other respects the Green Paper's concept of a regional spatial strategy seems little different to the current policy quoted at 10.37. The Department for Transport, Local Government and the Regions (DTLR) seems to think regional planning bodies have not yet responded adequately to that guidance. Specific criticisms are that they have devoted too much space to reproducing national policies and failed to identify and address the key issues facing the region, especially where these involve difficult choices. However, there has been relatively little time to put current policy into effect, and documents now emerging, such as the West Midlands draft, seem to indicate that progress is being made.

10.48 The Green Paper proposes that regional spatial strategies should be integrated more fully with other regional strategies, and in particular that they should 'provide the longer term planning framework for the Regional Development Agencies' strategies and those of other stakeholders, and assist in their implementation'.[36]

10.49 Regional planning guidance and regional economic strategies in their present form do not constitute integrated spatial strategies in the sense we have described. Although regional strategies and plans may share a commitment to sustainable development, there is concern that they are not necessarily consistent with each other. The concept of integrating economic, social and environmental objectives is now embedded in most regional strategies and plans. But that may often conceal the political choices that have to be made about priorities for the region and the directions that development ought to take. There is a confusing variety of documents produced, all the more so because several successive drafts of some of them are published as a basis for consultation. The discrepancies in the timetables for producing them is another reason why they are sometimes inconsistent with each other. A recent study has recommended that the regional economic strategy, regional planning guidance and regional sustainability frameworks should be merged into a single document in the medium term 'so economic, social and environmental objectives are considered in parallel rather than sequentially'.[37] If our concept of an integrated spatial strategy is adopted and applied at regional level, it would have a similar effect, but it seeks to go further.

THE LONDON PLAN

10.50 Following abolition of the Greater London Council, strategic planning guidance for London was prepared in broadly the same way as regional planning guidance elsewhere in England. It was drafted by a consortium of London borough councils, the London Planning Advisory Committee, and issued by the Secretary of State.[38] There is now a duty on the Mayor of London to prepare a spatial development strategy, which he has decided to call the London Plan.

10.51 The Mayor is also required to prepare strategies for economic development, transport, municipal waste management, noise, biodiversity, air quality and culture. Each strategy must take account of national policies and international obligations, and be consistent with the other strategies.[39] A state of the environment report must be produced, and updated every four years, but the first such report need not be produced until May 2003.[40] The draft spatial development strategy must be accompanied by a 'sustainability appraisal'. A further statutory requirement is that all the strategies must take account of three cross-cutting themes: the health of Londoners, equality of opportunity, and 'the contribution to sustainable development in the UK'.[41] The Mayor intends to produce three further strategies: on children, on housing (jointly with the London boroughs) and on energy.[42] All the strategies were scheduled to be published as drafts by March 2002.

10.52 The Mayor has said his vision is to develop London as an exemplary sustainable world city, based on three balanced and interlocking elements:

- strong and diverse economic growth

- social inclusivity to allow all Londoners to share in London's future success

- fundamental improvements in environmental management and use of resources.[43]

10.53 Some people have seen the legislation now being implemented in London as a prototype for the introduction of spatial planning in the UK. The progress made initially is described in appendix F. Unless there is a very close relationship between all the various strategies, the end result could be very similar to the plethora of plans we have found elsewhere. The signs so far are not promising. It seems no systematic analysis has yet been made of environmental problems and priorities, and that some aspects of the environment are getting short shrift. This confirms us in the view that the approach to spatial planning advocated earlier in this chapter is more robust.

STRUCTURE PLANS

10.54 Structure plans are strategic and statutory. The current position in England is that:

- 23 structure plans fall to be prepared under joint arrangements between neighbouring local authorities

- 15 structure plans fall to be prepared by a county council on its own responsibility

- in the remaining areas there is a unitary development plan, in which part I is regarded as fulfilling a similar function to a structure plan. These areas include the metropolitan areas, Herefordshire, the Isle of Wight and the national parks.[44]

In Scotland there are 17 structure plan areas, of which six cover more than one unitary authority. Joint arrangements reflect the realities of the situation on the ground. In many cases, however, it has yet to be seen how they will work in practice.

10.55 In many areas, structure plans have been evolving rapidly towards performing a spatial planning function. It was claimed in evidence to us that they operate at a level conducive to strategic decisions but 'close enough to communities to allow effective participation'.[45] The process of producing the current structure plans was strongly influenced both by pressure for economic development and by pressure to protect the environment. Those two pressures were often brought together, at least rhetorically, in a general commitment to 'sustainable development'.[46] The specific aims and objectives set out in individual structure plans show a wide variation, reflecting the different needs and problems of different areas; some typical examples are reproduced in appendix E.

10.56 The numerous policies in a typical structure plan (typically a hundred or more) include extensive coverage of environmental issues. The background papers produced in preparing a structure plan may include a state of the environment report (7.8).[47] There is a move, however, to extend such reports to cover a much wider range of issues and make them sustainable development reports.[48] The local planning authority is expected to carry out a full environmental appraisal of the plan,[49] and encouraged to consider extending this to cover the four sustainable development objectives (3.8).[50]

10.57 Despite explicit commitments to sustainable development, structure plans in their existing form are not ideal instruments for pursuing integrated policies, or for identifying and implementing proactive solutions to future problems of environmental sustainability. There are several reasons for that. First, they do not extend far enough into the future to provide an effective response to many environmental problems; typically, the nominal period covered is 15 years, but little more than 10 years usually remain by the time a plan is adopted. Second, they are not usually based on projections of the future effects of current pressures on the environment; even where the supporting documents include a state of the environment report, this is simply a description of the current position.

10.58 One factor limiting the effectiveness of structure plans is a lack of guidance from national government, an issue we discussed in chapter 8. For example, they typically contain policies for reducing carbon dioxide emissions, developing renewable energy sources and reducing traffic growth; but, in the absence of any measuring rods to indicate what it is reasonable for a particular area to achieve in these directions over a given period, such policies risk being little more than platitudes.

10.59 A further difficulty has often been a lack of effective dialogue between local planning authorities and the specialist agencies. The planning authority is aware of areas designated by the specialist agencies (for example, as Areas of Outstanding Natural Beauty or as flood plains). It may also quote the views of a specialist agency if they support its own policy of restricting the number of houses built.[51] There is little sign however that there is as yet a generally effective partnership. This is particularly true of the Environment Agency, which came into operation only in 1996, when most of the current structure plans were either approved or at an advanced stage, and did not in its early years attach priority to this work.[52] It intends to accord it a much higher priority in future. But this work is resource-intensive, especially if it has to extend to participating in an examination in public (for example, to express support for a policy proposed by the planning authority under the Agency's influence), and difficulties may therefore arise if there is general pressure on its resources. The countryside bodies also appear to be constrained in the amount of time and money they can afford to devote to the town and country planning system, although English Heritage has tended to give a high priority to this task.

10.60 There is also a legal limitation on the scope of structure plans: policy guidance is that the matters they address 'must be capable of being addressed through the land use planning system'.[53] This brings into consideration both what constitutes 'land use' for the purposes of the planning Acts and when the town and country planning regime is permitted to intervene. The courts have repeatedly warned against exclusive categories and have accepted that there can be a large overlap between different regulatory systems.

10.61 Although the statutory status of a structure plan places limitations on its scope, it also has considerable weight as part of the formal development plan for the area. In areas with two tiers of local government, the structure plan has provided district councils, not only with a clear and firm basis for preparing a more detailed local plan, but also, where a local plan is not yet in place, with the policies on which to determine most of the planning applications they receive.

10.62 It took a long time (14 years) to put the first generation of structure plans in place.[54] Although the present generation of structure plans were intended to be simpler, it has taken a decade to have them all in place. Current reviews, however, are taking only two to three years. That does not seem an unreasonable period of time, given the range of contentious issues dealt with in structure plans and the need for wide consultation and an examination in public.[55]

10.63 The structure plan process has achieved a good deal. The Green Paper proposes the abolition of structure plans; but, if this were to happen, an alternative process would in our view be necessary in order to ensure there is a strategic level of planning involving local authorities above the district level. Given major variations in local government organisation in different parts of the UK, we accept that there is no single consistent tier that could be charged with responsibility for the integrated spatial strategies we consider essential. The present statutory restrictions on structure plans prevent their serving as integrated spatial strategies. We could therefore agree to the Green Paper's proposal to abolish structure plans, in England, provided they are replaced by integrated spatial strategies with statutory force covering areas no smaller than those currently covered by structure plans.

LOCAL PLANS

10.64 Local plans are the more detailed statutory plans drawn up and adopted by district councils in England and unitary authorities in Scotland;[56] elsewhere in Britain the equivalent is part II of the unitary development plan. Local plans consist of a written statement and a map of the local authority's area defining sites for particular developments or land uses,[57] and have remained broadly similar to the original development plans produced under the 1947 legislation. If another authority has prepared a structure plan, it is asked to state whether the draft local plan conforms with it.[58] Where there is an up-to-date local plan, it may be the predominant factor determining the decisions on individual planning applications (2.10).

10.65 Coverage is still incomplete. After a decade many areas in England still do not have a local plan prepared under present legislation (2.12). This is partly a consequence of the procedures followed, which can include a sometimes lengthy public inquiry into objections, conducted by a planning inspector. Local authorities also have difficulty in finding resources simultaneously for the day-to-day work of development control and for the preparation or amendment of the local plan. Because of delays the policies in local plans are often out of date by the time the plan is approved; for example, they may be overtaken by revision of the structure plan, or by the development of land that had not been scheduled for development.

10.66 A large part of the present contents of local plans are not really necessary. They reproduce policies and designations which are decided and modified independently by other bodies, for example in regional planning guidance or in the structure plan. A substantial proportion of the objections to local plans relate to policies derived from elsewhere. Any argument that it is convenient for the public to bring all this information together in one place has been undermined by the delays in producing local plans, which mean that the information given is often more misleading than helpful. The Planning Portal now being constructed will ensure that in future anyone will be able to obtain all such information direct in up-to-date form. If our recommendation for an environmental information centre (6.36) is accepted, it will also be possible for anyone to check the current boundaries of all relevant designated areas in the more informative presentation of an electronic geographical information system.

10.67 Even for a planning authority's own proposals, we do not consider it is always necessary for the local plan to map the whole of the authority's area. Maps might be provided only for localities where development or environmental pressures are particularly intense; in other areas, the plan would lay down general criteria for development. The combined effect of these changes would be a much slimmer local plan focused on a local authority's own policies for the exercise of its development control functions.

10.68 The Green Paper proposes that local plans should be replaced by *local development frameworks* consisting of:

- a statement of core policies setting out the local authority's vision and strategy to be applied in promoting and controlling development throughout its area

- more detailed action plans for smaller areas of change

- a map showing existing designations such as conservation areas and the areas of change for which action plans are to be prepared,

together with a statement of community involvement (5.13). This framework would be continuously updated to reflect changes in national and regional planning policies, reissued in paper form once a year, and reviewed every three years or when the community strategy (see below) is reviewed.[59]

10.69 While we believe the local development frameworks proposed in the Green Paper represent, in general, a sensible approach, there are some serious practical issues which require further consideration, especially in view of some of the other tasks district and unitary authorities face. These include retaining all their current development control functions; fulfilling their new responsibility to prepare a community strategy (2.25); and under the Green Paper preparing action plans, including neighbourhood-based plans, especially in localities subject to major development. Rather than simplifying planning at the local level, the combined effect of these requirements threatens to create a more complex, less comprehensible, less effective and slower planning system than exists at the moment. It also represents a major challenge to many of the local authorities involved in terms of their capacity to undertake this work, given current limitations of resources and skills.

10.70 We are also concerned that the government proposes not to allow objections to draft local development frameworks or public inquiries: alternatives suggested range from 'wide public participation' to an informal hearing of representations by an inspector (whose report would then be binding on the local authority).[60] Irrespective of any arguments derived from effects on property rights, **we consider there should continue to be rights to object and provision for a public inquiry into a draft local plan or local development framework, on the ground that this kind of public challenge is fundamental to the purpose of the town and country planning system**. As local development frameworks would be much slimmer documents, handling objections should be a less onerous and costly process than at present; but the costs incurred for this should in any case be regarded as well justified in a wider perspective.

10.71 We discuss below the relationship between local plans/local development frameworks and spatial plans. The Planning Green Paper sees local development frameworks as being complementary to the community strategies local authorities are now required to prepare.[61] Community strategies and the associated local strategic partnerships (2.26) will set overall priorities for a local authority and its partners, some of which will be outside the scope of environmental planning and not spatially related. Local development frameworks will remain necessary as the basis for decisions taken at local authority level on planning applications, supplemented by the more detailed plans for smaller areas, worked out with the full involvement of the local community.

INTRODUCING A SYSTEM OF INTEGRATED SPATIAL STRATEGIES

10.72 From the discussion above, (10.13-10.33), it is evident that spatial plans that accommodate environmental priorities must have the following features:

- they must be strategic plans, inspired by a genuine vision of the long-term choices facing the area they cover, and the ways in which those choices can best be resolved;

- they must relate to areas that are large enough to integrate broad environmental issues and features of the town and countryside, and provide such resources as aggregates, water, and waste management facilities;

- the communities they affect must identify with the area defined and be directly involved in their preparation and ratification.

10.73 The area covered must also be sufficiently large to support the skill base of planners, engineers, environmental scientists and others needed to develop the plan. It should also be large enough to allow working links with the specialist environmental agencies and non-governmental organisations concerned with biological diversity, flooding and other factors that need to be included in integrated spatial strategies.

10.74 A spatial framework for the whole of the UK has been advocated in a report prepared by the Royal Town Planning Institute,[62] but the idea has not been taken up by government. We consider here how a system of integrated spatial strategies can best be established for areas within the UK.

10.75 The Planning Green Paper presents its proposed local development frameworks as 'in planning jargon … much more of a "spatial" strategy'. By this it means that the statement of core polices in the framework (10.68) will 'take full account of the land-use consequences of other policies and programmes relevant to the Community Strategy, including education, health, waste, recycling and environmental protection and consider how it can assist in the delivery of these and other economic, environmental and social objectives'.[63] However, we do not believe either local plans or local development frameworks could become integrated spatial strategies in the sense we are advocating. The areas they cover are not sufficiently large or self-contained to provide a satisfactory basis for strategic planning. There are no established links between preparation of local plans and the specialist agencies: the agencies are statutory consultees in the preparation of structure plans, but not local plans nor unitary development plans.[64] As we have seen, the authorities responsible for preparing local plans have often struggled to progress even plans of the present conventional type; it would hardly be sensible to impose on them the task of producing much more sophisticated plans of a novel kind which would require a wide range of new skills in their staff and elected members. Equally, the specialist agencies have problems in finding resources even for effective liaison with structure plan authorities, and liaison with the much larger number of authorities preparing local plans would require very much larger resources.

10.76 If local plans or local development frameworks are not to be integrated spatial strategies in the sense used here, it is nevertheless essential that they take environmental considerations fully into account. Some environmental objectives can be identified locally. We would expect to see these taking their proper place among the priorities identified by the local authority or local strategic partnership in the community strategy, as well as in the local plan. Objectives identified at local authority level, however, will not necessarily be mutually consistent. Nor will the sum total of those local objectives necessarily be compatible with sustainable development. On many matters, safeguarding environmental sustainability will require policies to be framed in a wider perspective. As well as giving careful attention to the local environment, therefore, local plans or local development frameworks should also incorporate whatever constraints or targets are needed as contributions to the realisation of the integrated spatial strategy. **It should be a statutory requirement that local plans or local deveeloopment frameworks must comply with the integrated spatial strategy. Wherever appropriate, the policies and targets in the integrated spatial strategy should also be reflected in the community strategy or plan**.

10.77 The best way of satisfying the general requirements for integrated spatial planning identified earlier in this chapter may vary with circumstances. Both the present institutions and the geographical conditions differ significantly in the different parts of the UK. In making recommendations about the appropriate level for establishing spatial planning, we have therefore distinguished between the different parts of the UK.

Northern Ireland

10.78 **In Northern Ireland we consider that drawing up a spatial development strategy for the whole province and more detailed spatial frameworks for the Belfast Metropolitan Area and the regional city of Derry/Londonderry represents a sensible approach to introducing spatial planning.**

10.79 The Scottish Executive has sought views on whether a 'national overview document' should be prepared for Scotland, and if so what form it should take; but has emphasised this is not intended to be a national plan, nor comprehensive.[65] It has also sought views on whether strategic plans should be prepared for the four largest cities and their hinterlands under the supervision of a joint committee serviced by a dedicated team. **We recommend that the strategic development plans the Scottish Executive has proposed for the conurbations centred on Glasgow, Edinburgh, Aberdeen and Dundee should take the form of the integrated spatial strategies we have recommended, and that consideration should be given to introducing integrated spatial planning in the remainder of Scotland.**

WALES

10.80 In Wales local government is too fragmented to undertake spatial planning at a sub-regional level unaided. The National Assembly is committed to producing a spatial planning framework 'to link together the Assembly's policies and set a vision for balanced development that benefits all parts of Wales'; although a national strategy, it is also envisaged as having 'a strong regional dimension'.[66] This commitment represented a victory for professional opinion over initial opposition from the Assembly; but progress towards producing the framework seems to be slow. National strategic frameworks for energy, waste and transport are being produced, with the intention that they will feed into the spatial planning framework;[67] and, if there is further delay, there must be a real danger that they will pre-empt any attempt at genuine spatial planning. **We urge the National Assembly for Wales to publish the promised national spatial planning framework for consultation at an early date. We also recommend that the Assembly take the initiative, in conjunction with the relevant local authorities, in preparing integrated spatial strategies for regions within Wales.**

ENGLAND OUTSIDE LONDON

10.81 In England the Planning Green Paper and the promised White Paper on regional governance complicate the task of deciding how integrated spatial planning can best be established. As noted previously, the Green Paper proposes that regional planning guidance should be replaced by regional spatial strategies (10.46-10.48) and that structure plans should be abolished (10.63). It looks forward to the prospect that elected assemblies will be established in English regions where a referendum supports that and unitary authorities predominate,[68] as promised in successive Labour Party manifestos.[69] It is difficult to imagine a situation persisting for long in which some regions of England have elected regional assemblies and others do not. The Greater London Assembly (which came into operation in 2000) could be regarded as the first such regional assembly, although in all probability not a typical one.

10.82 We noted in chapter 4 unsatisfactory features of the present hierarchy of documents in town and country planning which are a major obstacle to a coherent approach (4.17-4.18). Taken as a whole, the current system absorbs too many resources in producing largely out-of-date plans. That cannot be in the interests of environmental protection and enhancement. New policies and responses to growing environmental threats can take ten years or more to feed through into local plans.

10.83 Prior to the Planning Green Paper the Confederation of British Industry (CBI) and others urged that one layer of plans should be removed,[70] although without specifying which layer.[71] The Council for the Protection of Rural England (CPRE) has argued, on the other hand, for retaining two tiers of strategic planning; measures to strengthen regional planning should not undermine

> the distinct role of Structure Plans in facilitating democratic accountability, scrutinising county-level development objectives, and closely matching development patterns with identified needs. [Regional-level plans] should provide a policy framework for development plans rather than directly defining the scale and location of development or prescribing numerical targets.[72]

10.84 We have considered carefully whether it would be desirable and feasible to remove one layer. We support the government's aim of speeding up and simplifying local plans, provided adequate opportunities remain for public involvement (10.70); that will be an important contribution to producing a more effective town and country planning system, and we do not see any case for trying to dispense entirely with any form of local plan.

10.85 At the other end of the scale there is also consensus that the arrangements for promulgating national planning policies in England need to be rationalised. At regional level, the role of regional planning guidance has to be assessed against the other strategies and plans produced; it is essential to maintain, and indeed increase considerably, the spatial and environmental contribution to the overall process of regional planning.

10.86 As our objective is to bring together economic, social and environmental factors, one relevant consideration in designing a new system might be the areas over which environmental parameters can most effectively be assessed and controlled. In fact, no set of boundaries can satisfy all criteria. Natural areas do not coincide with administrative areas, and the Environment Agency regards different areas as appropriate for different aspects of the environment, for example air pollution and surface waters. Its regions are defined primarily in terms of water catchment areas. However, the Agency has adopted a pragmatic approach to facilitate liaison and defined 'public face' boundaries for its regions, adjusted to coincide with the border between England and Wales and follow the boundaries of local authority areas. There is still no connection in some areas with the boundaries of Government Office regions. The Agency has therefore designated one regional office to take the lead in relation to each of the Government Office regions; thus Southern Region takes the lead for the South East of England, even though about half that region lies within the Agency's Thames Region. The other specialised agencies have had less difficulty in relating their activities to the boundaries of Government Office regions, even though those do not necessarily coincide with the transitions between natural character areas.

10.87 One option for establishing integrated spatial planning is to extend the scope and role of regional planning guidance (or regional spatial strategies, if the proposal in the Planning Green Paper is implemented). The Government Office regions for which they are prepared are expected to provide the framework for elected regional authorities, but have disadvantages as the basis for spatial planning. The public does not necessarily identify with them. The South West Region, which starts a few miles south of Stratford-upon-Avon and stretches across the M4 corridor for over 200 miles to Penzance, has been widely criticised as not forming a single coherent area. There is certainly little public awareness in most regions of the work done to prepare regional planning guidance. Regions do not have a proper democratic structure and preparation of regional planning guidance is dependent at present on the skill base at county and unitary authority level. There is only a very small central capability in each region: regional planning guidance is drafted by staff from the local authorities in the region on behalf of bodies in which those authorities are at least predominant (2.50-2.51).

10.88 The position will change significantly if elected regional authorities are established. Regions will have a much higher public profile and much greater public recognition. It is envisaged the new bodies will take over responsibility for regional planning.[73] There will then be a much clearer line of accountability, and no longer a democratic deficit at regional level. There are some potentially serious weaknesses, however. The critical nature of many of the decisions required implies a need for active public engagement: arguably that could not be delivered by a remote regional body with possibly only a small membership. Many of the policies the integrated spatial strategy will seek to co-ordinate and integrate are likely to remain the responsibility of national government: if the lead is taken by the elected regional assembly, and Government Offices are less crucially involved, they will have less commitment to taking the actions required to give effect to the strategy. It is also important that transfer of responsibility for regional planning to an elected assembly does not reduce the effort devoted to direct consultation with stakeholders.

10.89 Another option for establishing integrated spatial strategies is to extend the role of structure plans. That might involve bringing together larger numbers of county or unitary authorities to co-operate on strategies at sub-regional levels. Legislation could remove the present legal limitation on the scope of structure plans and give the government powers to ensure the new style of plan will include appropriate environmental objectives and targets. The period covered by the plan would be extended to 25 years. Preparation of integrated spatial strategies for areas smaller than Government Office regions could attract more effective public participation, informed by local knowledge. In areas with two tiers of local government, the county council would be in close touch with district councils, and that could have an important effect in raising their awareness of the contents of the plan and facilitating its implementation. There are the same potential disadvantages as at regional level over commitment to the plan by government Departments and over direct involvement of stakeholders. A focus at sub-regional level would allow the specialised agencies to collaborate more easily than at county and unitary authority level.

10.90 Indeed, sub-regions are in many ways the most suitable areas for integrated spatial strategies, assuming that they are defined on the basis of functional coherence. The Planning Green Paper recognises this point, and emphasises the need for a strategic approach to major conurbations and to the planning of major towns and cities and their hinterlands. It envisages that in most regions a small number of sub-regional strategies will be prepared, as part of the regional planning process, and incorporated in the regional spatial strategy.[74]

10.91 If and when elected regional assemblies are established in England they are likely to provide the most satisfactory basis for integrated spatial strategies. It might be number of years, however, before that position is reached; and even then there is likely to remain a need to prepare strategies for some sub-regions, including some that cut across regional boundaries. The introduction of integrated spatial strategies ought not to wait that long. Experience with structure plans (10.62) and regional planning guidance (10.47) confirms the importance of the learning curve when a new approach to planning is introduced. In moving towards spatial planning in which environmental factors are fully integrated there will be many practical and conceptual difficulties to overcome, and many new working relationships will have to be established. This work should start as soon as possible. **We recommend that regional planning guidance and structure plans should both be converted into integrated spatial strategies with a comprehensive coverage of land use and environmental issues. There should be increasing co-operation between county and unitary authorities to develop integrated spatial strategies for sub-regions where these have greater functional coherence.**

LONDON AND THE SOUTH EAST

10.92 The dominance of London creates the most difficult problem in defining English regions. The wider South East region, for which planning guidance has been prepared hitherto, contains almost 30% of the UK's population, and an even higher proportion of economic activity. This is regarded by the government as too large and dominant an area to form a satisfactory basis for Government Office regions. It is split between three Government Offices, and for the future the areas covered by planning guidance are being modified to reflect the areas covered by those offices.[75] The areas thus created, however, fail to reflect economic and social realities, which have been recognised by successive governments since the South East Study in 1963, or the nature of the pressures on the environment. Splitting London from its hinterland conflicts with the general desirability of integrating planning for urban and rural areas. Co-ordination arrangements have been agreed for what will now in effect be the super region of the South East,[76] but it has yet to be seen how effective these will be.

10.93 The most appropriate solution for South East England is not necessarily the appropriate solution for the rest of England, or *vice versa*. In London we have some concerns about the approach the Greater London Authority is adopting in preparing the spatial development strategy for London, and we hope that approach will be significantly modified before the strategy is finalised. In broad terms that is an experiment which will have to be allowed to run its course, in the expectation that the present legislation and the way it has been implemented will be carefully evaluated. In the rest of the South East there could in theory be three tiers of strategic planning, with structure plans and regional planning guidance for the two Government Office regions overlain by the as yet unknown form of 'pan-regional' framework for the whole of the South East. That would clearly be nonsense. **In South East England the best solution, irrespective of whether elected regional authorities are created in England and given responsibilities for spatial planning, would be to concentrate strategic planning at only two levels: the South East super region (including London) and sub-regions no smaller than the areas for which structure plans are prepared at present.**

CONCLUSION

10.94 Provided they are on the lines we have advocated, and can be based on a holistic view of environmental processes, integrated spatial strategies will be a substantial step towards joining up government and integrating environmental considerations into economic and social policies. Those are necessary conditions if sustainable development is to be achieved and environmental sustainability safeguarded. Changes in planning procedures at regional, sub-regional and local levels are an essential complement to the clearer and firmer framework at national level which we have recommended in chapter 8 and the improvements in policies for town, country and coast we have recommended in chapter 9.

RECOMMENDATIONS

We bring together here all the recommendations which appear (in bold type) elsewhere in this report.

We recommend that the demonstrable capacity of public participation to improve plans and policies should be fostered by improving existing procedures and developing new deliberative processes. (5.18)

We recommend that the legislation on development control, conservation areas, scheduled monuments, listed buildings and control of advertisements should be consolidated and a single consent procedure introduced, provided this can be achieved without any weakening of the present safeguards. (5.21)

We recommend that pollution control authorisation and planning permission for industrial plants should be obtained through a single open process involving a common environmental statement (see 7.27-7.28 below) and, where appropriate, a joint public inquiry. (5.24)

We emphasise that there should be no reduction in the obligations on planning authorities to consult the agencies responsible for pollution control, flood defence, conservation of species and habitats, countryside and the built heritage. (5.29)

There will be some types of case in certain areas where the relevant specialist agency can provide the planning authority with standing advice in advance, and so dispense with the need for consultation on individual cases and we recommend that more effort be devoted to identifying such categories of cases. (5.29)

We recommend the establishment of Environmental Tribunals to handle appeals under environmental legislation other than the town and country planning system, including those now handled by planning inspectors. (5.36)

We recommend that third parties should have a right of appeal against decisions on planning applications in certain circumstances, and that similar rights of appeal for third parties should be introduced for other forms of environmental regulation. (5.46)

We recommend that the public planning register should contain, not only all section 106 agreements entered into, but also the heads of agreement between the local planning authority and the developer which provide the basis for negotiating the detailed terms. Local authorities should also be encouraged to consult the public on the terms of such agreements. (5.57)

Planning authorities must be properly resourced for their tasks so that they will not have the incentive to accept forms of funding which could prejudice their decisions. (5.58)

We recommend that, where a local authority might have a conflict of interest in relation to a planning matter it is considering, there should be a statutory requirement for it to make a formal public declaration of the nature and extent of its interest before taking a decision. We further recommend that the decision whether to grant planning permission for any development above a specified size promoted by a local authority or affecting local authority which is also the planning authority or affecting its land should be taken by an inspector appointed by the Secretary of State. (5.60)

We urge the government and the devolved administrations to review all categories of data withheld on grounds of commercial confidentiality, to see which can be safely released. In particular, we recommend that Agricultural Departments place agricultural returns in the public domain. (6.15)

We recommend that data which have been gathered in the public name and for the public good should be available electronically at no cost for public use. (6.20)

We recommend that the government adjust the financial model for public bodies holding and developing essential data sets (such as the Natural Environment Research Council and the Ordnance Survey) and replace income from sales of environmental information with direct grants. Consideration should be given to retaining a market element by relating the level of grant to the public use made of a body's data sets. (6.20)

We recommend that the government fund a feasibility study on the use of Grid technology in planning. (6.34)

We recommend the establishment of a virtual centre for environmental data, in order to overcome the barriers to presenting coherent and consistent environmental information in electronic form. (6.36)

All relevant public sector bodies whould be under a statutory obligation to give free access to their information. (6.39)

Where compliance with a numerical standard is the goal, the body setting the standard should give clear guidance on the appropriate methodologies for modelling and measurement. (7.20)

We recommend that consideration be given to introducing mandatory preliminary stage in environmental impact assessment in which the planning authority will prescribe the scope of a particular assessment after public consultation. (7.31)

We recommend that a counterpart of the Dutch Environmental Impact Assessment Commission should be established in the UK to provide a rigorous independent check on the assessment process. The commission could also carry out evaluations of a sample of statements and issue guidance on best practice. (7.35)

We recommend that human health issues be incorporated explicitly in the environmental impact assessment process. (7.38)

We recommend that the government, if it wishes to retain sustainability appraisal, strengthen the environmental component so that it will satisfy the legal requirements of the European Directive on strategic environmental assessment. We do not consider that sustainability appraisal as currently undertaken is adequate for this purpose. (7.48)

We recommend that a comprehensive and definitive statement of priority objectives for the environment be produced now for each part of the UK, and widely publicised. (8.7)

Wherever possible, this statement must include a quantified target or targets for movement towards the objective by a specified date. (8.7)

We recommend that the initial statements of priority environmental objectives should be reviewed at an early date through a process of extensive consultation and debate about environmental priorities. (8.8)

It will be necessary to produce a statement of priority environmental objectives for the UK as a whole, as well as for each component part. (8.9)

We recommend the statements of priority objectives should be prepared on the basis that sustainable development is achievable only if the environment is safeguarded and enhanced. (8.10)

It is essential that each objective is underpinned by a soundly based program for achieving it. (8.13)

We recommend that the town and country planning system should be given a statutory purpose, and that an appropriate purpose would be 'to facilitate the achievement of legitimate economic and social goals whilst ensuring that the quality of the environment is safeguarded and wherever appropriate enhanced'. (8.33)

We repeat the recommendation made by the Commission in 1996 that the diverse legislation the Environment Agencies inherited should be reviewed to give it coherence and relate it to consistent general principles, and the necessary changes should be enacted at the earliest practicable opportunity. (8.35)

We recommend that town and country planning legislation should stipulate key aspects of the environment and natural resources as material considerations that should be taken into account in considering planning applications. (8.36)

We recommend that planning policy guidance for England (the PPG series) should be condensed into a single document updated at frequent intervals, both on the Internet and in paper form; that consideration be given to a similar rationalisation of planning policy guidance for Scotland; and that the National Assembly ensure that the guidance documents for Wales sets out clear policies and is regularly updated. (8.41)

We emphasise that proposals for major infrastructure projects should always be put forward within the framework of carefully considered national policies, which should always be adopted after wide public consultation, and take full account of environmental considerations including the statement of environmental objectives we have recommended. (8.49)

The national need for additional infrastructure should be probed in an open and participatory process, which where practicable should engage local communities which may be affected. (8.50)

The issues involved in framing a national policy underlying major infrastructure projects may be better handled by a body which combines inquisitorial and adversarial elements, as a planning inquiry commission would. (8.56)

There must continue to be open hearings at which local people and others can express views about the local impacts of a proposed major infrastructure project and challenge claims by the developer. (8.58)

We recommend that, if under the government's proposals for major projects the inspector conducting the local inquiry concludes that the local impacts of a proposed project would be unacceptable, he should be permitted to recommend that the approval in principle should be reconsidered. (8.58)

We recommend that targets set for developing renewable energy at regional and local levels should have a firm and consistent basis in terms of the capacity for developing each of the main types of renewable energy without damage to the environment. (8.65)

We strongly support giving greater prominence to energy issues in regional planning guidance. (8.69)

We recommend that planning policy guidance on renewable energy in England, which is now nearly nine years old, should be revised and reissued as soon as possible. (8.72)

Mechanisms are needed to ensure that legitimate societal needs can be met in the face of preferences opposing the developments implied by those needs. The town and country planning system is intended to be such a mechanism but such developments must be essential parts of comprehensive and generally accepted policies, they must stem from transparent assessments of needs and environmental capacity, and there must be more imagination in countering any adverse effects on particular areas. (8.73)

We recommend that the overall policy objective for contaminated land should be to identify and seek to bring about the combination of remediation and subsequent use that represents the best practicable environmental option for each site. (9.10)

We recommend that the government and the devolved administrations set target dates for local authorities to complete their inspection of contaminated land, and provide the necessary finance for them to do so. (9.12)

We recommend that, once a clearer picture emerges of the extent of the problem posed by contaminated land and the possible uses for remediated sites, the government and the devolved administrations should set targets for the total area to be brought back into beneficial use over ten years and should plan to provide the necessary finance. They should also report on the feasibility of the 2030 goal for dealing with contaminated land proposed by the Urban Task Force. (9.14)

We urge the government to put in place mechanisms to replace the Partnership Investment Programme for land remediation. (9.16)

Government should inject more public finance into site investigations and remediation not covered by the statutory regime for contaminated land, and develop means of recovering at least a proportion of the cost of these investigations from any subsequent commercial scheme. (9.17)

There should be a single web portal that would allow local authorities, developers, their professional advisers and the public to access information on contaminated land throughout the UK, and through which all relevant public documents, including research findings, would be freely available. This should also include the public registers maintained by local authorities. (9.18)

We recommend that the government and the devolved administrations review the respective roles of the town and country planning system and the building regulations in order to design and implement an effective system for achieving substantially better environmental performance in new or refurbished buildings. (9.21)

We recommend that the government and devolved administrations include in their guidance to planning authorities targets for the maximum distance any urban household should be from a green space of specified size open to the public. (9.23)

We consider production subsidies to agriculture should be phased out as soon as possible. While they remain part of the Common Agricultural Policy (CAP), we recommend that farmers receiving such subsidies should be required to maintain a defined level of environmental protection on the land they manage. We urge the government to take full advantage of the existing scope for cross-compliance under the CAP to support the protection and enhancement of the environment, and to seek to widen the scope for cross-compliance as part of the reform of the CAP. (9.32)

We believe there is justification for the state to continue payments to rural land managers, including arable and livestock farmers, for achieving well defined, measurable environmental and social objectives. We recommend that the Department for Environment, Food and Rural Affairs and the devolved administrations launch a wide debate on rationalising the support for owners and managers of rural land through the introduction of schemes that serve environmental and, where appropriate, other objectives. (9.34)

We recommend the withdrawal of the permitted development rights that currently apply to building conversions and the construction of new buildings, roads and vehicle tracks when these activities are associated with agriculture or forestry. (9.42)

We recommend that the impact of new planning guidance on rural diversification is monitored for its effectiveness in protecting the environment and to ensure that it does not block beneficial diversification projects. We also recommend that information is collected on the rate at which diversification is proceeding in rural areas, the quantity and type of employment created and maintained, and the overall environmental impact of diversification including its effect on travel patterns. (9.45)

We call on DEFRA and the devolved administrations to ensure that the rural environment enjoys the best possible protection under the EIA Directive. In particular, they should not hesitate to refuse consent to schemes that would cause significant environmental damage, nor miss such schemes at the initial screening stage. Screening should be carried out by staff with appropriate environmental training using rigorous criteria. (9.49)

We recommend that local planning authorities should be added to the list of statutory consultees for environmental impact assessment of intensive agriculture. (9.50)

We recommend that there should be a thorough review of controls on environmental impacts of agriculture. This should include measures for protecting the conservation value of the countryside and for controlling agricultural pollution. We further recommend that the specialist environmental agencies should co-operate to conduct an independent assessment of the efficacy of the new EIA regulations and the other measures mentioned above in five years' time. (9.53)

We recommend that in future each agricultural holding in the UK receiving public subsidy should be required to prepare a farm plan containing actions to improve the environment which can be readily monitored; and that, to simplify the existing arrangements, all bodies giving grants, exercising regulatory functions or requiring certification of environmental performance should accept the plan as meeting their requirements for information. (9.54)

We recommend that DEFRA move swiftly to bring forward proposals for legislation for a farm plan scheme, following wide consultation, and produce guidance on the format and content of such plans with an emphasis on securing environmental protection and simplifying current administrative procedures. The Rural Payments Agency and its counterparts should have responsibility for all grant payments made pursuant to the plan, including payments made in respect of management of SSSIs or for farm woodland or afforestation schemes. (9.55)

We therefore recommend that DEFRA and the devolved administrations take the lead in ensuring that sponsor bodies co-operate to make data from the second round of shoreline management plans for the UK publicly available in their entirety through a central point. (9.61)

We recommend that planning protection is extended below the high water mark and to the sea-bed. (9.62)

We recommend that allocations for development should not be made until it has been established that water supply and sewerage can be provided in an environmentally sustainable manner. (9.67)

We recommend that all relevant planning guidance contain comprehensive advice on the risks of inland and coastal flooding under current conditions and following a period of climate change. We further recommend that the Environment Agency should be made a statutory consultee on flooding issues. (9.70)

We recommend that climate change, its effect on natural resources and the managed environment, the scope for adaptation and the scope for reducing emissions of greenhouse gases is specifically taken into account in spatial strategies, and that planning departments receive guidance and training in dealing with climate change issues. (9.74)

We recommend that the use of land for agriculture, forestry and countryside recreation should be issues covered in all spatial planning in future. (10.16)

We recommend the introduction of integrated spatial strategies which take account of all spatially related activities and all spatially related aspects of environmental capacity. They should be four-dimensional, covering the atmosphere and groundwater as well as the land surface, and looking at least 25 years ahead. (10.21)

An integrated spatial strategy must specify exactly what contributions are expected from local development plans and from the activities of other public bodies. (10.28)

To ensure that all the relevant bodies contribute fully to preparation of the integrated spatial strategy, and are committed to its implementation, it should have a firm statutory basis, and the lead body should be clearly designated. All other public bodies should be placed under a duty to co-operate in its preparation and comply with it where it affects their activities. (10.29)

We consider there should continue to be rights to object and provision for a public inquiry into a draft local plan or local development framework, on the ground that this kind of public challenge is fundamental to the purpose of the town and country planning system. (10.70)

It should be a statutory requirement that local plans or local development frameworks must comply with the integrated spatial strategy. Wherever appropriate, the policies and targets in the integrated spatial strategy should also be reflected in the community strategy or plan. (10.76)

In Northern Ireland we consider that drawing up a spatial development strategy for the whole province and more detailed spatial frameworks for the Belfast Metropolitan Area and the regional city of Derry/Londonderry represents a sensible approach to introducing spatial planning. (10.78)

We recommend that the strategic development plans the Scottish Executive has proposed for the conurbations centred on Glasgow, Edinburgh, Aberdeen and Dundee should take the form of the integrated spatial strategies we have recommended, and that consideration should be given to introducing integrated spatial planning in the remainder of Scotland. (10.79)

We urge the National Assembly for Wales to publish the promised national spatial planning framework for consultation at an early date. We also recommend that the Assembly take the initiative, in conjunction with the relevant local authorities, in preparing integrated spatial strategies for regions within Wales. (10.80)

We recommend that regional planning guidance and structure plans should both be converted into integrated spatial strategies with a comprehensive coverage of land use and environmental issues. There should be increasing co-operation between county and unitary authorities to develop integrated spatial strategies for sub-regions where these have greater functional coherence. (10.91)

In South East England, the best solution, irrespective of whether elected regional authorities are created in England and given responsibilities for spatial planning, would be to concentrate strategic planning at only two levels: the South East super region (including London) and sub-regions no smaller than the areas for which structure plans are prepared at present. (10.93)

ALL OF WHICH WE HUMBLY SUBMIT FOR
YOUR MAJESTY'S GRACIOUS CONSIDERATION

Tom Blundell *Chairman*

Brian Follett

Martin Holdgate

Michael Marmot

Michael Banner

Roland Clift

John Flemming

Ian Graham-Bryce

Brian Hoskins

Richard Macrory

Cheryl Miller

Susan Owens

Jane Plant

John Roberts

David Lewis   *Secretary*

Howard Morrison }
John Rea   }   *Assistant Secretaries*

REFERENCES

Place of publication is not given where it was London or in the case of European Commission or European Council documents.

Key messages

1   Department for Transport, Local Government and the Regions (DTLR) (2001). *Planning Green Paper – Planning: delivering a fundamental change.* See paragraphs 1.3-1.4.

2   Green Paper, paragraph 1.3.

3   Green Paper), paragraph 1.4.

4   Twenty-second Report, chapter 2 and paragraphs 4.13-4.28.

5   Green Paper, paragraph 1.8.

6   Evidence from, among others, Council for the Protection of Rural England, June 2000; East Sussex County Council, June 2000; Institute of Wastes Management, June 2000; UK Environmental Law Association Planning Law Working Party, July 2000.

Chapter 1

1   Commission of the European Communities (1999). *Europe's environment: what directions for the future?* COM(1999)543 final (the Global Assessment of the Fifth Environment Action Programme);

European Environment Agency (1999). *Environment in the European Union at the turn of the century.* Copenhagen;

Environment Agency (2000). *Environment 2000 and beyond.* Bristol.

2   Fifth Report, chapter XI and recommendations 75-94.

3   Through the introduction of integrated pollution control in the Environmental Protection Act 1990, and through the establishment in 1996 of the Environment Agency and the Scottish Environment Protection Agency.

4   The Commission discussed the changing nature of environmental concerns and some of the implications in its Twenty-first Report, *Setting Environmental Standards*: see paragraphs 1.11-1.13.

5   Twenty-first Report, paragraph 1.10.

6   Centre for Environment and Planning, University of the West of England. *A comparison of environmental planning systems legislation in selected countries. A background paper prepared for the Royal Commission.* April 2000. The countries were New Zealand, Germany, the Netherlands, Sweden, France, the Republic of Ireland and the USA.

7   Environment Agency (2001). *An environmental vision: the Environment Agency's contribution to sustainable development.* Bristol. See appendix 1 on page 26. In total 21 targets are listed; but 2 of them relate to the electronic handling of government business and are therefore not counted here as environmental targets.

8   European Environmental Advisory Councils (2001). *Greening sustainable development strategies: proposals for the EU Sustainable Development Strategy.* Wiesbaden, Focal Point of EEAC.

9   World Humanity Action Trust (2000). *Governance for a sustainable future*;

German Advisory Council on Global Change (WBGU) (2001). *World in transition: conservation and sustainable use of the biosphere.* Earthscan.

Chapter 2

1   At the time of the 1947 Town and Country Planning Act and for several years afterwards there was a separate Ministry of Town and Country Planning. The two fields of policy have subsequently been combined in the same Department, though not in the same directorate, until June 2001. Over that period the range and nature of environmental policies has of course evolved considerably.

2   Department for Environment, Food and Rural Affairs (DEFRA) (2001). DEFRA's Aim and Objectives available at www.defra.gov.uk/corporate/aims/aimobjs.pdf.

3   In a response to DEFRA (2001), which can be seen on www.rcep.org.uk.

4   Government of Wales Act 1998, section 121.

5   Cynulliad Cenedlaethol Cymru/National Assembly for Wales (2000). *Learning to live differently. The Sustainable Development Scheme of the National Assembly for Wales/Dysgu byw'n wahanol. Cynllun Datblygu Cynaliadwy Cynulliad Cenedlaethol Cymru*. Cardiff.

6   Commission discussions with Scottish Ministers and officials, April 1999 and April 2000.

7   Scotland Act, section 58.

8   Scotland Act, section 57.

9   Policy guidance which emphasises this role includes PPG12 on development plans (December 1999), PPG11 on regional planning (October 2000), PPG3 on housing (March 2000) and PPG13 on transport (March 2001). There has also been a good practice guide: Department of the Environment, Transport and the Regions (DETR) (1998). *Planning for sustainable development: towards better practice.*

10   Welsh Office (2001). Consultation on 'Draft Planning Policy Wales'. Cardiff. February 2001. 'Planning Policy Wales' will replace 'Planning Guidance (Wales): Planning Policy, First Revision 1996.

11   www.wales.gov.uk/subiplanning/content/minerals/minerals-planpol-e.htm

12   Evidence from Local Government Association, June 2000; evidence from National Farmers Union, July 2000.

13   Evidence from Environment Agency, July 2000; initial submission from Scottish Environment Protection Agency, October 1999; initial submission from Friends of the Earth, November 1999; initial submission from National Trust, November 1999; initial submission from Royal Society for the Protection of Birds, November 1999.

14   Initial submission from English Nature, November 1999; initial submission from National Trust, November 1999; initial submission from Royal Society for the Protection of Birds, November 1999.

15   It is the latter element in development plans that brings them within the primary meaning of 'plan' given in *Chambers 20th Century Dictionary*: 'a figure or representation of anything projected on a plane or flat surface, especially that of a building, floor, etc., as disposed on the ground'. In this definition 'projected' is a term from geometry; a 'plan' in this sense can be merely a representation of the existing position, but a development plan is clearly more than that.

16   In England, currently PPG 12, issued in December 1999.

17   Department for Transport, Local Government and the Regions (DTLR) (2001). *Planning Green Paper – Planning: Delivering a Fundamental Change.* Cited as 'Green Paper'.

18   Scottish Executive (2001). *Development plan progress.* Edinburgh.

19   This is the Camber Town Map, for which the local planning authority is Rother District Council. See East Sussex County Council (2001). *Development Plan Index.* Lewes.

20   DETR (1998). *Modernising planning: a policy statement by the Minister for the Regions, Regeneration and Planning.*

21   *The Times*, 15 January 1998, under the headline 'Businesses to help to shape planning law'.

22   See endnote 17.

23   Thompson, R. (2001) 'Spatial Planning – the big picture'. Speech delivered at the Royal Town Planning Institute Annual Conference, Glasgow, 13-15 June 2001.

24 As well as not being responsible for town and country planning, local authorities in Northern Ireland have fewer other functions than local authorities elsewhere in the UK. This section of our report, on the wider local government picture, does not apply to Northern Ireland.

25 Home Energy Conservation Act 1995; Twenty-second Report, paragraph 6.75. The indicated reduction was 34% in Northern Ireland; but housing there is a responsibility of regional boards rather than district councils.

26 Cabinet Office, Performance and Innovation Unit (2000). *Reaching out: the role of central government at regional and local level.*

27 Road Traffic Reduction Act 1997, ISBN 0 10 545497.

28 House of Commons Select Committee on Public Administration (2001), Sixth Report – Innovations in Citizen Participation in Government, 26 March 2001.

29 DETR (2000) Preparing Community Strategies, Government Guidance to Local Authorities. 8 December 2000.

30 In 2001/02 88 local authorities qualified for such funding.

31 Scottish Executive (2000). *A power of community Initiative: community plannings.* Edinburgh.

32 In Welsh the Environment Agency Wales is Asiantaeth yr Amgylchedd Cymru.

33 DEFRA (2001). *Environment Agency Financial, Management and Policy Review. Stage 1 Report.* August 2001.

34 House of Commons Select Committee on Environment, Transport and Regional Affairs (2000) Sixth Report 3 May 2000.

35 Environment Act 1995, section 31.

36 Environment Agency (2001). *An environmental vision: the Environment Agency's contribution to sustainable development.* Bristol.

37 Environment Agency (2000). *Environment 2000 and beyond.* Bristol.

38 A government review of the funding of flood and coastal defence is now in train.

39 Department of the Environment, Transport and Regional Affairs (2000). *Environment Agency Financial, Management and Policy Review.* December 2000.

40 Oral evidence from Environment Agency, 31 May 2001.

41 Oral evidence from Environment Agency, 31 May 2001.

42 DEFRA (2001). *The Environment Agency's objectives and contribution to sustainable development: statutory guidance. Consultation Document.* January 2002.

43 Information provided by Scottish Environment Protection Agency, November 2001.

44 English Nature (2001). Corporate Plan 2001-2005. Peterborough.

45 Environment and Heritage Service ([1996]). Framework Document. Belfast.

46 The Planning Service (undated). Corporate and Business Plans 1999/2000-2001/02. Belfast.

47 Cabinet Office (2000).

48 Cullingworth, B. and Nadin, V. (2002). *Town and Country Planning in the UK.* 13th Ed. Routledge. See page 78.

49 For example, *A sustainable development strategy for the South East: public consultation,* published in May 1998 by SERPLAN (London and South East Regional Planning Conference) was followed by SERPLAN. *Draft RPG 9 – a sustainable development strategy for the South East.* December 1998; and then, after a public examination by an independent panel, by Government Office for the South East/Government Office for East of England/Government Office for London. *Draft regional planning guidance for the South East (RPG 9) – proposed changes. Public consultation document.* March 2000; and by Government Office for the South East/Government Office for East of England/Government Office for London. *Reasons for proposed changes to draft regional planning guidance for the South East (RPG 9).* March 2000. The outcome has now been Government Office for the South East/Government Office for East of England/Government Office for London. *Regional planning guidance for the South East (RPG 9).* TSO, March 2001.

50 Green Paper, paragraph 4.44. Regional chambers have been formed in North West, South East. South West, and Yorkshire and the Humber regions.

51 See for example Dungey, J. and Newman, I. (eds) (1999). *The new regional agenda.* Preface by the Minister for the Regions, Regeneration and Planning. Local Government Information Unit and South East Economic Development Strategy.

52 The single regeneration budget, the rural development programme, redundant building grants, rural challenge, the competitiveness development fund, the skills development fund and the rapid response fund (to respond to large-scale redundancies), together with support from the Invest in Britain Bureau for promoting inward investment and most of the industrial premises provided in the region by the government agency English Partnerships.

53 Regional Development Agencies Act 1998. Part 1.

54 DETR (2000) Guidance on Preparing Regional Sustainable Development Frameworks, February 2000.

55 For example, preparation of *Action for sustainability*, the framework for the North West, was initiated by the Government Office in 1997 and was adopted by the North West Regional Assembly in 1999-2000.

56 The framework for the South East was published in June 2001, after the regional planning guidance (see endnote 49). The South East Regional Assembly (SEERA) (2001) 'A Better Quality of Life in the South East: Framework for a Sustainable Future, February 2001.

Chapter 3

1   International Union for the Conservation of Nature and Natural Resources (IUCN)/United Nations Environment Programme (UNEP)/World Wide Fund (WWF) (1980). *The World Conservation Strategy. Living resource conservation for sustainable development.* IUCN, Gland (Switzerland).

2   World Commission on Environment and Development (1987). *Our common future.* Oxford University Press, Oxford and New York.

3   Meadows, D H, Meadows, D L, Randers, J and Behrens,W.W. (1972). *The limits to growth.* Universe, New York.

4   IUCN/UNEP/WWF (1991). *Caring for the Earth. A strategy for sustainable living.* IUCN, Gland (Switzerland).

5   United Nations (UN) (1993). Report of the United Nations Conference on Sustainable Development, Rio de Janiero, 3-14 June 1992. Volume I, Resolutions adopted by the Conference. UN publication E.93.1.8. New York.

6   Holdgate, M. (1996). *From care to action: making a sustainable world.* Earthscan.

7   United Kingdom (1994a). *Sustainable Development. The UK Strategy.* Cm 2426. HMSO. See summary, page 6.

8   United Kingdom (1994b). *Climate Change, The UK Programme.* Cm 2427. HMSO.

9   Department of the Environment (1994). *Biodiversity, The UK Action Plan.* Cm 2428. HMSO.

10 United Kingdom (1994c). *Sustainable Forestry: the UK Programme.* Cm 2429. HMSO.

11 Cotter, B. and Boer, B. (1994). Local conservation strategies in Australia. Paper delivered to General Assembly of IUCN in Buenos Aires.

12 Department of the Environment, Transport and the Regions (DETR) (1999). *A better quality of life, A strategy for sustainable development for the UK.* Cm 4345. TSO.

13 Cynulliad Cenedlaethol Cymru/National Assembly for Wales (2000). *Learning to live differently. The Sustainable Development Scheme of the National Assembly for Wales/Dysgu byw'n wahanol. Cynllun Datblygu Cynaliadwy Cynulliad Cenedlaethol Cymru.* Cardiff.

14 Information supplied by Department of the Environment Northern Ireland, January 2002.

15 www.sustainable.scotland.gov.uk/strategy; Worldwide Fund for Nature (WWF) (2001). *Reality check: a review of Scottish Executive activity on sustainable development.*

16   DETR (1999), paragraph 8.3.

17   Institute of Medicine, Committee on Environmental Justice (1999). *Toward environmental justice: research, education, and health policy needs*. National Academy Press, Washington D.C.

18   Commission of the European Communities (2001). *A sustainable Europe for a better world. A European Union Strategy for Sustainable Development*. The Commission's proposal to the Gothenburg European Council, May 2001.

19   Council Directive on the quality of fresh waters needing protection or improvement in order to support fish life (78/659/EEC). *Official Journal of the European Communities*, **L222**, 14.8.78.

20   Ramade, F. and Hodgson, J. (1987). *Ecotoxicology*. Paris.

21   Twenty-second report, paragraph 2.36. John Wiley and Sons, Chichester.

22   Owens, S. and Cowell, R. (2002). *Land and limits: interpreting sustainability in the planning process*. Routledge.

23   Health of Londoners Project (2000). *Mapping health for primary care groups*.

24   Nineteenth Report, paragraph x.xx. One form of stewardship might be a system of *usufruct*, if that idea is properly understood.

25   Policy Commission on the Future of Farming and Food [chaired by Sir Don Curry] (2002). *Farming and food: a sustainable future*. Available at www.cabinet-office.gov.uk/farming.

26   Holdgate, M. (1996). The ecological significance of biological diversity. Carl Gustaf Bernhard Lecture to the Royal Swedish Academy of Sciences. *Ambio* **25/6**, 409-416.

27   PPG1. *General policy and principles*. 1997.

28   NPPG1. *The planning system*. Revised 2000.

29   New Zealand was included in a survey commissioned of a number of countries: Centre for Environment and Planning, University of the West of England. *A comparison of environmental planning systems legislation in selected countries. A background paper prepared for the Royal Commission*. April 2000. The Commission had discussions with Mark Southgate of the Royal Society for the Protection of Birds, who had visited New Zealand to study the Resource Management Act; subsequently Professor Macrory and Sir Tom Blundell had discussions with officials about the operation of the Act during visits to New Zealand.

30   That has been blamed, at least in part, on an absence of guidance from central government.

31   Council Directive on the conservation of natural habitats and of wild fauna and flora (92/43/EEC). *Official Journal of the European Communities*, **L206**, 22.7.92.

32   DETR (1999). *Quality of life counts. Indicators for a strategy for sustainable development for the UK: a baseline assessment*.

33   The first such report is DETR (2001). *Achieving a better quality of life: review of progress towards sustainable development. Government annual report 2000*.

34   Organisation for Economic Co-operation and Development (OECD) (2001). *Policies to enhance sustainable development*. SG/SD(2001)5/FINAL.

35   House of Commons Environmental Audit Committee (2000) Environmental Audit. 'The First Parliament', First Report Session. 2000-01, 13 December 2000.

36   Twenty-first Report, chapter 8.

37   Initial submission by OXERA Environmental Ltd, October 1999.

38   OECD (2001), page 18.

39   OECD (2001), page 13 and box 3.

Chapter 4

1   As an example see Best Foot Forward and Environmental Policy and Management Group, Imperial College of Science, Technology and Medicine (2000). *Island state: an ecological footprint analysis of the Isle of Wight.* Best Foot Forward, Oxford.

2   Eighteenth Report, table 2.1, page 11. Leisure accounted for 40% of total distance travelled in Great Britain, other personal business for 15%.

3   Department for Transport, Local Government and the Regions (DTLR) (2001). *Planning Green Paper – Planning: delivering a fundamental change.* Cited as 'Green Paper'. See for example paragraph 1.2.

4   Owens, S. and Cowell, R. (2002). *Land and limits: interpreting sustainability in the planning process.* Routledge. See chapter 7;

    Plant, J. A., Turner, R. K. and Highley, D. E. (1998). Minerals and the environment. In Institution of Mining and Metallurgy. *Proceedings of the Conference in Minerals, Land and the Natural Environment.*

5   The Commission's Eighteenth Report (paragraph 4.69) proposed targets for the use of recycled material in road construction and reconstruction.

6   For example, recycled materials may have to be stored until an opportunity arises to incorporate them in roads. County councils have been encouraged by the government to sell off land, and lack of land for storage may limit their ability to reuse materials (Elghali, L. EngD portfolio, University of Surrey, 2002).

7   'Plan' is used in this discussion as a generic term, although not all the documents in question are plans in a strict sense.

8   Prior to the most recent round of local government reorganisation, Peterborough formed part of the county of Cambridgeshire. As in many other parts of England. the Department of the Environment ruled that the structure plan should continue to be produced for the former area.

9   See appendix E.

10   'The scale and pattern of new development in the County is to be *environmentally sustainable.* Environmentally sustainable development is defined as development which meets the needs of the present without compromising the ability of future generations to meet their own needs, and which *avoids irreparable or long-term damage to the environment'* (structure plan, page 6, emphasis added).

11   Government Office for the South East/Government Office for East of England/Government Office for London (2001). *Regional Planning Guidance for the South East (RPG 9).* TSO. See paragraphs 12.66-12.68. Cited as 'RPG 9'. The current regional planning guidance, for East Anglia, proposes a study of development options in the Cambridge sub-region. Independent analysts have seen Cambridge's most significant relationships as possibly being with another Government Office region, East Midlands (The ESPRIN UK Team (2000). *European spatial planning and urban-rural relationships: the UK dimension.* Final Report. Department of the Environment, Transport and the Regions. See page 10).

12   The local plan has been deemed to be 'in general conformity' with the 1995 structure plan (Cambridge local plan, paragraph 1.11).

13   Green Paper, paragraph 4.38.

14   So too at regional level. In the minerals chapter of RPG 9, the final sentence of policy M1 (page 83) reads 'The regional contribution to the supply of aggregates shall be reassessed in an early review of this chapter of RPG 9 following the publication of the revised MPG [Minerals Planning Guidance Note] 6.'

15   Quoted in Bulkeley, H. and Rayner, T. (2001). New realism and local realities: local transport planning in Leicester and Cambridgeshire, Working Paper, University of Cambridge Department of Geography.

16   Cambridgeshire Transport Plan Monitoring Report, appendix A, page xxv. At the same time, it is suggested traffic may grow in the immediate area of Cambridge because development pressures there are so strong.

17   Counsell, D. and Bruff, G. (2001). Treatment of the environment in regional planning: a stronger line for sustainable development? *Regional Studies* **35** (5), 486-492.

18   Government Office for East of England (1999). *Draft Regional Planning Guidance for East Anglia. Report of the Panel conducting the public examination.* Bedford.

19   (RPG p. 56)

20   Evidence from Edinburgh College of Art, Herriot-Watt University, May 2000.

21   Local Environment Agency Plan, 1st Annual Review, pages 4, 9 and 12.

22   Evidence from the Council for the Protection of Rural England (CPRE), June 2000, paragraphs 55 and 70.

23   Evidence from English Nature, July 2000, paragraph 4.3.1.

24   Oral evidence from Environment Agency, 31 May 2001.

25   Evidence from English Nature, July 2000, paragraph 4.2.2.

26   Evidence from English Nature, July 2000, paragraph 4.1.6.

27   Evidence from CPRE, June 2000, paragraph 30.

28   The guidance includes a detailed *Biodiversity Checklist for Land Use Planners in Cambridgeshire and Peterborough* (carrying a sticker saying 'GO-East endorsed – GO-East strongly encourage local authorities to adopt this document'). This covers considerations for different kinds and scales of development, offers case studies, and provides references and contacts. Shorter leaflets provide guidance for developers and for householders seeking planning permission.

29   Evidence from East Sussex County Council, July 2000..

30   Rt Hon Tony Blair MP in a speech to the United Nations Commission on Sustainable Development in New York.

31   Local Government Management Board (1997), *LA21 in the UK: the first five years.*

Chapter 5

1   Evidence from Royal Society of Edinburgh, July 2000.

2   Department for Transport, Local Government and the Regions (DTLR) (2001a). *Planning Green Paper – Planning: Delivering a Fundamental Change.* Cited as 'Green Paper'.. See foreword by the Secretary of State.

3   Green Paper, paragraph 4.7.

4   Green Paper, paragraph 5.2; Town and Country Planning Act 1947, section [X].

5   Green Paper, box on page 58. In practice most decisions are taken by local authority officials under delegated powers: the target set for the Best Value regime in 2002/03 is that 90% of decisions should be delegated to officials.

6   Green Paper, paragraphs 2.2-2.8.

7   Evidence from Professor Patsy Healey, June 2000; Herriot-Watt University, Edinburgh College of Art, July 2000.

8   An example is the exercise to produce a vision for the Belfast area, beginning in 1997, and resulted in 'Belfast 2025: The Core Vision' see http//:www.belfastvision.com

9   As in the Planning for Real exercise undertaken by West Sussex County Council, (1999-2000) as preparation for their structure plan, in which people were invited to pick locations within the county for additional housing.

10   UK Local Issues Advisory Group (1997). *Guidance for local biodiversity action plans: an introduction. Guidance Notes.* DETR, UK Biodiversity Secretariat.

11   Evidence from Professor Patsy Healey, June 2000; Professor Judith Petts, July 2000; University College London, Bartlett School of Planning, July 2000.

12 Levett, R. (1999). *Environmental planning, people's values and sustainable development.* Background Paper for the Royal Commission on Environmental Pollution. CAG Consultants. See paragraphs 4.20-4.21;

Kitchen, T. (1997). *People, politics, policies and plans.* Paul Chapman.

13 Levett, (1999), paragraph 5.18.

14 Green Paper, paragraph 1.3.

15 Green Paper, paragraphs 4.21-4.24.

16 Green Paper, paragraph 4.28.

17 Green Paper, paragraphs 5.55-5.56 *cf.* paragraphs 4.22-4.23 and box on page 31.

18 Green Paper, paragraphs 5.58-5.59.

19 Green Paper, paragraph 4.10.

20 Green Paper, paragraph 4.6.

21 Green Paper, paragraph 4.24.

22 Green Paper, paragraphs 5.39-5.42.

23 Levett, (1999). See paragraphs 4.20-24;

Kitchen. (1997).

24 Twenty-first Report, paragraph 7.6.

25 Evidence from Professor Patsy Healey, June 2000.

26 Twenty-first Report, paragraph 7.26 and appendix F.

27 Society for Advanced Legal Studies, Planning and Environmental Law Reform Group (2001). *The simplification of planning legislation.*

28 Green Paper, paragraph 5.17.

29 Evidence from East Sussex County Council, July 2000, citing an animal carcass incinerator at Ringmer for which it gave planning permission in December 1997.

30 Green Paper, paragraphs 5.18-5.19.

31 A report produced by the Department of the Environment, Transport and the Regions (DETR) contained (annex A) a comprehensive list of the requirements on local planning authorities to consult other bodies about planning applications: DETR (2001). *Statutory and non-statutory consultation report.* Available on DTLR website.

32 Oral evidence from the Environment Agency, 31 May 2001.

33 Green Paper, paragraphs 5.32-5.34.

34 Green Paper, paragraph 5.34.

35 Green Paper, paragraph 5.35.

36 Development Control Statistics, England 2000/01, available on the DTLR website at: www.planning.dtlr.gov.uk/devcon/devcon01/index.htm. In Wales, call-ins and recovered appeals are considered and determined by a cross-party committee of the National Assembly.

37 The Planning Inspectorate currently handles appeals concerning water discharge consents, water abstraction licences, IPPC consents, waste management licences, hazardous substance consents and hedgerow retention orders, together with appeals concerning Codes of Practice under the Environmental Protection Act 1990 and the Water Resources Act 1991. According to the annual statistics of the Planning Inspectorate, in 1989/90 there were 185 appeals falling into these categories, and 60 in 1999/2000.

38 See the judgement by Lord Slynn in the Alconbury case.

39 R v Secretary of State for Environment, Transport and the Regions *ex parte* Alconbury Developments Ltd and Others, 9 May 2001 [2001] UKHL 23.

40 Lord Woolf (1991). Are the judiciary environmentally myopic, *Journal of Environmental Law,* **4** (1), page 1.

41 Lord Woolf (2001). Environmental risk: the responsibilities of the law and science. The Environmental Law Foundation Professor David Hall Memorial Lecture, 24 May 2001.

42   Grant, M (2000). *Environmental Court Project*. DETR.

43   Review on Tribunals (2001). *The Tribunal System and Its Costs. Consultation Paper.*

44   Green Balance *et al.* (2002). *Third party rights of appeal.* Council for the Protection of Rural England.

45   Green Paper, paragraph 6.20.

46   Green Paper, paragraph 6.7.

47   Green Paper, paragraph 6.8.

48   Green Balance *et al.* (2002).

49   Cullingworth, B. and Nadin, V. (2002). *Town and Country Planning in the UK.* 13th edition. Routledge. See page 21.

50   For example, where the local planning authority revokes planning permission given previously.

51   Cullingworth and Nadin (2002), page 26.

52   In particular, conditions attached to a planning permission cannot at present require the recipient to take actions which do not relate directly to use of the relevant site.

53   Committee on Standards in Public Life (1997). *Standards of conduct in local government.* Third Report. Cm 3702-1. TSO;
Local Government Association (2000). *Planning obligations.* An LGA Policy Paper.

54   DETR (1997). *Planning obligations.* Circular 1/97. Available on DTLR website.

55   DTLR (2001b). *Planning obligations: delivering a fundamental change. Consultation Paper.* Available on DTLR website.

56   Town and Country Planning Association (TCPA) (1999). *Inquiry into Planning.* Warburton quoted by Land Use Consultants (1999). *The use of the land use planning system to achieve non-land use policy objectives.* Background Paper for the Royal Commission on Environmental Pollution. December 1999.

57   DTLR (2001b), paragraph 1.13.

58   Monbiot, G. (2000). *Captive state: the corporate takeover of Britain.* Macmillan. See pages 134-140.

59   Evidence from the Central Council of Physical Recreation, July 2000.

Chapter 6

1   Evidence from Professor Patsy Healey, June 2000.

2   Evidence from Bedford Borough Council, July 2000; Local Government Association, July 2000.

3   National Environmental Monitoring Programmes database; available from the Environment Agency on behalf of the Collaborative Forum for Environmental Monitoring.

4   Data on groundwater movements are not available for Scotland. Information supply by Scottish Environment Protection Agency (SEPA), January 2002.

5   Flood Plain Surveys are not available for Scotland. Information from SEPA, January 2002.

6   European Commission (1990). Directive 90/335 on Freedom of access to information. OJ L158 23.06.90.

7   UNECE Convention on access to information, public participation in decision-making and access to justice in environmental matters, June 1998.

8   *Public Access to Environmental Information: Guidance on the Implementation of the Environmental Information Regulations 1992.* Statutory Instrument SI 1992 No. 3240. HMSO.

9   Stec, S. and Casey-Lefkowitz (2000). *The Aarhus Convention – An Implementation Guide.* United Nations, Geneva and New York.

10   The UK is committed to ratifying the Aarhus Convention as soon as possible. The Freedom of Information Act 2000 contains a power to enable Regulations to be made to bring the existing regime into line with the Aarhus regime ahead of action at the Community level. These Regulations are now being drafted. A similar power will be taken in Scotland in due course to allow implementation across the whole of the UK. See www.defra.gov.uk.

11   European Commission (2000). *Proposal for a Directive of the European Parliament and of the Council on public access to environmental information,* COM (2001)402, final 29.6.00, OJ C337, 28.11.00.

12   Department for Environment, Food and Rural Affairs (DEFRA) (2000). *Proposals for a Revised Public Access to Environmental Information Regime, Consultation Paper.*

13   DEFRA (2001).

14   Pira International (2000). *Commercial exploitation of Europe's public sector information.* Report by Pira International for the European Commission, September 2000.

15   Environment Agency. *Viewpoints on the environment,* Available on Environment Agency website, www.environment-agency.gov.uk

16   National Environmental Monitoring Programmes database, available from the Environment Agency on behalf of the Collaborative Forum for Environmental Monitoring.

17   Environment Agency (2000). *Environment 2000 and beyond.* Bristol.

18   See www.environment-agency.gov.uk.

19   Royal Town Planning Institute (RTPI) (2000). *IT in local planning authorities.*

20   Presentation to the Commission by Mr Mike Allen, Environment Department, London Borough of Newham, 5 October 2000.

21   Information supplied by Scottish Environment Protection Agency, January 2002.

22   Evidence from the Council for British Archaeology, July 2000; Environmental Services Association, July 2000; Institute of Waste Management, July 2000; Natural Environment Research Council, July 2000; Royal Society of Edinburgh, July 2000.

23   The British Geological Survey manages DEAL for UKOOA. The DEAL website (www.ukdeal.co.uk) contains spatially based metadata about information held by a variety of public and private organisations with interests in the hydrocarbons in the UK Continental Shelf. Many millions of items of information are available through the site, yet all of these information items remain with the owners or creators of the information. No attempt is made to physically bring the information together. Internet technology is used to bring the knowledge about the information to any user of the web.

24   Social Exclusion Unit (1998). *Bringing Britain Together: a national strategy for neighbourhood renewal.* Cabinet Office.

Chapter 7

1   See, for example, European Environment Agency (1998). *Europe's Environment: The Second Assessment.* Office for Official Publications of the European Union, Luxembourg.

2   Department of the Environment, Transport and the Regions (DETR) (1999). *Quality of Life Counts, Indicators for a strategy for sustainable development for the United Kingdom: a baseline assessment.* HSMO, London.

3   See for example Scottish Environment Protection Agency (2001). *State of the Environment, Soil Quality Report.* SEPA Corporate Office, Stirling.

4   Suffolk Local Planning Authorities (2001). *Suffolk's Environment…towards Sustainable Development, Third Monitoring Report.* May 2001.

5   Lancashire County Council (1997). *Green Audit 2 Results.* Available at www.la21net.com/ga2.htm.

6   Hertfordshire Environmental Forum (2000). *Quality of Life Report 2000* (Formerly the State of Hertfordshire's Environment Report). Copies obtainable from Hertfordshire County Council Environment Department.

7   Cambridgeshire County Council (1994). *Cambridgeshire's Environment 1994.* Printed by Cambridgeshire County Council on behalf of the Cambridgeshire's Environment Steering Group.

        Cambridgeshire County Council (1998). *Cambridgeshire and Peterborough's State of the Environment Report 1998.* Printed by Cambridgeshire County Council on behalf of the Cambridgeshire's Environment Steering Group.

8   Hertfordshire Environmental Forum (2000). *Quality of Life Report 2000* (Formerly the State of Hertfordshire's Environment Report). Copies obtainable from Hertfordshire County Council Environment Department.

9   DETR (2000a). *Local Quality of Life Counts, A Handbook for a menu of local indicators of sustainable development.* 19 July 2000. Available on DETR website.

10   For example see Environment Agency (2000). *The State of the Environment of England and Wales: The Land.* The Stationary Office.

11   ENDS Report 'Birmingham sent back to the drawing board or Air Quality' February 2001, Issue no. 313, page 14.

12   *Air Quality Management magazine* West Midlands: DETR replies. February 2001, Issue no. 62, page 1.

13   Information supplied by Scottish Environment Protection Agency, January 2002.

14   Wood, C. (2001). 'Environmental Assessment' in Miller, C.E. (ed), *Planning and Environmental Protection.* Hart, Oxford.

15   Council Directive 85/337/EEC of 27 June 1985 on the assessment of the effects of certain public and private projects on the environment. Official Journal of the European Communities L176,5/7/85.

16   Environmental Impact Assessment (EIA) is for the most part integrated into the British Planning System but some types of projects listed in the EIA Directive lie outside this system. Accordingly, additional regulations are in place which are broadly similar to those in the Town and Country Planning System. Those relating to highways, for example, require the Secretary of State for Transport, Local Government and the Regions to publish an ES for the preferred route at the time when the draft orders are published. Others require the EIA of afforestation projects in any case where, in the opinion of the Forestry Commission, the project is likely to have significant environmental effects.

17   In the case of Forestry see The Environmental Impact Assessment (Forestry) (England and Wales) Regulations 1999 [SI 1999/2228] and the Environmental Impact Assessment (Forestry) (Scotland) Regulations 1999 [SI 1999/43].

18   Council Directive 97/11/EC of 3 March 1997 amending Directive 85/337/EEC on the assessment of the effects of certain public and private projects on the environment. Official Journal of the European Communities L073,14/3/97.

19   Council Directive 97/11/EC.

20   Council Directive 85/337/EEC of 27 June 1985 on the assessment of the effects of certain public and private projects on the environment. Official Journal of the European Communities L176,5/7/85.

21   A formal decision about whether an EIA is required and an explanation for that decision is now needed from Local Planning Authorities or Secretary of State for all Schedule 2 development proposals.

22   The Town and Country Planning (Environmental Impact Assessment) (England and Wales) Regulations 1999, SI 1999 NO. 293.

23   British Medical Association (1998). *Health and Environmental Impact Assessment: an integrated approach.* Earthscan, London.

24   Council Directive 97/11/EC.

25   Wood, C., Dipper, B. and Jones, C. (2000). Auditing the assessment of the environmental impacts of planning projects. *Journal of Environmental Planning and Management* **43**: 23-47.

26   Statutory consultees according to the Town and Country Planning (Environmental Impact Assessment) (England and Wales) Regulations 1999: (1) any principal council for the area where the land is situated, if not the relevant planning authority, (2) the Countryside Commission and English Nature (where the land is situated in England), (3) the Countryside Commission for Wales (where the land is situated in Wales), (4) the Environment Agency, (5) the Secretary of State for Wales (where the land is situated in Wales), (6) the bodies which would be statutory consultees under Article 10 of the Town and Country Planning (General Development Procedure) Order 1995 (GPDO) for any planning application for the proposed development.

27   Wood, C. (2001), page 166.

28   Weston (2000) quoted in Wood, C (2001) page 161, found that two thirds of planning authorities reported that developers consulted them in all the EIA cases they dealt with and that another quarter of planning authorities were consulted in seventy-five per cent of the EIA cases they dealt with.

29   Jones, C. E., Wood, C. M. and Dipper, B. (1998). Environmental assessment in the UK planning process. *Town Planning Review* **69**:315-339.

30   DETR (1998). *Environmental Assessment*, 27 March 1998, London. Available on DTLR website. DETR (2000b). *Environmental Impact Assessment, A Guide to Procedures.* November 2000. DETR London and National Assembly for Wales, Cardiff.

31   Wood, (2001), page 159.

32   Information supplied by Scottish Environment Protection Agency, January 2002.

33   Wood, C. (2001).

34   The source of box 7C is: Environmental Impact Assessment Commission (1998). *Information for Members of Working Groups of the Commission for Environmental Impact Assessment in the Netherlands.* EIAC, Utrecht. Quoted in Wood, C. M. (2002). *Environmental Impact Assessment: a Comparative Review.* Pearson, Harlow (2nd edition).

35   Arts, E. J. M. M. (1998). *EIA Follow-up: On the Role of Ex-post Evaluation in Environmental Impact Assessment.* Groningen, Geo Press.

36   This intention is stated alongside other objectives including 'quality of life', 'maintenance of the diversity of species and reproductive capacity of the ecosystem as a basic resource of life' Council Directive 97/11/EC.

37   DETR (2000b).

38   British Medical Association (1998). *Health and Environmental Impact Assessment: an integrated approach*, page 207. Earthscan, London.

39   British Medical Association (1998), page 32.

40   DETR Circular 02/99 , 12 March 1999 states in Paragraph 46; that "in judging whether the effects of a development are likely to be significant, local planning authorities should always have regard to the possible cumulative effects with any existing or approved development".

41   Directive 2001/42/EC of the European Parliament and the Council of 27 June 2001 on the assessment of the effects of certain plans and programmes on the environment, Official Journal L 197, 21/07/2001 P. 0030 –0037.

42   Directive 2001/42/EC (Preamble 14).

43   Therivel, R and Partidario, R (1996), *The Practice of Strategic Environmental Assessment*, London: Earthscan.

44   DETR (1999). Planning Policy Guidance Note 12: Development Plans, December 1999, London, paragraph 4.66. DETR (2000). Planning Policy Guidance Note 11: Regional Planning, October 2000, London, paragraphs 2.23-2.38.

45   DETR (2000c). Proposals for a Good Practice Guide on Sustainability Appraisal of Regional Planning Guidance (GPG 25). October 2000, DETR. ISBN 011 753568 0.

46   DETR (2000c).

47   DETR (2000c).

48   Evidence from the University of Hull, Centre for City and Regional Studies, July 2000.

49   Baker and Associates (1999). *Regional Planning Guidance for the South East (RPG9), Sustainability Appraisal of the Proposed Changes to Draft RPG9.* Final Report, May 2000, page 20. Baker and Associates, Bristol.

50   Evidence from Professor Chris Wood, University of Manchester, January 2002.

51   Counsell, D. and Haughton, G. (2001). *Sustainability Appraisal of Regional Planning Guidance: Final Report*, November 2001, Centre for City and Regional Studies, University of Hull.

52   Counsell, D and Haughton, G (2001).

Chapter 8

1   Twenty-first Report, paragraph 6.31.

2   See for example United Kingdom (1995). This Common Inheritance; UK Annual Report 1995. Reporting on the UK's Sustainable Development Strategy of 1994 (including the Environmental Strategy of 1990). Cm 2822. HMSO. This recorded and reported on 601 commitments.

3   Department of the Environment, Transport and the Regions (DETR) (1999). *A better quality of life, A strategy for sustainable development for the UK.* Cm 4345. TSO.

4   Oral evidence from Environment Agency, 31 May 2001. list that was compiled appears in Environment Agency (2001). *An environmental vision: the Environment Agency's contribution to sustainable development.* Bristol.

5   Netherlands (2001). Where there's a will there's a world. Working on sustainability. 4th National Environmental Policy Plan – Summary. Ministry of Housing, Spatial Planning and the Environment, The Hague.

6   Sweden, Ministry of the Environment (1998). *Swedish environmental quality objectives: a summary of the Swedish government's Bill 1997/98:145.* Stockholm. The proposal presented to the Riksdagen in May 1998; European Environmental Advisory Councils (2001). *Greening sustainable development strategies: proposals...for the EU Sustainable Development Strategy.* Wiesbaden, Focal Point of EEAC. See box on page 13. The Committee set up worked in parallel with a Commission for Measures against Climate Change.

7   DETR (1999), paragraph 8.3.

8   Cabinet Office, Performance and Innovation Unit (2001). *Resource productivity.*

9   Controversially, a recent study for the World Economic Forum, by the Yale Center for Environmental Law and Policy and the Center for International Earth Science Information Network at Columbia University ranked the UK 98th out of 142 countries for environmental sustainability, and lower than any other country in Europe apart from Belgium (*The Observer*, 3 February 2002). Factors contributing to this low ranking were said to be 'serious air pollution, … eco-system stress derived from an inadequate land protection program, habitat destruction, significant waste and consumption pressures'.

10   A Public Service Agreement concluded with the Ministry of Agriculture Fisheries and food for the period 2001-04 was to 'care for our living heritage and preserve natural diversity by reversing the long term decline in the number of farmland birds by 2020, as measured annually against underlying trends' (Treasury (2000). *Spending Review: Public Service Agreements White Paper*).

11   DETR/Scottish Executive/National Assembly for Wales/Department of the Environment in Northern Ireland (2000). *Climate Change: the UK Programme.* Cm 4913. TSO.

12   Criticisms of the draft climate change programme published in March 2000 were made in the twenty-second Report, paragraphs 5.46-5.60.

13   See, in particular, Scottish Executive (2000). *Scottish Climate Change Programme.*

14   Grant M. (1980), *Urban planning law.* Sweet and Maxwell. See page 5.

15   Town and Country Planning Act 1990, section 70.

16   Town and Country Planning Act 1990, section 54, as amended by Planning and Compensation Act 1991.

17   The classic modern ruling, still quoted, is that of Mr Justice Cooke in Stringer v Minister of Housing and Local Government (1971) 1 All ER 65 at 77: 'In principle it seems to me that any consideration which relates to the use and development of land is capable of being a planning consideration. Whether any particular consideration falling within that broad class is material in any given case will depend on the circumstances.'

18   Examples include section 16(1) of the Food and Environment Protection Act (pesticide controls), which specifies as a general objective '(i)(a) to protect the health of human beings, creatures and plants, (b) to safeguard the environment, (c) to secure safe, efficient and humane methods of controlling pests and (ii) to make information about pesticides available to the public'. This general objective was introduced to provide a context for the large degree of discretion given to the government to make regulations about pesticides. Other examples of statutory objectives include section 7 of the Environmental Protection Act 1990 (for authorisation for integrated pollution prevention and control) and section 36(3) of the same Act, which specifies as criteria governing refusal of waste management licences 'preventing (a) pollution of the environment; (b) harm to human health; or (c) serious detriment to the amenities of the locality'. See also section 1 of the Pollution and Prevention Control Act 1989, which says that regulations to be made under the Act are for the purpose of '(a) implementing Council Directive 96/61/EC concerning integrated pollution prevention and control; (b) regulating, otherwise than in pursuance of that Directive activities which are capable of causing any environmental pollution; (c) otherwise preventing or controlling emissions capable of causing any such pollution'.

19   '...the securing of proper sanitary conditions, amenity and convenience, and the preserving of existing buildings or other objects of architectural, historic or artistic interest and places of natural beauty'.

20   The Commission commented on this in its Fifth and Tenth Reports.

21   Department of the Environment. (1980). *Development control: policy and practice.* Circular 22/80. See paragraph 3.

22   The 1992 version of PPG 1 *(General Policy and Principles)* first included reference to sustainable development.

23   McAuslan, P. (1979). The ideologies of planning law. *Urban Law and Policy* **2**, 1-23.

24   Grant (1980), page 36.

25   Article 1, First Protocol. The implications of the Human Rights Act for the town and country planning system are discussed at 5.32.

26   Nineteenth Report, recommendation 4.

27   Lord Hoffman in Tesco Stores v Secretary of State for the Environment [1995] 1 WLR 759 at 780.

28   Scottish Office (1974). *North Sea Oil and Gas: Coastal Planning Guidance*

29   Green Paper, paragraph 2.3.

30   Green Paper, paragraph 6.3.

31   PPGs covering issues of current controversy, such as transport and retailing, have been revised more frequently than others.

32   National Assembly for Wales, *Draft Planning Policy Wales*, Cardiff: NAW, 2001.

33   Foresight Built Environment and Transport Panel. (2001). *The Physical World in a Virtual Age.*

34   A consultation document covering this aspect was published in December 2001.

35   RCEP 2000, Para 7.106, p. 146.

36   RCEP 2000, Para 7.106, p. 146.

Royal Commission on Environmental Pollution
23rd Report Environmental Planning

Cm 5459 (Session 2001-2002)

ISBN 0 10 154592 4

CORRECTION

Please note the following correction to the 23rd Report on Environmental Planning:

On page 186 endnotes 28-36 should be deleted and replaced by the following:

28   Cullingworth, B. and Nadin, V. (2002). *Town and country planning in the UK.* 13th edition. Routledge. See page 131.

29   The latest version is National Assembly for Wales (2001). *Draft Planning Policy Wales.* Cardiff.

30   Department for Transport, Local Government and the Regions (DTLR) (2001a). *Planning Green Paper – Planning: delivering a fundamental change.* Cited as 'Green Paper'. See paragraph 2.3.

31   PPGs covering issues of current controversy, such as transport and retailing, have been revised more frequently than others. The Green Paper (paragraph 4.61) lists PPG1 among the priorities for revision.

32   Green Paper, paragraph 6.3.

33   Green Paper, paragraph 4.60.

34   Green Paper, paragraph 4.63.

35   Green Paper, paragraph 4.62.

36   Green Paper, paragraph 4.60.

37   DTLR (2001b). *New Parliamentary procedures for processing major infrastructure projects.* December 2001. See paragraph 4.

38   Other procedures apply to trunk roads and large power stations (see 10.7 below); to ports under the Harbours Act 1964; and to major railways and tram systems and inland waterways under the Transport and Works Act 1992.

39   DETR (1999b). *Streamlining the processing of major projects through the planning system.*

40   DTLR news release of 20 July2001 and Parliamentary Written Answer.

41   DTLR (2001b).

42   DTLR (2001c). *Compulsory purchase and compensation – the government's proposals for change*. December 2001.

43   DTLR (2001b), paragraphs 10-18.

44   House of Commons Environmental Audit Committee (2001). *Evidence*. HC 326-II. See Q166 at the session on 22 November 2001.

45   DTLR (2001b), paragraphs 19-21.

46   DTLR (2001b), paragraph 28.

47   The House of Commons Procedure Committee and the Transport, Local Government and the Regions Select Committee are examining the proposals: Parliamentary Office of Science and Technology. Appraising major infrastructure projects. *postnote* **173**. February 2002.

48   House of Lords Science and Technology Committee (1999). *Management of nuclear waste*. Third Report Session 1998-99, HL Paper 41.

49   DTLR(2001b), paragraph 7.

50   Twenty-first Report, chapter 8.

51   This would probably not be a requirement of the EC Directive on strategic environmental assessment because that covers plans and programmes, but not policies (7.43 and box 7D).

52   Foresight Built Environment and Transport Panel. (2001). *The physical world in a virtual age*. Department of Trade and Industry. The Planning Major Infrastructure Task Force was set up by the Built Environment and Transport Panel.

53   House of Lords Science and Technology Committee (1999).

54   Radioactive Waste Management Advisory Committee (1999). *The Radioactive Waste Management Advisory Committee's response to the House of Lords Select Committee on Science and Technology report on the management of nuclear waste, May 1999.* DETR.

55   There has been provision for planning inquiry commissions in town and country planning legislation since 1968, but it has never been used.(Cullingworth and Nadin (2002), page 365).

56   DTLR (2001b), paragraph 22.

57   Twenty-second Report, paragraph 7.106.

58   Cabinet Office, Performance and Innovation Unit (2002). *The Energy Review*. February 2002. Cited as 'Energy Review'. See paragraph 7.144 and the surveys cited there.

59   Twenty-second Report, paragraph 7.117.

60   Energy Review, paragraph 7.145.

61   Twenty-second Report, paragraph 7.34.

62   Energy Review, paragraph 7.144.

63   Twenty-second Report, paragraphs 7.117-7.120.

64   Department of Trade and Industry (DTI) (2000). *New and renewable energy: prospects for the 21st century. Conclusions in response to the public consultation.* See page 20.

65   Energy Review, paragraph 8.42.

66   *ENDS Report* **316** (May 2001), page 10.

67   The methodology was described in the Twenty-second Report, paragraphs 7.4-7.9 and box 7A.

68   The Northern Energy Initiative (1999). *Energy for a new century: an energy strategy for the North East of England.* Sunderland.

69   United Utilities news release, 13 February 2002.

70   PPG22 *Renewable energy* (February 1993).

71   Information supplied by Scottish Enterprise and Lifelong Learning Department, January 2002.

72   NPPG6, *Renewable energy developments.* See paragraph 16.

73   NPPG6, paragraphs 46-60.

74   Green Paper, paragraph 4.61.

75   This has been proposed by the Performance and Innovation Unit (Energy Review, paragraph 8.41).

March 2002
LONDON: THE STATIONERY OFFICE

Chapter 9

1   The combined population of Manchester, Liverpool and Inner London fell by more than a quarter between 1961 and 1994 against a background of a rise in the overall population of the UK. Office for National Statistics. *Regional Trends 32*, 1997. HMSO.

2   In England, over 60% of local authorities have areas of low demand or unpopular local authority housing stock95 and private dwellings in some areas are difficult to sell. (DETR. *National Strategy for Neighbourhood Renewal. Report of Policy Action Team 7: Unpopular Housing.* DETR, 1999). Over three quarters of a million homes are standing empty across England.96omes Agency for 1999/2000. DETR (1999) *Final Report of the Urban Task Force Chaired by Lord Rogers of Riverside.* TSO. Schoon, N. (2001). *The Chosen City.* E and FN Spon Press.

3   Ministry of Agriculture, Fisheries and Food and Department of Transport, Environment and the Regions (2000). *Our Countryside: the Future a Fair Deal for Rural England.* The Stationary Office, November 2000.

4   Department of the Environment, Transport and the Regions (DETR) (2000a). *Our Towns and Cities: the Future – Delivering an Urban Renaissance.* The Stationary Office, November 2000. Cited as DETR (2000a).

5   DETR (2000b). *(PPG3) Planning Policy Guidance Note 3: Housing.* The Stationary Office.

6   DETR (2000b). See paragraph 8. DETR (1999) *Final Report of the Urban Task Force Chaired by Lord Rogers of Riverside.* TSO. Schoon, N. (2001). *The Chosen City.* E and FN Spon Press.

7   Department for Environment, Food and Rural Affairs (DEFRA) (2001a). *The environment in your pocket 2001.* DEFRA. See page 46.

8   Scottish Executive (2000). *National Planning Policy Guideline 1 Revised 2000, The Planning System.* Edinburgh, Scottish Executive. See paragraphs 6 and 3.

9   National Assembly for Wales (2001a). *Draft Planning Policy Wales (Public Consultation – February 2001).* Cardiff, National Assembly for Wales. See pages 7, 9, 55, 75-80.

10 Northern Ireland Department for Regional Development (NIDRD)(2001a). *Shaping Our Future – Regional Development Strategy for Northern Ireland 2025.* Belfast, Department for Regional Development. See page.56. Cited as *(NIDRD 2001a)*; and Department of the Environment for Northern Ireland Planning Service (1998). *Planning Policy Statement 1 – General Principles.* Belfast, Planning Service. See pages 7-8, 10-11.

11 Evidence from Mr David Rogers, Scottish Executive, November 2001.

12 NIDRD (2001a).

13 Eighteenth Report, Chapter 9.

14 Eighteenth Report, paragraph 6.105.

15 Large-scale redevelopment in urban areas could lead to increased traffic congestion and more air pollution; the quality of transport and other services will be crucial. Furthermore, if urban living remains unpopular at a time when green-field house building is under tighter restraint, housing is likely to become more expensive in desirable areas, intensifying social polarization. Schoon, N. (2001). *The Chosen City.* E and FN Spon Press.

16 DETR (2000b). See paragraph 5.

17 British Geological Survey / LCG. (2000). *Summary on Land Quality in the UK, Summary R&D Report 25.* Environment Agency, Bristol 2000.

18 Nineteenth Report, paragraph 2.33.

19 Nineteenth Report, paragraph 8.19.

20 Nineteenth Report, paragraph 8.69.

21 Nineteenth Report, paragraph 8.4.

22 DETR (1999) See page 244.

23   House of Commons Select Committee on Environment, Transport and the Regions (2000). *The Implications of the European Commission Ruling on Gap Funding Schemes for Urban Regeneration in England,* Sixteenth Report. The Stationary Office, 2000.

24   See *www.regeneration.dtlr.gov.uk.* Accessed 01/02/2002.

25   DETR (1999). See p242.

26   Department of Transport, Local Government and the Regions (DTLR)(2001a). *Compulsory purchase and compensation – the government's proposals for change.* DTLR. See paragraph 1.6. Cited as *(DTLR 2001a).*

27   Town and Country Planning Act 1990. See section 226.

28   DTLR (2001a). See chapter 2.

29   Twenty-second Report, paragraph 6.97.

30   DETR (2001a). *The Building Regulations 2000, Conservation of Fuel and Power, Interim Draft L Approved Document.* DETR.

31   Society for Advanced Legal Studies (2001). *The Simplification of Planning Legislation,* Planning and Environmental Law Reform Group, May 2001.

32   House of Commons Select Committee on Environment, Transport and Regional Affairs (1999). *Twentieth Report, Town and Country Parks.* TSO, 1999. Cited as *(HoC ETR Committee 1999a).*

33   HoC ETR Committee (1999a). See paragraphs 23-30.

34   DETR (2000 a). See pages 74 to 76.

35   DETR News Release 033, 29 January 2001. *Regeneration Minister breathes fresh life into urban green space.*

36   English Nature (1996). *A Space for Nature.* English Nature, Peterborough.

37   Greater London Authority, Mayor's Housing Commission (2000). *Homes for a World City.* GLA..

38   DETR (2000b).

39   Department of the Environment (1997). *Planning Policy Guidance 1: General Policy and Principles.* London, DOE, 1997.

40   Burningham K and Thrush D (2001). *Rainforests are a long way from here: the environmental concerns of disadvantaged groups.* York, Joseph Rowntree Foundation/York Publishing Services, 2001.

41   *DETR 2000a.*

42   Broadleaf and coniferous woodlands account for 12% of the UK's land and urban areas about 10%. R.H. Haines-Young, et al (2000). *Accounting for nature: assessing habitats in the UK countryside,* DETR. Cited as Countryside Survey (2000).

43   MAFF, SERAD, DARDNI & NAWAD (2001). *Agriculture in the United Kingdom 2000.* The Stationary Office, London, 2001.

44   Policy Commission on the Future of Farming and Food [chaired by Sir Don Curry] (2002). *Farming and food: a sustainable future.* Available at www.cabinet-office.gov.uk/farming.

45   Labour force survey, Office of National Statistics website www.statistics.gov.uk/statbase. Accessed 28/01/02.

46   Countryside and Rights of Way Act 2000.

47   Countryside Survey 2000.

48   National Statistics. 'Summary of UK Food and Farming', Updated 15 March 2000. Available on DEFRA website at www.defra.gov.uk/esg/m_overview.htm.

49   Forestry Commission et al (1998). *England Forestry Strategy: A new focus for England's woodlands; and Woodlands for Wales; and Draft Strategy Forestry Strategy for Scotland* (1999).

50   Scottish Executive (1999). *Land use planning under a Scottish Parliament: Overview of Responses to Consultation.* Edinburgh, Scottish Executive.

51   Evidence from the National Farmers Union, July 2000.

52   DoE, MAFF, WO (1997). *The Hedgerow Regulations 1997: a Guide to the Law and Good Practice.*

53   Oral evidence from Forestry Commission, April 2001.

54   Evidence from the Country Land Owners Association, June 2000.

55   Cabinet Office Performance and Innovation Unit (1999). *Rural Economies*. London, The Stationary Office.

56   Land Use Consultants et al (2001). *The Implementation of National Planning Policy Guidance (PPG7) In Relation to the Diversification of Farm Businesses*. DTLR, 2001. Cited as Land Use Consultants et al (2001).

57   DLTR Planning Policy Guidance Notes, (1997). *PPG7: The Countryside: environmental quality and economic and social development;* and (1994) *PPG13: Transport.*

58   Scottish Office (1999). NPPG15: *National Planning Policy Guidance 15: Rural Development.* Edinburgh, Scottish Office.

59   This research found that the proportion of planning applications related to farm diversification which were approved (83 %) was only slightly below the approval rate for all types of planning application in England (88 %). The researchers concluded that the majority of local planning authorities were not 'proactively assisting farm diversification', but neither was there any evidence that they were proactively hindering it. One of their recommendations was that 'government should consider the feasibility of providing a clearer, but flexible, definition of sustainable farm diversification.' Land Use Consultants et al (2001).

60   Policy Commission on the Future of Farming and Food, 2002. *Farming and Food: a sustainable future*, January 2002. See page 54.

61   Pollution Prevention and Control (England and Wales) Regulations 2000. Statutory Instrument SI 2000 No. 1973 HMSO. Pollution Prevention and Control (Scotland) Regulations 2000. Statutory Instrument SI 2000 No. 323.

62   DEFRA (2001b) *The protection of waters against agricultural nitrate pollution in England. How should England implement the 1991 Nitrate Directive?* Consultation Paper (PB 6269). DEFRA. Scottish executive (2002). *Protection of Scotland's Water Environment. Consultation on further Scottish Nitrate Vulnerable Zones.* Edinburgh, Scottish Executive, January 2002.

63   Council Directive 2000/60/EC establishing a framework for Community action in the field of water policy. Official Journal of the European Communitie L327 22.12.2000. Council Directive 1991/156 EEC Amended Framework Directive on Waste. Official Journal of the European Communities L78, 26.3.91.

64   *Environmental Impact Assessment (Uncultivated land and semi-natural areas) Regulations (England) 2001.* Statutory Instrument S.I. 2001 3966. HSMO.

65   *Environmental Impact Assessment (Uncultivated land and semi-natural areas) Regulations (Scotland) 2002.*

66   National Assembly for Wales (2001b). *Implementation of the uncultivated land and semi-natural areas provisions of the Environmental Impact Assessment Directive,* Second Consultation Paper, September 2001. NAW, Cardiff.

67   *Environmental Impact Assessment (Uncultivated land and semi-natural areas) Regulations (Northern Ireland) 2001.* S.R. 2001 No 435.

68   DEFRA website www.defra.gov.uk/erdp/schemes/landbased/esas/esaindex.htm. Accessed 28/12/2001.

69   Countryside Survey (2000).

70   Countryside Survey (2000). See page 3.

71   English Nature website. Report on *SSSI Statistics/ damage.* www.english-nature.gov.uk/special/sssi/default.htm. Accessed 3 January 2002.

72   Department of the Environment and the Welsh Office (1992). *Planning Policy Guidance 20: Coastal Planning.* DOE. Cited as DOE (1992).

73   Scottish Office (1997). *NPPG13: National Planning Policy Guidance 13: Coastal Planning.* Edinburgh, Scottish Office. Cited as NPPG13.

74   Evidence from the Wildlife Trusts and WWF UK, June 2000.

75   Evidence from Scottish Natural Heritage, July 2000.

76   Evidence from the Marine Conservation Society, June 2000.

77   Forthcoming set of Environmental Impact Assessment and Habitats (extraction of minerals by marine dredging) Regulations for, respectively, England, Wales, Northern Ireland and Scotland. These are planned for 2002.

78   UK Climate Change Programme, The Meteorological Office and the Climatic Research Unit (1998). *Climate Change scenarios for the UK – Scientific Report, UKCIP Technical Report No. 1.* Norwich, CRU, 1998. Cited as UKCIP (1998).

79   Department of Transport, Local Government and the Regions (2001b). *Planning Policy Guidance Note 25: Development and Flood Risk.* DTLR. Cited as DETR (2001b).

80   DEFRA (2001c). *National Appraisal of Assets at Risk from Flooding and Coastal Erosion, including the potential impact of climate change, DEFRA Flood Management July 2001* (www.defra.gov.uk/environ/fcd/policy/flrptv2.pdf). Cited as DEFRA (2001c).

81   DEFRA (2001c).

82   Evidence from the Environment Agency, June 2000.

83   DETR (2001b). *Consultation on flood and coastal defence managed realignment: Land purchase, compensation and payment for alternative beneficial use. Consultation paper.* DEFRA, September 2001.

84   Environment Agency. Press Release 'Environment Agency warns that climate change is causing serious problems'. 5 July 2001. Document Reference 142/01.

85   Oral Evidence from the House Builders Federation, July 2001.

86   UKCIP (1998).

87   Insurance claims estimated to total £700 million, of which £389 million was for private homes and £251 million for commercial properties. Association of British Insurers. Press Release, 'Floods Costs Push Up Cost of Property Insurance Claims in 2000', 7 March 2001.

88   Centre for Hydrology & The Meteorological Office (2001). *To what degree can the Oct/Nov 2000 floods be attributed to climate change?* DEFRA Final Report, FD2304. DEFRA.

89   UKCIP (1998).

90   Environment Agency Thames Region (2001). *Autumn 2000 Floods Review Regional Report.* Bristol, Environment Agency (2001).

91   Environment Agency evidence to *ETR Select Committee on Climate Change,* 1998.

92   DETR (2000b), (DOE 1992) and Department of the Environment (1996). *Planning Policy Guidance 14: Development on unstable land: landslides and planning.*

93   Scottish Office (1995). *National Planning Policy Guidance 7 : Planning and Flooding; and National Planning Policy Guidance 13: Coastal Planning.* Edinburgh, Scottish Office.

94   Scottish Office (2001). A Forward Strategy for Agriculture. Scottish Office, Edinburgh. National Assembly for Wales (2001b). *Draft Strategy Document for the Future of Farming in Wales: Consultation Exercise.* July 2001. Cardiff. Department of Agriculture and Rural Development, Northern Ireland (2001). *Vision for the future of the agri-food industry.* Belfast, October 2001.

Chapter 10

1   University of the West of England (1999). *Subsidiarity and proportionality in spatial planning activities in the European Union.* Report for the Department of the Environment, Transport and the Regions (DETR).

2   European Union. Committee on Spatial Development (1999). *European Spatial Development Perspective.*

3   'Spatial planning' and 'physical planning' are alternative translations of the same term in Dutch.

4   Twenty-second Report, paragraph 10.37. As well as generating plants with a capacity of 50 MW or more, the recommendation also covered overhead transmission lines.

5   Eighteenth Report, paragraph 9.50; the Commission's preference was to abolish trunk roads as a separate category.

6   Department for Transport, Local Government and the Regions (DTLR) (2001a). *Planning Green Paper – Planning: Delivering a Fundamental Change.* Cited as 'Green Paper'.
     See paragraphs 6.5-6.6.

7   Cardiff University, Department of City and Regional Planning and ECOTEC Research and Consulting (2001). *Comparative Spatial Planning Methodologies Research Study. Final Report.*

8   *Ibid,* page 2.

9   ECOTEC Research and Consulting Ltd (1997). *Encouraging sustainable development through Objective 2 programmes: guidance for programme managers.* Final report to the European Commission;
     Environment Agency Wales/Countryside Council for Wales/Welsh Development Agency (2000). *Maximising the environmental sustainability of the West Wales and the Valleys Objective 1 Programme. A guide for project applicants and programme managers prepared by Environmental Resources Management.* ERM UK, London. See page 9 and table 2.2 (page 11) 'Progressing towards a sustainable growth model'.

10   Nineteenth Report, paragraph 5.174.

11   Department of the Environment/Welsh Office (1992). *Indicative forest strategies.* DOE Circular 29/92, Welsh Office Circular 61/92. This followed Scottish Development Department Circular 13/1990, with the same title.

12   Nineteenth Report, recommendation 47.

13   The Commission previously recommended that aspects of soil capacity, vulnerability and sensitivity which represent constraints on development should be incorporated in development plan maps (Nineteenth Report, recommendation 43), but no action has resulted (Barron, E.M. (2001). *A review of the Royal Commission on Environmental Pollution's Nineteenth Report,* Sustainable Use of Soil. See paragraph 2.122.).

14   In oral evidence (on 31 May 2002) the Environment Agency used the term 'reconciliation sheet' for this kind of statement of resource requirements.

15. Initial submissions from National Trust, November 1999; Royal Geographical Society, November 1999; Water UK, October 1999; Wildlife and Countryside Link, October 1999. Evidence from Energy from Waste Association, July 2000; Environmental Services Association, July 2000; Royal Society of Edinburgh, July 2000.

16   The need to address the relationships in which activities in urban and rural areas are embedded, and avoid treating urban and rural policy in separate compartments, is one of the key themes to emerge from the European Spatial Development Perspective: The ESPRIN UK Team (2000). *European spatial planning and urban-rural relationships: the UK dimension.* Final Report. DETR.

17   For comparative data for the English regions and Wales, covering the economic, social and environmental aspects of sustainability, see DETR (2000). *Regional quality of life counts: regional versions of the national 'headline' indicators of sustainable development.*

18   Evidence from Council for the Protection of Rural England, June 2000.

19   Such links must be more than rhetorical, they must be consistent, reliable and operational. One approach worth developing is regular secondments of staff between local planning authorities and the other agencies involved.

20   Twenty-first Report, *Setting environmental standards.* See especially chapter 7.

21   Department for Regional Development Northern Ireland (2001) S*haping Our Future. Regional Development Strategy for Northern Ireland 2025.* Belfast.

22   PPG 11, issued in October 2000, paragraph 1.3.

23   Owens, S and Cowell, R (2001), *Land and limits: interpreting sustainability in the planning process,* London: Routledge: 113

24   Eighteenth Report, chapter 9.

25   DETR (1998). *Government response to the Royal Commission on Environmental Pollution's Twentieth Report,* Transport and the Environment – Developments since 1994. Cm 4066. See paragraphs 89-92.

26   Government Office for the South East/Government Office for East of England/Government Office for London (2001). *Regional Planning Guidance for the South East (RPG 9).* TSO. Policy INF3 on page 77.

27   See for example English Nature (1999). *Sustainable development and regional biodiversity indicators for the South West.* Peterborough.

28   Biodiversity Steering Group (1995). Biodiversity: The UK steering group Report. Vol 1: Meeting the Rio Challenge. Vol 2: Action Plans. HMSO

29   Research by Commission Secretariat.

30   Hewett, C. (ed) (2001). *Sustainable development and the English regions.* Institute for Public Policy Research and Green Alliance.

31   Research by Commission Secretariat

32   Research by Commission Secretariat

33   Research by Commission Secretariat

34   West Midlands Regional Planning Guidance Review. *Draft Regional Planning Guidance November 2001.* West Midlands Local Government Association, Birmingham.

35   Green Paper, paragraph 4.42.

36   *Ibid.*

37   Hewett (2001), page 1.

38   The most recent version is DETR (1996). *Strategic guidance for London planning authorities.*

39   Greater London Authority, Mayor of London (2001). *Towards the London Plan. Initial proposals for the Mayor's spatial development strategy.* See paragraphs 5-6.

40   Greater London Authority Act 1999, section 351.

41   Greater London Authority Act 1999, section x.

42   Greater London Authority, Mayor of London (2001), paragraph 5.

43   Greater London Authority, Mayor of London (2001), paragraph 1.20.

44   These are the structure plans for Cornwall, Cumbria, Gloucestershire, Hertfordshire, Lincolnshire, Norfolk, Northamptonshire, Northumberland, Oxfordshire, Somerset, Suffolk, Surrey, Warwickshire, West Sussex and Worcestershire; in large parts of the areas of Cumbria and Northumberland, planning functions are exercised by a national park authority, not by the county council. The joint arrangements in other areas are shown in Cullingworth, B. and Nadin, V. (2002). *Town and Country Planning in the UK.* 13th edition. Routledge. See table 4.1, pages 101-2. For Scotland see table 4.2, page 104.

45   Evidence from Council for the Protection of Rural England, June 2000.

46   Davoudi, S. *et al* (1997). Rhetoric and reality in British structure planning in Lancashire, 1993-5. In Healey, P. *et al* (edd). *Making strategic spatial plans: innovation in Europe.* UCL Press.

47   Berkshire County Council (1995). *The Berkshire environment: a first state of the environment report*. Reading;
      Cambridgeshire and Peterborough's State of the Environment Report Steering Group (1998). *Cambridgeshire and Peterborough's State of the Environment Report 1998*. Cambridge, Cambridgeshire County Council

48   That is likely to happen in the case of the Cambridgeshire and Peterborough Structure Plan (information supplied by Cambridgeshire County Council Planning Department, April 2001).

49   PPG12 (1999), paragraphs 4.16-4.22; DOE(1993). *Environmental appraisal of development plans*.

50   PPG12 (1999), paragraph 4.16; DETR(1998). *Planning for sustainable development: towards better practice*.

51   For example, the Berkshire Structure Plan (2.15) referred to the view of the then National Rivers Authority that 'levels of development will need to be restrained within current sustainable water resource limitations until such time as new water resource schemes are proved and appropriate infrastructure can be guaranteed'.

52   Oral evidence from the Environment Agency, 31 May 2001.

53   PPG12 (1999), paragraph 3.5.

54   Cullingworth and Nadin (2002), page 95.

55   In South East England the regional planning body has proposed that local authorities should complete the next round of structure plan reviews by the end of September 2003, that is within 30 months of publication of new regional planning guidance. The review of the Cambridgeshire structure plan was completed within three years (1992-95).

56   In the legislation minerals and waste plans are also 'local plans', but the term is used here to refer solely to geographically based, rather than topic-based, plans.

57   PPG12 (1999), annex A, paragraphs 23-28.

58   PPG12 (1999), annex B, paragraph 5.

59   Green Paper, paragraphs 4.29-4.31.

60   Green Paper, paragraph 4.26.

61   Green Paper, paragraph 4.7

62   Royal Town Planning Institute (2000). A UK spatial framework.

63   Green Paper, paragraph 4.12

64   PPG12 (1999), annex C.

65   Scottish Executive, Development Department (2001). *Review of Strategic Planning. Consultation Paper*. Edinburgh. See paragraphs 20-21 and page 17.

66   National Assembly for Wales (NAW 2001). Strategic statement on the Preparation of "Plan for Wales 2001", July 2001, Cardiff.

67   Strategic Statement, pages 14-15 (NAW 2001).

68   Green Paper, paragraphs 4.52-4.53.

69   Green Paper, paragraphs 4.46-4.47. Planning for productivity, A ten point action plan, July 2001.

70   Confederation of British Industry (2001).

71   Confirmed by CBI, December 2001.

72   CPRE I(2001), page 24.

73   Green Paper, paragraph 4.53.

74   Green Paper, paragraphs 4.49-4.51.

75   RPG9, paragraph 1.8.

76   RPG9, paragraph 1.9.

.

Appendix A

ANNOUNCEMENT OF THE STUDY AND INVITATION TO GIVE EVIDENCE

The Commission study which has led to this report was announced on 22 July 1999 in the following terms:

ROYAL COMMISSION TO STUDY ENVIRONMENTAL PLANNING

The Royal Commission on Environmental Pollution is going to investigate whether present arrangements for environmental planning are capable of achieving environmental policy objectives. This will involve looking at the current land use planning system, at other relevant legislation and procedures, and at the interactions between them. The aim is to produce a report by the end of 2000.

The use of land is linked to environmental change on many different scales, and is increasingly implicated in strategies for sustainable development. Changes in land use are regulated through the development control system under Town and Country Planning legislation, but land use is also influenced by other policies and other statutory and non-statutory arrangements. Equally, the success of policies in such fields as transport, energy, water and nature conservation depends to a significant extent on decisions about land use.

The interrelationship between measures to combat pollution and the system of statutory land use plans under the Town and Country Planning Acts has long been recognised. It formed a major theme of the Commission's Fifth Report, published in 1976. Since then, the land use planning system has changed significantly. It is continuing to evolve in response to new pressures. There are indications of problems arising, or missed opportunities, at some of the interfaces. It is not clear whether the present combination of procedures is adequate to bring about sustainable development.

In inquiring into this subject, the Royal Commission intends to consider a broad range of relevant topics, including how democratic control and people's values influence decisions, potential conflicts between national environmental strategies and local interests, whether there are gaps or duplications in the current arrangements, and the robustness of present arrangements in the face of trends such as climate change.

In the first phase of the new study the Royal Commission will concentrate on identifying more specific issues for investigation. In the second phase, beginning early next year, it will invite evidence on the issues it has identified. To help select the key issues, it is consulting widely, and anyone who wishes to propose specific issues for investigation is invited to bring these to the Commission's attention.

At the same time the following, more detailed description of the study was sent to some 80 organisations, as an invitation to submit views about the issues it should address:

STUDY OF ENVIRONMENTAL PLANNING

The Royal Commission has decided to undertake a study of Environmental Planning. The preparatory phase of this new study is overlapping with completion of the current study of Energy and the Environment. In the second phase of the new study, beginning early next year, the Commission will invite evidence on specific issues. The purpose of this letter is to help the Commission identify issues for detailed investigation in the second phase. It summarises the background to the new study, indicates the broad topics the Commission intends to cover, and invites views on what are the key issues.

BACKGROUND TO THE NEW STUDY

The use of land is connected to environmental change at many different scales and is increasingly implicated in strategies for sustainable development. Development is regulated directly through the development control system (under Town and Country Planning legislation) but land use is influenced by other policies and by a range of statutory and non-statutory arrangements. Furthermore, the success of policies in diverse sectors (such as transport, energy, water and nature conservation) depends to a significant extent on decisions about land use.

Measures to combat pollution and the system of statutory land use plans under the Town and Country Planning Acts have been recognised for a long time as being inter-related. This formed a major theme of the Commission's Fifth Report, published in 1976. Since then, the land use planning system has seen significant changes and continues to evolve in response to new pressures.

In many cases that system now requires the environmental implications of development to be assessed. It is explicitly plan-led. It is no longer concerned solely with the uses of land. The government has produced guidance on how to incorporate sustainable development principles into the preparation of plans and into development control. It has gone on to point out that sustainable development is not only about protecting the environment but is also concerned with achieving economic growth, employment, and social progress. In some respects changes of this kind echo European moves towards a more comprehensive spatial development strategy.

At the same time, the government has continued to advise, and the Courts have confirmed, that the planning system should not be operated so as to duplicate controls which are the statutory responsibility of other bodies (or of local authorities in their non-planning functions). And some significant forms of human intervention in the environment are not subject to the planning system.

Within environmental protection, partly under the influence of European Community legislation, the trend has been towards an increasingly strategic approach. A wide variety of regulatory mechanisms, strategies and plans has been put in place to achieve environmental goals at every level from the international to the local. These take many forms. Examples include the Kyoto Protocol on reducing emissions of carbon dioxide, the EC Acidification strategy, the UK's national and local biodiversity action plans, the National Air Quality Strategy, water resource plans produced by water companies in England and Wales, and Local Environment Agency Plans. Where targets are set nationally, it is not always clear how they should be translated into local plans and action. Conversely, decisions reflecting local priorities may sometimes be inconsistent with national aims.

Unless planning processes (in the widest sense) engage adequately with the public and take due account of the values of the wider public as well as the views of stakeholders, the outcome can be a loss of confidence in the system. Practice in this respect varies. Plans may also provide a framework within which companies are able to develop their own measures to reduce the environmental effects of their activities and products.

Legislation has brought together many environmental functions in the Environment Agencies but some policy goals are achievable only through the concerted actions of more than one body. Air quality, for example, is affected by development patterns, industrial and domestic emissions, transport sources and topographical and climatic conditions. Environmental policies have been given a strong spatial dimension by such concepts as 'environmental footprint' and 'environmental capacity', the impetus of Local Agenda 21, and the duties in relation to sustainable development which have been placed on bodies at different geographical levels (such as the Welsh Assembly, the Regional Development Agencies, the Scottish Environment Protection Agency and the Environment Agency). The full implications of devolution have yet to become apparent.

There may be good reasons for not attempting to cover all aspects of the environment in a single comprehensive procedure. Nevertheless there are indications of problems arising, or missed opportunities, at some of the existing interfaces, and it is not clear that the present procedures, taken together, are adequate to achieve sustainable development. It is these concerns which the Commission wishes to investigate.

BROAD TOPICS TO BE COVERED

In its study the Commission intends to include the following broad topics:

a) how democratic control should be exercised over land use decisions, and priorities established, in the light of subsidiarity and devolution, regard for people's values, openness, transparency and accountability;

b) the potential conflict between national environmental strategies and local interests, and when private rights are limited in the public interest (including the interest of future generations);

c) how environmental planning systems take account of needs for particular types of development as well as the need to manage and conserve resources; concepts of 'national needs' and their alignment with local and regional environmental aspirations; the use of Parliamentary procedures to examine, and where appropriate sanction, decisions of national significance;

d) the proper roles for statutory procedures and less formal arrangements in environmental management, the appropriateness of the present statutory framework, and the extent of public confidence in the appeals systems;

e) the extent to which the quest for 'sustainable development' might jeopardise the effectiveness of present arrangements for achieving environmental objectives;

f) the extent of gaps, duplication, co-ordination and conflict in present arrangements;

g) the resilience of present arrangements in coping with foreseeable major developments such as climate change;

h) the relationships between underlying environmental processes and the geographical areas to which plans and decisions at present relate;

i) the knowledge base, including the location and availability of expertise, training, the use of environmental impact assessment, and the adequacy of data.

INVITATION TO SUBMIT VIEWS ON THE KEY ISSUES

The list of topics given above is not intended to be comprehensive and the Commission would be glad to have other significant topics drawn to its attention. The Commission also invites interested organisations and individuals to provide examples of practical difficulties, or of good practice, in operating the present arrangements. Information on gaps, duplication etc (sub-paragraph (e) above) in the present arrangements would be especially welcome.

In parallel with this consultation, the Royal Commission's secretariat is assembling information on the regimes which help protect the environment and analysing existing material on relevant topics. The Commission has also asked for some reports from consultants to provide background information and help it to define more sharply the questions to which it should direct its attention later in the study (see annex A).

The Commission would welcome views at this stage on the more specific questions to which it should investigate later in the study.

After considering the responses to the original announcement the Commission wrote to over a thousand organisations and individuals on 11 April 2000 inviting the submission of written evidence, and also issued a news release. The invitation was in the following terms:

ROYAL COMMISSION STUDY OF ENVIRONMENTAL PLANNING: ISSUES ON WHICH EVIDENCE IS SOUGHT

KEY THEMES

The aim of this study is to assess whether the various regimes at different levels for setting and achieving environmental goals provide an effective, accountable and transparent way of protecting the environment. To this end, there are five key themes below on which the Commission is seeking evidence. Each theme has a number of questions associated with it.

The scope of the study goes much wider than land use planning (although that aspect is central) and will encompass other environmental planning regimes, such as pollution control, air quality, waste, water, agri-environment and biodiversity. Most of the questions below are intended to address environmental planning in general, but some are specific to regimes such as land use planning or pollution control.

The Commission does not expect those responding to address all of the questions – many respondents may wish to comment on only a few of the issues raised below. The list of questions is not intended to be exhaustive and respondents are welcome to address other issues relevant to the key themes that they wish to draw to the Commission's attention.

1. Environmental sustainability

The Commission recognises that sustainable development has economic, social and environmental components. Within that framework the Commission sees its particular function as to ensure that environmental sustainability is not being prejudiced. In this case the Commission wishes to investigate the extent to which current environmental planning systems promote or prejudice environmental sustainability.

a. Has the pursuit of sustainable development as the broad objective of policy had favourable or unfavourable consequences for protection of the environment? To the extent that consequences have been unfavourable, how could that best be remedied?

b. Can environmental objectives always be balanced against other issues or are there environmental imperatives? If so, how are they (or how should they be) determined?

c. What regulatory approaches are likely to be the most effective and practicable to protect the environment, in both measurable terms, e.g. water, soil and air quality, and less tangible aspects, e.g. landscape and amenity?

d. In practice, to what extent does land use planning still embody a presumption in favour of development? Has the legislative change to a plan-led system given land use planning the potential to become a more effective instrument for achieving environmental sustainability? Is any further change necessary, and, if so, what?

e. In practice, how far have planning regimes in general moved from "predict and provide" to "plan, monitor and manage" to avoid environmentally unsustainable outcomes?

f. Do current arrangements for environmental planning sufficiently take into account the cumulative impacts of developments?

g. To what extent is effective environmental planning hindered by a lack of resources within central government and local government, statutory agencies and advisory bodies? Have the procedures become too complex for any institution to cope adequately?

h. What are the implications of long-term risks, such as those posed by climate change or persistent waste, for environmental planning? Can planning systems become drivers for limiting the extent of damage from unavoidable climate change?

i. To what extent does the achievement of environmental sustainability depend on permitted uses being time limited?

2. Boundaries

The Commission wishes to investigate whether administrative boundaries and the way environmental planning is sub-divided between policy areas are hindering the pursuit of environmental sustainability.

a. To what extent does a mismatch between administrative areas and environmental processes contribute to environmentally unsustainable planning, for instance in river catchments or along coastlines? What should be done about it?

b. What problems arise from different plans being produced and implemented for overlapping geographical areas?

c. Should the land use planning system be responsible for helping to deliver policy targets in other areas such as transport, energy, water provision, flood protection, climate change and nature conservation?

d. How might geographical information systems (GIS) contribute to environmental planning in both the short and long term? What problems are associated with data accessibility and quality, and how might they be addressed?

e. Does the lack of control over certain activities, such as forestry and agriculture, prejudice the achievement of environmental goals? If so, what would be the effect of introducing such controls?

3. INTEGRATION OR COORDINATION?

Different environmental planning regimes have grown up over time to serve different objectives. The Commission is interested in how well the current arrangements work as a whole.

a. Does the current system need "fixing"? What gaps, unnecessary duplication and conflicts exist in present arrangements for environmental planning?

b. Is there in practice a hierarchy in the formulation of different types of environmental plans? Would there be advantages in establishing a clearer hierarchy?

c. Should the process of environmental planning be further integrated or rationalised, e.g. as in New Zealand? Or would better coordination be sufficient to ensure an efficient and effective system?

d. Are present arrangements for environmental planning efficient and cost-effective? Can the wish to speed up the land use planning process be reconciled with effective environmental protection?

e. Are the mandates and procedures of the pollution control bodies appropriate to their environmental planning responsibilities? Are these responsibilities appropriate? Is it practical to have parallel decisions on land use planning and pollution control?

f. Has a satisfactory integration of transport planning and land use planning been achieved? If not, what more needs to be done?

g. To what extent could economic instruments, non-statutory procedures, or informal arrangements complement environmental planning regulation, and how effective would they be at providing environmentally sustainable solutions? Would there be implications for openness, transparency and accountability?

h. One possible economic instrument could be a "betterment tax" aiming to increase public ownership of development gain. Is such a tax feasible and desirable? Might there be some way of linking the rate of tax to environmental impact?

i. Does the adoption of sustainability as the focus of policy intensify disagreements about the boundary between public and private development rights and obligations? To what extent does the current system enable such issues to be resolved?

4. Subsidiarity and democracy

The Commission is interested in the accountability and transparency of environmental planning regimes. There is often an inherent tension between delivering national policy targets and ensuring adequate local accountability in the vicinity of a development. Indeed policy targets themselves may be controversial. National targets may impose local environmental degradation against the wishes of the local population. On the other hand, the sum of local planning decisions across the country may not deliver national environmental protection targets. The Commission is also keen to ensure that decisions are taken at the most appropriate level with an appropriate range of inputs to the decision making process.

a. Is the current balance between elected leadership, expert assessment and public participation in environmental planning decisions appropriate?

b. How do we ensure that all levels of decision-making processes are sufficiently open, transparent and accountable to gain public acceptance? What are the best ways to reflect the range of public opinion whilst maintaining an appropriate procedural timetable? When should local public opinion be overridden in the interest of a broader common goal?

c. What should be the relationship between international, national, regional and local goals? Should environmental planning take place at the lowest level consistent with the common good (the principle of subsidiarity)? How far do current arrangements depart from that principle?

d. Are new regional planning arrangements, or other measures such as strengthening the strategic planning role of local government, needed to ensure greater coherence between national and local planning regimes? If so, what should these be and how should they be made accountable?

e. To what extent do the principles of the environmental planning regimes in England, Scotland, Wales and Northern Ireland need to differ from each other? What are the specific drivers for these differences?

f. Does the present form of planning inquiry offer the best way of resolving disputes? Should it be extended to permit a third party right of appeal? If so, should such rights be restricted to prevent abuse?

g. Would environmental tribunals or courts enhance public confidence in the land use planning appeals process? If so, would they impose significant extra costs and delays?

5. Assessment approaches

There are many different approaches to assessing the impact of plans and developments. The Commission wishes to determine the most appropriate approaches to safeguard environmental sustainability while maintaining efficient planning systems.

a. What are the most appropriate appraisal methodologies for use in drawing up environmental plans and assessing the environmental impact of plans prepared for other purposes? Do appraisal methodologies applied to individual cases provide sufficient information about their implications for the achievement of wider environmental goals?

b. Could increased use of such methodologies dovetail effectively with the efficient operation of environmental planning systems? How widely applicable should environmental appraisal be? What level of detail is appropriate for the various plan types? Who should be responsible for: i) undertaking environmental appraisal, and ii) judging its quality?

c. What would be the value of increased use of other assessment tools, e.g. sustainability appraisal, environmental capital, environmental footprint, environmental space, and health impact assessment?

d. Are there good examples of comparisons between the actual environmental, social and economic effects predicted when a case was being considered and what the actual effects were? In addition, is there evidence of the effectiveness of pre-development mitigation and compensation agreements at avoiding unsustainable outcomes?

e. How adequate is the knowledge base, including the location and availability of expertise, provision of training for practitioners, and the accessibility and quality of data? How far are any of these elements in the knowledge base constrained by the lack of resources or suitable institutions, and, if appropriate, how could that be remedied?

Appendix B

CONDUCT OF THE STUDY

In order to carry out this study Commission Members sought written and oral evidence, commissioned studies and advice on specific topics, and made a number of visits.

EVIDENCE

In parallel with the news releases inviting evidence, which are reproduced in appendix A, the Secretariat wrote direct to a large number of organisations.

The organisations and individuals listed below either submitted evidence or provided information on request for the purposes of the study or otherwise gave assistance. In some cases, indicated by an asterisk, meetings were held with Commission Members or the Secretariat so that oral evidence could be given or particular issues discussed.

Government Departments
Department for Environment, Food and Rural Affairs*
Department for Transport, Local Government and the Regions*
Department of the Environment, Northern Ireland*
Department of the Environment, Transport and the Regions*
Department of Trade and Industry*
National Assembly for Wales*
Scottish Executive*

European and international bodies
European Commission, Research Directorate General
Organisation for Economic Co-operation and Development*

Other organisations
Aberdeen City Council
Association for the Protection of Rural Scotland
Association of Electricity Producers
Association of London Government
Audit Commission
Bedford Borough Council
BG Property Holdings Ltd
BG Transco Plc
BP Amoco Chemicals
British Geological Survey*
British Medical Association
British Property Federation
Central Council of Physical Recreation
Chapter 7, The Land is Ours

Chartered Institution of Water and Environmental Management

City and County of Swansea

Composting Association

Confederation of British Industry

Council for British Archaeology

Council for National Parks

Council for Nature Conservation and the Countryside

Council for the Protection of Rural England*

Council for the Protection of Rural England (North Lincolnshire Branch)

Country Land and Business Association (formerly the Countryside Landowners Association)*

Countryside Agency* (formerly the Countryside Commission)

Countryside Council for Wales*

Coventry County Council*

Dundee City Council

East Riding of Yorkshire Council

East Sussex County Council*

Economic and Social Research Council

Energy from Waste Association

English Heritage*

English Nature*

Environment Agency*

Environmental Analysis Co-operative

Environmental Services Association

Enviros Aspinwall

Foresight Programme*

Forestry Commission*

Friends of the Earth

Hart District Council

Heriot-Watt University/Edinburgh College of Art, School of Planning and Housing

Horsham District Council

Horticultural Trades Association

House Builders Federation*

Institute of Wastes Management

Institution of Environmental Sciences

Institution of Mechanical Engineers

Lancashire County Council

Landscape Institute

Leicester City Council

Local Government Association

Local Government Association Special Interest Group on Coastal Issues

London Green Belt Council

Marine Conservation Society

National Farmers Union*

National Farmers' Union of Scotland

National Housing Federation

National Retail Planning Forum

National Society for Clean Air and Environmental Protection*
National Trust
National Wind Power Ltd
Natural Environment Research Council
Norfolk County Council
Office of Water Services (OFWAT)
OXERA Environmental Ltd
Oxfordshire County Council
Planning Officers Society
Quarry Products Association
Radioactive Waste Management Advisory Committee
Renfrewshire County Council
ROOM, National Council for Housing and Planning
Round Table on Sustainable Development
Royal College of General Practitioners
Royal Geographical Society
Royal Institute of Chartered Surveyors
Royal Society*
Royal Society for the Protection of Birds*
Royal Society of Edinburgh*
Royal Town Planning Institute*
Scottish Environment LINK*
Scottish Environment Protection Agency*
Scottish Natural Heritage*
Somerset County Council
South Lanarkshire Council
Southwark Borough Council
Surrey County Council*
Timber Growers Association
Town and Country Planning Association
Transport Research Laboratory
UK Environmental Law Association, Planning Law Working Party
Ulster Farmers' Union
University College London, Bartlett School of Planning
University of Hull, Institute of City and Regional Studies
University of the West of England
Warwickshire County Council
Water UK
West Berkshire County Council
West Sussex County Council
Wildlife and Countryside Link
Wildlife Trusts joint with World Wide Fund for Nature UK
Woolley & Company
Yorkshire Water

Individuals

Mr Mike Allen, London Borough of Newham*

Mr Andrew Bennett, MP*

Dr A J Bond, University of Wales, Aberystwyth

Mr W R Butterworth, Land Network International Ltd

Professor David Crichton

Professor Bob Evans, South Bank University*

Ms Nicky Gavron*

Professor Malcolm Grant, University of Cambridge*

Professor Sir Peter Hall, University College London*

Professor Patsy Healey, University of Newcastle upon Tyne*

Ms Samantha Heath*

Mr John Horam, MP*

Professor David Johns

Professor Jeffrey Jowell, University College London

Lord Justice Keene*

Ms Diana Kershaw*

Professor Nathaniel Lichfield

Professor Jim Longhurst, University of the West of England*

Professor Patrick McAuslan, Birkbeck College, University of London*

Mr Richard Mills*

Mr George Monbiot*

Mr James Page

Professor David Pearce, University College, London*

Professor Judith Petts, University of Birmingham*

Professor Michael Purdue, City University

Mr Keith Reed*

Professor Paul Selman, Cheltenham & Gloucester College of Higher Education

Professor Jim Skea, University of Sussex*

Professor Andy Stirling, Science Policy Research Unit, University of Sussex*

Mr Justice Sullivan*

Mr John E Thackray, Policy and Enterprise Services

Mr Robin Thompson*

Mr Paul Tomlinson

Dr Jo Treweek

Mr Robert Upton*

Rt Hon Simon Upton*

Mr Vangelis Vitalis*

Mr Peter Wilks, Iwade Parish Council

Dr Elizabeth Wilson, Oxford Brookes University

COMMISSIONED STUDIES

The following papers were commissioned in the course of the study:

Environmental Planning, People's Values and Sustainable Development. Roger Levett, CAG Consultants. November 1999.

Environmental Planning in the UK. Institute for European Environmental Policy. November 1999.

The Use of the Land Use Planning System to Achieve Non-Land Use Planning Objectives. Land Use Consultants. December 1999.

Planning and Pollution Revisited. Dr Chris Miller, University of Salford. October 1999.

A Comparison of Environmental Planning Legislation in Selected Countries. Centre for Environment and Planning, University of the West of England. April 2000.

VISITS

In the course of its work on environmental planning, Members of the Commission and its Secretariat made a series of visits:

2-3 September 1999 – Northern Ireland
Dinner with representatives from the Department of the Environment for Northern Ireland, the Environment and Heritage Service for Northern Ireland, and the Planning Service.

6-7 April 2000 – Scotland
Visit to and discussions with representatives at Seafield Wastewater Treatment Plant, Edinburgh;
Visit to a large greenfield development featuring a sustainable drainage scheme, Dunfermline, Fife;
Discussions with Mr Vincent Goodstadt, Dr Chris Himsworth, and representatives from the Scottish Environment Protection Agency and the Scottish Executive;
Dinner with Ms Sarah Boyack MSP, Minister for Transport and the Environment, and representatives from the Friends of the Earth Scotland, Macauley Land Use Research Institute, Royal Society of Edinburgh, and Scottish Natural Heritage.

5-7 July 2000 – Wales
Visit to the Cardiff Bay barrage and discussions with representatives from Cardiff Bay Development Corporation, the Countryside Council for Wales, and the Environment Agency Wales;
Visit to regeneration sites in the Merthyr Valley and discussions with a representative from the Welsh Development Agency;
Discussions with Professor Martin Lowson, Professor John Whitelegg, and representatives from the Department of City and Regional Planning, Cardiff University, the Countryside Agency, the Countryside Council for Wales, the Department of Trade and Industry Foresight programme, and the National Assembly for Wales;
Dinner with Ms Sue Essex AM, Assembly Secretary for Planning, Environment and Transport, and representatives from the Environment Agency Wales, the Royal Society for the Protection of Birds, Wales Wildlife Link, and the Wales Worldwide Fund for Nature.

2-3 November 2000 – Northern Ireland

Discussions with Mr Sam Foster MLA, Minister for the Environment, Northern Ireland Executive and representatives from the Department of the Environment for Northern Ireland, the Department of Regional Development, and the Environment and Heritage Service for Northern Ireland;

Dinner with Professor Malachy McEldowney, and representatives from Belfast City Council, the Department of the Environment for Northern Ireland, and Northern Ireland Environment Link.

5-6 April 2001 – Scotland

Oral evidence sessions with representatives from the Scottish Executive, and Scottish Natural Heritage.

Dinner with Mr Ross Finnie MSP, Minister for the Environment and Rural Development, and representatives from the Scottish Executive;

26 November 2001 – Birmingham

Visit and discussion with representatives from Advantage West Midlands, the Council for the Protection of Rural England, Environment Agency, Local Government Association, Government Office for the West Midlands, and the Regional Round Table on Sustainable Development.

19 December 2001 – The Hague, the Netherlands

Discussions with representatives from Advisory Council for Research on Spatial Planning, Nature and Environment (RMNO), the Council for Housing, Spatial Planning and the Environment (VROM-raad), the Ministry for Housing, Spatial Planning and the Environment (VROM), Society for Nature and the Environment (Stichting Natuur en Milieu), Syzygy (an environmental NGO), and the University of Nijmegen.

SECRETARIAT

Other Members of the Secretariat who made a significant contribution to the content of the report at various stages were Keith Allott, David Aspinwall, Sally-Ann Gannon, Cathy Garretty, Nicholas Schoon and Diana Wilkins.

Appendix C

JOINING UP ENVIRONMENTAL PLANNING – A ROYAL COMMISSION SEMINAR

To assist the Commission in defining specific issues on which it would invite evidence, a seminar under the title 'Joining up Environmental Planning' was held on 3 February 2000 at the Institute of Materials in London, with a wide range of invited participants and the following programme:

SESSION 1: CHAIRED BY SIR TOM BLUNDELL

Chair – Sir Tom Blundell, Chairman of the Royal Commission on Environmental Pollution

What is environmental planning?
Dr Susan Owens, Member of the Royal Commission on Environmental Pollution

The changing policy context
John Benington, Warwick University

SESSION 2: PLANNING TODAY

Chair – Richard Macrory, Member of the Royal Commission on Environmental Pollution

Panel Discussion: Current environmental planning regimes: complementary or conflicting?
Malcolm Grant, Cambridge University
William Sheate, Imperial College
Richard Mills, National Society for Clean Air and Environmental Protection
Patricia Henton, Scottish Environment Protection Agency

SESSION 3: PLANNING TOMORROW

Chair – Sir Tom Blundell

Views of the Round Table on Sustainable Development
Graham Wynne, Royal Society for the Protection of Birds

Environmental planning – sustainability and public values
Roger Levett, CAG Consultants

The contribution of economic instruments to planning objectives
Bob Evans, South Bank University

English Nature's vision of the future
Sue Collins, English Nature

Planning and long-term risk
Andy Blowers, Open University

Environment Agency's vision
Jan Pentreath, Environment Agency

Panel Discussion: Constraints and opportunities for delivering a sustainable future
(The speakers from Session 3)

Concluding remarks
Sir Tom Blundell

In addition to the speakers and Members of the Commission, the other participants were:

Keith Allott *(ENDS)*

Mike Ash (Department of the Environment, Transport and the Regions)

Stephen Batey (Department of the Environment, Transport and the Regions)

Graeme Bell (Town and Country Planning Association)

Andy Blowers (Open University)

Pamela Castle (Cameron McKenna Solicitors)

Philip Dale (UK Round Table on Sustainable Development)

Tom de Castella (*Planning* Magazine)

Paul Ekins (Forum for the Future)

Nick Evans (Scottish Executive)

John Hawkins (Chartered Institution of Water and Environmental Management)

David Harrison (House of Commons Select Committee on Environment, Transport and Regional Affairs)

Jeff Jacobs (Department of the Environment, Transport and the Regions)

Rob Jarman (National Trust)

David Jones (Ministry of Agriculture, Fisheries and Food)

Mark Jones (Country Landowners Association)

Alistair Keddie (Department of Trade and Industry)

Wendy Le-Las (UK ELA Planning Law Working Party)

Nathaniel Lichfield (Dalia & Nathaniel Lichfield Associates)

Richard Longman (Department of the Environment, Transport and the Regions)

Jeff Maxwell (Macaulay Land Use Research Institute)

Duncan McLaren (Friends of the Earth)

Brian McLaughlin (National Farmers Union)

Laura Merrill (OXERA Environmental Ltd)

Vincent Nadin (University of the West of England)

Henry Oliver (Council for the Protection of Rural England)

Derek Osborn (UK Round Table on Sustainable Development)

Judith Petts (University of Birmingham)

Michael Purdue (City University)

Louise Rees (Economic and Social Research Council)

Sam Richards (Local Government Association)

Libby Street (Royal Town Planning Institute)

Sue Slack (Kelda Group Plc [formerly Yorkshire Water])

David Stathers (Boots the Chemist)

Geoff Steeley (National Retail Planning Forum)

Paul Tomlinson (Transport Research Laboratory)

Jane Topliss (Confederation of British Industry)

Roger Vallance (Environment Agency)

Geoff Vigar (University of Newcastle)

Walter Wehrmeyer (University of Surrey)

Jeremy Worth (Countryside Agency)

A report of the Seminar is on the Commission's website: www.rcep.org.uk/ep-semin.html

Appendix D

Greening sustainable development strategies – proposals by the European environmental advisory councils for the EU sustainable development strategy

Executive Summary

The European Union urgently needs to commit itself wholeheartedly to sustainable development. Adoption of a Sustainable Development Strategy for the EU will therefore mark a major step forward. This must be a substantial and influential document, which will provide a framework for integrating environmental considerations into EU policies in every sector.

The national and regional advisory bodies which make up the network of European Environmental Advisory Councils (EEACs) are putting forward detailed proposals for the scope and content of the EU Sustainable Development Strategy, drawing on the experience of putting sustainable development into effect already gained in Member States. More than 20 advisory councils from 15 countries support this statement.

EEACs acknowledge that sustainable development must fulfil economic, social and environmental objectives. Because survival of the natural environment is crucial for economic and social development in the long run, they have focused on the environmental dimension of sustainability.

Many current trends are not sustainable. They include the rising level of greenhouse gases in the atmosphere; other forms of pollution from diffuse sources; the effects of congestion and pollution on the quality of life for people in towns and cities; disruption of the water cycle; degradation of soils and terrestrial ecosystems; increasing concentrations of hazardous chemicals in the environment; increasing quantities of wastes for disposal; losses of biodiversity, and of natural and cultural landscapes; and over-exploitation of marine ecosystems. These environmentally unsustainable trends are driven by the high, and increasing, use of basic natural resources that results from traditional patterns of economic growth.

The basic principle of sustainability, EEACs believe, is that the natural environment has critical and unique values that can seldom be substituted by, or traded for, the economic or social products of civilisation. Sustainable development can be achieved only if the EU adopts a new concept of development, involving far-reaching modifications in patterns of both production and consumption. This new concept of development will acknowledge economic needs and social aspirations, but accept protection of the environment and natural resources as a fundamental constraint.

By taking the lead in technological and social innovations that decouple economic development from resource use and pollution, the EU can not only improve the quality of life for all its peoples, but also increase the competitiveness of its industries and stimulate employment.

There are many barriers to achieving such a new concept of development. One major barrier is a general lack of coherence in the EU's existing policies, especially with respect to long-term effects. Notable examples include perverse subsidies given under the Common Agricultural Policy and Structural Funds. Fundamental transformations in policies will therefore be required.

EEACs identify the essential elements for success. A sustainable development strategy must have both wide political support and strong backing at the highest levels of government. It needs to be supported by approaches to learning which make full use of people's experiences and creativity. It must look at least 20-25 years into the future. It must address the most important long-term environmental problems, and establish clear objectives for resolving them, utilising quantified indicators and targets. It has to bridge the gap between global and local levels, and incorporate carefully designed mechanisms that will ensure effective implementation. A sustainable development strategy should have a strong research base. Once it has been adopted, its effectiveness must be monitored continuously and it must be reviewed at regular intervals.

The EU Sustainable Development Strategy must have tangible content. There must be significant changes in the procedures of all European institutions. EEACs believe that:

- The *Cardiff Process* for integrating environmental considerations into other policy areas must continue and be reinforced. The *Lisbon Process*, which aims to integrate social and economic policies through an annual report to the spring EU summit, must be extended to include environmental considerations.

- There should be an *annual review* of the Strategy at the spring EU summit. Each part should be reviewed in detail at least every four years, not least to extend the scope of the Strategy beyond the six initial policy areas identified by the European Commission.

- To secure better co-ordination of policies, the directorates-general of the European Commission should establish a programme of *joint policy reviews*.

- A *Sustainable Development Committee of the European Parliament* should keep under review the extent to which EU policies are environmentally sustainable.

- Where international obligations have been allocated between Member States, the *European Court of Justice* should have powers to impose penalties on any Member State which fails to meet its obligation.

EEACs also propose far-reaching changes to policies in particular sectors. These include:

- *Energy*: The Strategy must focus on the need for very large reductions in carbon dioxide emissions in the long term. That will require a carbon tax, with a minimum rate applying throughout the EU, and demanding energy efficiency standards for products and buildings. Energy markets must be structured to encourage low-carbon technologies.

- *Transport*: More ambitious targets are needed to reduce fuel consumption of vehicles. A high minimum rate of road fuel taxation must be set at EU level, and backed by other measures to promote less environmentally damaging forms of transport. Market-based instruments should be applied to air transport.

- *Agriculture*: The Common Agricultural Policy needs radical reform. Financial support should only be given to farmers who go beyond legal requirements to protect the environment.

- *Industry*: The main focus must be on the use of materials and energy over the entire life cycles of products, and on a new strategy for chemicals.

- *Nature conservation*: Promoting biodiversity should be an objective in all forms of land use. In the case of marine ecosystems, an integrated approach must be adopted in order to maintain their biodiversity and overall productivity.

EEACs will draw on the present paper in giving advice to their national and regional governments. They also intend to use it as the basis for a continuing dialogue with the European institutions and other actors about the best ways of moving towards sustainability.

The full text of this statement can be found at www.EEAC-network.org

It was adopted at a conference held by European Environmental Advisory Councils at Stockholm in February 2001. It was endorsed by 23 advisory councils from 15 Member States and accession countries, including the Royal Commission on Environmental Pollution.

February 2001

Appendix E

EXAMPLES OF AIMS AND OBJECTIVES IN STRUCTURE PLANS

BERKSHIRE (1995)

The overall strategy of the Plan is to seek sustainable development and improvement to the quality of life in Berkshire by pursuing the following objectives:

(i) to restrain development to levels that respect the limits set by environmental, infrastructure and other constraints upon the development of land

(ii) to give priority within (i) to meeting Berkshire's economic and social needs, including the provision of low-cost housing and wider employment opportunities

(iii) to protect and enhance the character and quality of Berkshire's landscape, environment and heritage

(iv) to steer development to locations which minimise the need for travel and can be well served by public transport

(v) to conserve natural resources

(vi) to minimise pollution

(vii) to seek improvements to infrastructure, services and amenities

(viii) to promote an appropriate balance between all forms of transport by continuing to develop an integrated transport strategy

BRIGHTON AND EAST SUSSEX (1999)

In order to meet the needs for development and change in the plan area in a way that is more environmentally sustainable in the longer term, all planning activities and development decisions should take account of the following criteria. Where appropriate, local planning authorities may require proposals for development to demonstrate how far they contribute to the achievement of these criteria.

The criteria are:

(a) meeting needs for a balance between homes, jobs and a range of facilities and services in order to improve the quality of life for all sections of the community, but not necessarily meeting all demands for development

(b) minimising impact on the environment, including residential areas, and compensating for the loss of environmental resources where their loss is acceptable and unavoidable in order to achieve other policies in the plan

(c) reducing the need to travel, particularly by car, and improving accessibility of all to a range of services and facilities by more environmentally friendly means of transport (including public passenger transport, walking and cycling)

(d) not creating or perpetuating unacceptable traffic or transport conditions

(e) efficient and effective renewal and re-use of existing premises and "brown" sites, particularly in the urban areas to reduce the need for greenfield sites

(f) protecting and enhancing the attractiveness and individual character of urban and rural areas for residents, businesses and visitors

(g) protecting and enhancing water quality and maintaining groundwater and river levels for human consumption, industrial and agricultural water supply and to support local biodiversity

(h) avoiding the development of land which is unstable, at risk to flooding or which would be likely to increase the risk of flooding elsewhere

(i) protecting and enhancing air quality, including the reduction of air pollution and the emission of greenhouse gases

(j) according with the objectives of and not causing damage to the Sussex Downs and High Weald Areas of Outstanding Natural Beauty (AONB), Ashdown Forest, downland, wetland, open heathland, ancient woodlands, undeveloped coast (including Heritage Coast), Sites of Special Scientific Interest (SSSI), Special Protection Areas (SPA), Special Areas of Conservation (SAC), Ramsar sites, nature reserves, ancient monuments, conservation areas, historic parks and gardens, battlefields and other areas of designated or recognised important landscape, archaeological, geological, ecological or historical character and their settings

(k) preventing development which would reduce strategic and other important gaps of valued countryside between settlements

(l) protecting and enhancing the provision of open and green spaces and community facilities in towns and villages where these are recognised as being of importance for environmental and/or community purposes

(m) protecting and enhancing conservation areas, other areas of acknowledged townscape importance, listed buildings and other buildings of acknowledged importance and their settings

(n) protecting agricultural land and preventing development on the best and most versatile (grades 1, 2 and 3a)

(o) disposing of waste in an environmentally acceptable and economically practical manner by reducing waste generation, increasing the re-use and treatment of waste, and minimising disposal to land

(p) protecting mineral resources and land with potential for filling with waste

(q) making efficient and effective use of existing or planned infrastructure and services

(r) being energy efficient and taking advantage of ambient sunlight

(s) avoiding and reducing unnecessary noise and artificial lighting

(t) safeguarding environmentally acceptable sites which are identified as having potential for renewable energy production from prejudicial development, and

(u) promoting the principles of sustainable development among residents, businesses and visitors.

GLASGOW AND CLYDE VALLEY (1999)

The Structure Plan for Glasgow and the Clyde Valley aims to:

- increase economic competitiveness by enhancing the attractiveness of the area for investment

- improve the quality of life and identity of local communities in terms of jobs, housing services and environmental conditions, particularly for the most disadvantaged in society, to assist social inclusion

- sustain and enhance the natural and historic environment, in particular by the re-use of existing urban land and buildings

- improve access between work, home, leisure and shops, and the distribution of goods, in particular by public transport and the greater integration of land use and transportation.

Appendix F

PLANNING FOR LONDON

F.1 The statutory requirements for strategic planning in London are described in chapter 10 (10.50-10.53). On the basis of the consultation document published by the Mayor of London in May 2001[1] it is difficult to be sure what form the London Plan will take. But the general character of the initial proposals can be seen in the concluding paragraph of the summary:

> The London Plan will interpret the spatial dimensions of all the Mayor's strategies. In doing so it will not set out a prescriptive plan for London's future. Rather it will focus on providing an adequate supply side response to the demands placed on London by a growing economy and population. In particular it will aim to facilitate the projected growth in the economy by guiding new commercial development and ensure the provision of more housing, including affordable housing to accommodate London's growing population. Its aim will be to achieve rejuvenation in town centres and the regeneration of deprived areas and to address the need for improved public transport and to reduce dependence on the car. In supporting economic growth in a sustainable way, by focusing development around the public transport system, it will facilitate an improved quality of life for Londoners.[2]

F.2 There is therefore a strong bias towards economic development and major transport projects. The transport and economic development strategies have already appeared.[3] In both fields the Mayor has the support of a powerful executive body, Transport for London and the London Development Agency (which has produced the economic development strategy[4]). That these were the first two strategies to appear seems to be further evidence of the emphasis the spatial development strategy is likely to have, rather than reason to hope the balance will be corrected in due course.

F.3 The initial proposals for the spatial development strategy are not based on an overall assessment of London's environment; the first state of the environment report will not be available until 2003. Nor do the initial proposals refer to the assessment of the state of London's environment which the Environment Agency has produced.[5] They point in many desirable directions for improvements in the urban environment and open spaces.[6] They go on to refer to the issues raised by climate change, waste management and air quality, and the further strategies due to be produced,[7] but their coverage of these latter issues is in very general terms and unquantified. Of the issues the Environment Agency has highlighted for London,[8] the initial proposals for the spatial development strategy make no mention of land quality, water resources or water quality. It is striking that, although planning issues centring on the river Thames have been recognised as of major importance for London,[9] and the Environment Agency has primary responsibility for water management, there is no mention of its role either in the section on 'The Thames and London's waterways' or in the context of flooding.[10]

F.4 The initial proposals conspicuously decline to take into account the environment beyond London's boundaries, and we hope that like the Mayor's Policy Commission on the Environment recommends.[11] As an example, although the development wedges defined outside central London are all focused on airports (three of which are outside London), the proposed policy for airports is summarised as 'identifying preferred options for expansion of airports around London, to maximise social and economic benefit and minimise environmental impact *within London*' (our italics).[12] Another example is that, while reference is made to the proximity principle for waste (that it should be processed and disposed of as close as possible to where it is produced), the only part of the principle endorsed is the rider that, where waste has to be transported, that should be done by the most environmentally friendly means.[13]

F.5 The Mayor has only limited powers to intervene in individual cases under the town and country planning system. The unitary development plans of the London Boroughs and the way in which they exercise their development control functions will therefore be crucial in determining whether the London Plan can be implemented successfully.[14] It remains to be seen whether, without a lead role in its preparation, the London Boroughs will be sufficiently committed to the London Plan to co-operate full-heartedly in its implementation.

REFERENCES

1   Greater London Authority, Mayor of London. *Towards the London Plan. Initial proposals for the Mayor's spatial development strategy.* May 2001. Cited as GLA (2001a).

2   Greater London Authority, Mayor of London. *Summary: towards the London Plan. Initial proposals for the Mayor's spatial development strategy.* May 2001. Cited as GLA (2001b). See page 14. Similarly the only diagram included in the summary is titled 'Indicative transport improvements and development interactions'.

3   Greater London Authority, Mayor of London. *The Mayor's transport strategy.* July 2001.

4   Greater London Authority (2000) Success Through Diversity – the Mayor's Economic Development Strategy, July 2001.

5   Environment Agency Thames Region. *State of the environment report for London 2001.* Reading.

6   GLA (2001a), paragraphs 2.89-2.99 and associated text boxes.

7   Some of these strategies have now been produced in final or draft form:
    GLA (2001) Draft Air Quality Strategy for public consultation, September 2001.
    GLA (2001) The Mayor's Draft Municipal Waste Management Strategy, July 2001.
    GLA (2001) Connecting with Londons Nature: The Mayor's Draft Biodiversity Strategy, September 2001.

8   Environment Agency Thames Region, page 68.

9   To such an extent that supplementary regional planning guidance, *Strategic planning guidance for the river Thames* (RPG3B/9B)was issued in 1997, in addition to the 1995 *Thames Gateway Planning Framework* (RPG9A).

10 GLA (2001a), paragraphs 2.110-2.112 and text box; 2.100.

11 Environment and Sustainability – a report from the Mayor's Policy Commission on the Environment. Available on GLA website The Policy Commission encourage the Mayor's London Plan to address London's responsibilities in terms of use of resources and its effects on the wider UK environment, especially climate change but welcome the Mayor's decision to implement sustainability approvals and health impact assessments of all GLA strategies and the Mayor's decision to set up a Round Table on sustainable development.

12 GLA (2001b), challenge 4 (page 7).

13 GLA (2001a), paragraph 2.104.

14 GLA (2001a), paragraph 4.12.

Appendix G

SPATIAL PLANNING IN NORTHERN IRELAND

G.1 Northern Ireland can be regarded as having pioneered spatial planning in the UK The Department of the Environment for Northern Ireland (DOENI) has the statutory function of securing the orderly and consistent development of land and the planning of that development.[1] It is also responsible for integrating sustainable development into government policies and activities. In 1998 DOENI published a draft strategic framework for Northern Ireland which was comprehensive but concise.[2] This followed extensive consultations, in which 116 organisations were contacted direct,[3] a further 477 voluntary and community groups took part in facilitated consultation[4] and two major conferences were held for young people.[5] Accompanying the draft framework were a baseline report, a strategic environmental appraisal (showing how the evolving strategy had been 'tested against current best environmental practice'), a statistical report showing how future housing needs had been estimated, and the Family of Settlements Report containing profiles of individual towns and their future potential.

G.2 The strategic framework was presented as providing a long-term perspective on the development of Northern Ireland over the next 25 years and a spatial framework for action. It thus provides the framework for development plans within the town and country planning system and for Planning Policy Guidance Statements; but it is not limited to land use, and recognises that 'policies for physical development have an important bearing on other matters'.[6] It set out 30 'strategic planning guidelines. covering all aspects of economy, society and the environment. Each guideline was subdivided into several aims, and these in turn into specific objectives, although the only quantified targets were for housing in the main urban centres to 2010.[7] The spatial development strategy was summed up in a key diagram. This was supplemented by six diagrams summarising the strategy in particular fields of policy and two diagrams on a larger scale showing spatial frameworks for the Belfast and Derry/Londonderry areas.

G.3 A sustainability assessment of the draft framework was carried out by DOENI with the assistance of CAG Consultants. An overall conclusion was that the strategy

> seeks to provide an integrated approach in which negative environmental impacts arising from social and economic advancement are minimised as much as possible. Potential negative impacts will need detailed appraisal at the local level and particularly the implementation stage…. Environmental enhancement should, if possible, be the ultimate goal of any project.[8]

G.4 Production of a comprehensive spatial plan for Northern Ireland was undoubtedly helped by its particular political situation and administrative arrangements. Until 1999 almost all executive responsibilities, including physical planning, were brought together in a single administration provided by the UK government. That greatly simplified the task of bringing all aspects of development together in a single document; there was not the same difficulty as in England over aligning the views and actions of different tiers of government. Moreover, the framework was produced in a period when there was an unusually high degree of civic engagement, and presented as the fulfilment of commitments given by the UK government in the Belfast Agreement on the future of Northern Ireland in April 1998.[9] Despite this high level of political commitment the draft framework warned that:

> nothing contained in this document should be read as a commitment that public resources will be provided for any specific project, as all proposals for expenditure will be subject to economic, social, financial and environmental assessment and will also have to be considered having regard to the overall availability of resources.[10]

G.5 The relevance of this warning is illustrated by the subsequent evolution of policy on rail transport: strategic policy guideline 13.2 was that the regional rail system should be strengthened, and covered a range of specific objectives; yet a couple of years later consideration was being given to abandoning the rail system outside the Belfast area.[11]

G.6 Devolution to the Northern Ireland Assembly in April 1999, and establishment of multi-party government, made the situation more complicated, and the momentum seemed to be lost. Although a public examination of the draft framework was held in October-November 1999 [and it was subsequently revised], it was not until September 2001 that the Northern Ireland Assembly approved of the strategy. Moreover; decisions still have to be taken on an action plan to implement the strategy, with benchmarks against which progress can be measured and with review arrangements to ensure appropriate remedial action is taken where targets are not achieved'.[12] In terms of public profile the strategy has been overtaken by the Programme for Government, a budget-based document covering a period of three years and supplemented by public service agreements. The strategy is mentioned in the initial version of the Programme for Government adopted in April 2001,[13] but relatively briefly and only under the headings 'Creating the infrastructure for competitive regional development' and 'We will create a more co-ordinated and efficient planning process', not under the heading 'We will work to ensure the protection and enhancement of the environment'.

G.7 One repercussion of devolution was that responsibility for the regional strategic framework passed to the Department of Regional Development (DRDNI), while DOENI remained responsible for land use planning and for promoting sustainable development. DOENI is now preparing a separate sustainable development strategy for Northern Ireland, with the aim of going to consultation in March 2002 and finalising it in 2003. The purpose is to commit the entire Northern Ireland Executive to the principles of sustainable development and ensuring that structures and procedures exist to deliver it. These will include a set of indicators of sustainability, which will then provide a means of checking that the regional strategic framework is consistent with sustainable development. It has yet to be decided how compliance with the sustainable development strategy will be monitored and enforced.[14]

REFERENCES

1   The Planning (Northern Ireland) Order 1991, article 3.

2   Department of the Environment for Northern Ireland (DOENI) (1998). *Shaping our future: towards a strategy for the development of the region. Draft regional strategic framework for Northern Ireland.* TSO.

3   DOENI, page 96.

4   Queen's University of Belfast (School of Environmental Planning)/University of Ulster (Urban Institute)/Rural Community Network (Northern Ireland)/Community Technical Aid (Northern Ireland) ([1998]). *Shaping our future: public consultation on a regional strategic framework for Northern Ireland.* TSO.

5   The basis for consultation was\provided by DOENI (1997a). *Shaping our future: towards a strategy for the development of the region* (launched by the Secretary of State in June 1997); and DOENI (1997b). *Shaping our future: a discussion paper* (November 1997, on which 207 formal submissions were received).

6   DOENI (1998), page 2.

7   DOENI (1998), page 42 and diagram 5.

8   DOENI, Regional Planning Division ([1998]). *Shaping our future. Strategic environmental appraisal report: a sustainability assessment of the draft regional strategic framework for Northern Ireland.* Belfast.

9   DOENI (1998), page iii.

10   DOENI(1998), page 7.

11   Commission visit to Belfast, November 2000.

12   DOENI (1998), pages 92-93.

13   On Northern Ireland Executive web site: 'This Programme for Government sets out the Executive's proposed strategic aims and priorities which will be pursued working with and for all the people. It will provide an important focus of co-operation, to enable us to create a better future for ourselves and for our children.'

14   Information supplied by DOENI, August 2001.

Appendix H

MEMBERS OF THE ROYAL COMMISSION

CHAIRMAN
Sir Tom Blundell FRS FMedSci

Sir William Dunn Professor and Head of Department of Biochemistry, University of Cambridge and Professorial Fellow of Sidney Sussex College

Director General, Agricultural and Food Research Council 1991-94

Chief Executive, Biotechnology and Biological Sciences Research Council 1994-96

Member, Advisory Council on Science and Technology 1988-90

Honorary Director, Imperial Cancer Research Fund Unit in Structural Biology, Birkbeck College, University of London 1989-96

Professor of Crystallography, Birkbeck College, University of London 1976-90

MEMBERS
*The Reverend Professor Michael Banner MA DPhil

FD Maurice Professor of Moral and Social Theology, King's College London

Chairman, Home Office Animal Procedures Committee

Chairman, CJD Incidents Panel, Department of Health

Chairman, Government Committee of Inquiry on Ethics of Emerging Technologies in the Breeding of Farm Animals 1993-95

Dean, Fellow and Director of Studies in Philosophy and Theology, Peterhouse, Cambridge 1988-94

Member, Agriculture and Environment Biotechnology Commission

Professor Roland Clift OBE MA PhD FREng FIChemE FRSA

Professor of Environmental Technology and Director of the Centre for Environmental Strategy, University of Surrey

Visiting Professor, Chalmers University of Technology, Göteborg, Sweden

Member, UK Ecolabelling Board 1992-99

Chairman, Clean Technology Management Committee of Science and Engineering Research Council 1990-94

John Flemming CBE MA FBA

Warden, Wadham College, Oxford

Chief Economist, European Bank for Reconstruction and Development 1991-93

Chief Economist, Bank of England 1980-91

Member, Advisory Board on Research Councils 1977-90

Chairman, National Academies Policy Advisory Group Working Party on Energy and the Environment 1993-95

Chairman, Hansard Society/Economic Policy Forum Commission on the Regulation of Privatised Utilities 1995-97

Treasurer, British Academy

Chairman of Management Committee, National Institute of Economic and Social Research

Sir Brian Follett FRS

Chair, Arts and Humanities Research Board

Professor, Department of Zoology, University of Oxford

Chair, Inquiry into Infectious Diseases of Livestock 2001-02

Chair, Review into Research Library Provision 2001-02

Vice-Chancellor, University of Warwick 1993-2001

Professor of Zoology and Head of Biological Sciences, University of Bristol 1978-93

Vice-President and Biological Secretary, The Royal Society 1987-93.

Dr Ian Graham-Bryce CBE DPhil FRSC FRSE

President, Scottish Association for Marine Science

Chairman, East Malling Trust for Horticultural Research

Principal and Vice-Chancellor, University of Dundee 1994-2000

Convener, Committee of Scottish Higher Education Principals 1998-2000

President, British Crop Protection Council 1998-2000

Head of Environmental Affairs Division, Shell International 1986-94

Director, East Malling Research Station 1979-86

Member of Natural Environment Research Council 1989-96

*Sir Martin Holdgate CB PhD FIBiol

President, Zoological Society of London

Chairman, Energy Advisory Panel 1993-96

Director General, International Union for Conservation of Nature and Natural Resources 1988-94

Chief Scientist, and Deputy Secretary, Department of the Environment 1976-88

Chairman, International Institute for Environment and Development 1994-99

Professor Brian Hoskins CBE FRS

Royal Society Research Professor

Professor of Meteorology, University of Reading (Head of Department 1990-96)

Chairman, Expert Panel on UK Strategy in Global Environmental Research 1996

President of the Royal Meteorological Society 1998-2000

President, International Association of Meteorology and Atmospheric Sciences 1991-95

Royal Society Council and Chair of its Global Environmental Research Committee

Chair, Meteorological Office Science Advisory Committee

Vice-Chair, Joint Scientific Committee for the World Climate Research Programme

Member of Scientific Review Committees for Hadley Centre, Max Plank Institute for Meteorology and European Centre for Medium Range Weather Forecasts (Chair 1985-88)

Professor Richard Macrory CBE Barrister MA

Professor of Environmental Law, University College London

Board Member, Environment Agency

Former Specialist Adviser, House of Commons Select Committee on the Environment, Transport and Regional Affairs

First Chairman of UK Environmental Law Association 1986-88

Editor-in-Chief, *Journal of Environmental Law*

Chairman, Merchant Ivory Productions Ltd

Honorary Vice-President, National Society for Clean Air and Environmental Protection

Chairman, Steering Committee, European Environmental Advisory Councils

*Sir Michael G Marmot MB BS PhD FMedSci FRCP FFPHM

Professor of Epidemiology and Public Health, University College London, and Director, International Centre for Health and Society

Medical Research Council Research Professor

Member, Committee on Medical Aspects of Food Policy and Chair of the Cardiovascular Review Group 1989-99

Member, Scientific Advisory Group, Independent Inquiry into Inequalities in Health 1997-98

Member, Department of Health Prevention and Inequalities Task Force

Mrs Cheryl Miller BA FRSA

Chief Executive of East Sussex County Council

Non-Executive Director, Sussex Enterprise

Non-Executive Director, Wired Sussex

Member of the Advisory Panel to the South East England Development Agency

Executive Committee Member, Society of Local Authority Chief Executives

Dr Susan Owens OBE FRGS FRSA

Reader in Environment and Policy, University of Cambridge and Fellow of Newnham College

Member, Countryside Commission 1996-99

Member, UK Round Table on Sustainable Development 1995-98

Member of Deputy Prime Minister's Panel during preparation of 1998 Transport White Paper 1997-98

Member of Foresight Agriculture, Natural Resources and Environment Panel, Office of Science and Technology 1994-96

Professor Jane Plant CBE FIMM FGS FRSA CEng

Chief Scientist, British Geological Survey (Natural Environment Research Council)

Professor of Geochemistry, Imperial College of Science Technology and Medicine

Visiting Professor, Universities of Liverpool and Nottingham

Member, Parliamentary Science and Technology Committee

*John Roberts FIEE FCCA CEng CIMgt

Chief Executive, United Utilities plc

President, Electricity Association 1997-99

Chief Accountant, Merseyside and North Wales Electricity Board 1984-90

Managing Director (1991-92) and Chief Executive (1992-95), Manweb plc

Chief Executive, South Wales Electricity 1996

Chief Executive, Hyder Utilities 1997-99

*Leaves the Commission on completion of the Environmental Planning Study.

INDEX

232

Printed in the UK for The Stationery Office Limited
on behalf of the Controller of her Majesty's Stationery Office
03/02, 65536, C82718